Light from Heaven

Light from Heaven

... *the light that led astray,*
    Was light from Heaven.   <small>BURNS</small>

... *happy will our nature be,*
When love is an unerring light.   <small>WORDSWORTH</small>

... *Love indeed is light from heaven.*   <small>BYRON</small>

Love in British Romantic Literature

Frederick L. Beaty

Northern Illinois University Press / DeKalb

Library of Congress Cataloging in Publication Data

Beaty, Frederick L   1926–
    Light from heaven.
    Includes bibliographical references.
        1. English literature — 18th century — History and criticism.   2. English litera-
ture — 19th century — History and criticism.   3. Love in literature.   4. Romanticism — England.   I. Title.
PR447.B37   820.9′14   70-157649
ISBN 0-87580-028-9

Copyright © 1971 by Northern Illinois University Press
Published by the Northern Illinois University Press, DeKalb, Illinois
Manufactured in the United States of America
All Rights Reserved
Design by John B. Goetz

To Martha

Contents

Preface

So CONCERNED did British authors of the Romantic age become with every facet of human affection that only a work of encyclopedic dimensions could encompass all their treatments. My method, however, has been selective in several respects. Since the development of love in European civilization has already been extensively traced, I have concentrated upon major British writers as representatives of a common spirit and upon their specific depictions of love, often interrelated with other contemporary preoccupations, as reflections of a pervasive Romanticism. Though I have interwoven history, biography, letters, philosophy, and criticism where they seemed most relevant, I have focused upon love primarily as a literary phenomenon. Since the Romantics did not usually argue love as though it were the substance of philosophical disquisitions, what they assumed about it must be extracted from their creative works, most of which are narrative in nature. Consequently I have not approached the subject from the cultural historian's point of view, as just one aspect among many, and I hope to have avoided the pitfalls of those *Geistesgeschichten* that stray far from literature. Broad generalizations about love cannot be applied with equal validity to all writers, nor do some of the traditional conclusions survive close scrutiny of individual texts. The dynamic nature of love, which often needs for its comprehensive literary development either a narrative vehicle or some presentation allowing for passage of time, is so intricately bound up with specialized circumstances, character, and sequence of events that its meaning is easily distorted unless one examines it in context. Usually I have not endeavored to employ yardsticks of particular critical or psychological schools in order to determine the validity of erotic themes. A number of such evaluations have already been rendered, though judgment of that sort has sometimes been comparable to training heavy artillery on a butterfly. Rather, I should like to think that my specimens were presented alive.

To facilitate interpretation of Romantic concepts within their original matrices, I have divided my study into five basic sections, the first delineating the comic approach and the remaining four dealing with more serious attitudes toward a variety of amatory relationships. Where a number of authors have similar stances, these related treatments are incorporated under the same heading. Where one author has depicted several types of love, discussion of his works and ideas is divided among the appropriate chapters. Within this organization, I have particularly striven to present the individual development of each writer's attitude because such analysis reveals both a unity and a progression that cannot be achieved through an aggregation of motifs. However, it has also seemed profitable to group together certain themes infrequently used by any one writer yet sufficiently current to be typical of the Romantic age, and these have usually been arranged to show their evolution within the period. Obviously it has not been possible to follow any rigid system of classification for the many literary representations of love, which are so diverse and individualistic as to be almost living organisms, but I believe that my method has certain advantages over others I might have chosen for disclosing the vital character of Romanticism.

The preparation of this study has been advanced in many instances by the influence, interest, and cooperation of others, whom I wish to thank for their valuable contributions. Since it would be impossibly tedious to commend all those whose ideas I tacitly endorse or to refute all those with whom I disagree, I can only express general gratitude to the numerous critics, scholars, and students who have stimulated my thoughts. Particularly deserving of acknowledgment for their substantive aid in the composition of this manuscript are Irvin Ehrenpreis, John H. Fisher, William R. Parker, and Donald H. Reiman. My sincere appreciation is also due the editors of *Publications of the Modern Language Association,* the *Journal of English and Germanic Philology,* and the *Keats-Shelley Journal,* in which portions of this book have appeared in somewhat different form. I am very grateful to the editorial staff of the Northern Illinois University Press for many helpful suggestions and to the librarians of Indiana University and Harvard for untiring labors. To my wife I am especially indebted for both editorial assistance and faithful encouragement.

Introduction

I<small>T IS APPARENTLY</small> difficult in the present day for anyone to write about love in the Romantic age without being either defensive or condescending. Too often even apologists have interpreted it as an elongated shadow of the Marquis de Sade's erotic sensibility or an adumbration of Freud's psychopathology of sex. Not surprisingly therefore the emphasis has usually been on its negative aspects. In the view of many modern critics Romantic love is basically self-deception — the worship of an illusion that, when shattered by the encroachment of reality, must come to an unhappy end. Allied with the instabilities of youth, it is often condemned as basically irrational and so egocentric that it uses the beloved primarily as an instrument for achieving a higher emotional pitch. In its most deplorable form, beset by "overvaluation" of the beloved because of the uniqueness of maternal attachment in childhood, such emotion is said to be no more than a longing for an image of love whereby new objects of desire must be fitted into a preconceived mold.

On the contrary, much less has been made of the positive aspects of Romantic love, including that balance between sensuality and affectionate respect which Freud himself postulated as the normal attitude, and even sympathetic recent criticism usually reflects a twentieth-century coloring of the earlier concepts. Since little attention has been paid to the Romantics' own self-image, an examination from a more contemporaneous viewpoint seems needed to portray their work from within and reveal their original intentions. Therefore, with the conviction that the Romantics do offer something permanently worthy of consideration, I have tried to present, as nearly as possible after a century and a half, their treatments of love as these would likely have been interpreted in their own time — in short, to let authors speak for themselves on a subject which they regarded more highly than did preceding generations.

The belief that Romantic writers introduced a radically new approach to love is of course myopic, for Denis de Rougemont, C. S. Lewis, M. C. D'Arcy, Paul Kluckhohn, Maurice Valency, and J. B. Broadbent have demonstrated that the basic elements we call "romantic" have persisted in European literature since the twelfth-century Renaissance. Nevertheless, there is also some truth to André Gide's assertion in *The Counterfeiters* that every great school, other than the symbolist, has brought with it "a new way of looking at things, of understanding love, of behaving oneself in life." What the British Romantics inherited from native literary traditions of the eighteenth century was by no means cast overboard, though its elements were often used eclectically and reassembled into different patterns of thought. Chaste love, for example, that feeling grounded in spiritualized friendship and leading to matrimony, continued to be admired, especially among the middle classes, as much as it had been when Thomson and Richardson advocated it. Nor did hedonistic gratification, practiced in contempt of marriage by the heirs of Restoration profligates, cease to exist after any given date, as the novels of Smollett in particular show. Moreover, the synthesis of tender esteem and passion, which the Romantics are sometimes credited with having effected, had already been cogently argued by Fielding both in the prefatory essay to Book VI of *Tom Jones* and in the central character of that novel. During the eighteenth century, doctrines of benevolence showing sympathy triumphant over self-love were so extensively developed by sentimental philosophers like Shaftesbury, Hutcheson, and Butler that Romantic writers had only to select from various theories on universal love. Even without a "renascence of wonder," amatory revenants, at least in literature, survived the Age of Reason without any effective exorcism by Newtonian physics or Lockian philosophy. And in contradistinction to the growing trends of sensibility, there was a depedestalization of insipid love by Sterne, as well as the *comédie larmoyante*, sufficient to allow a comic perspective. One might well ask, then, wherein Romantic attitudes toward love differed from preceding ones.

The answer to that query is best found in what the Romantics refused to accept from their eighteenth-century heritage. A revealing instance is Madame de Staël's attack on neoclassicists in *De l'Allemagne* (1813), which deplored their inability to comprehend the "tender passion" as it had been convincingly depicted in chivalric romances. Indeed there was much in the Gothic revival, including renewed interest in poetical story-telling, that was congenial with the Romantics' anti-intellectual acceptance of emotions so intense as to lead only to death. Yet above all, British writers of the early nineteenth century rejected the implicit assumption, associated with both bourgeois-puritanical and aristocratic-epicurean traditions in their own country, that love and reason were necessarily incompatible. To understand what they most strenuously objected to one has only to examine some of Dr. Johnson's pronouncements on the detrimental effect of passion. In his preface to Shakespeare (1765), he especially praised the dramatist for a representation of love on the stage that accurately reflected its inconsequential role in the total scheme of human affairs. According to the critic, Shakespeare was aware that any emotion might produce either happiness or misery depending on whether it was rationally controlled. By the same principle, Johnson subsequently condemned Dryden's *All for Love; or, the World Well Lost* for its egregious moral flaw of conceding passion's omnipotence. Particularly in comparison with Shakespeare's redaction, as Johnson compared them in his *Lives of the English Poets*, Dryden's treatment of the love of Antony and Cleopatra appeared to extol behavior that the good invariably associate with vice and the bad with folly.

Contrary to such a rationalistic view, the Romantics wished to reunite the physical and the spiritual in such a way that reason and emotion would not confront each other destructively but would bolster one another in unison. In an idealized portrait of Byron as poetical redeemer, Shelley asserted that Maddalo, instead of curbing his passions with his extraordinary intellectual powers, allowed each to strengthen the other. Similarly Blake in *America* had his character Orc imagine rejuvenated man with heart and head of the same metal rather than, like the antecedents of that imaginary figure in the book of Daniel and Dante's *Inferno*, with a breast inferior to his head. To justify this belief in emotions as a valid guide to life it was necessary to formulate a new religion as well as a new epistemology. Whereas Continental Romantics turned increasingly to authoritarian churches for solution of their personal dilemmas, those in Britain inclined toward individualistic faiths based primarily on love. Every independent thinker, without any mediation other than the spirit of love itself, was expected to strive in Protestant fashion for direct contact between his own inner life and the Divine Being. Hence it was highly appropriate that virtually all the British Romantics conceived of love as "light from heaven," and quotations incorporating that phrase can be found in abundance.

In the tradition of Christian Platonism, of which Dante's *Paradiso* is possibly the most eloquent expression, earthly beauty, since it could be perceived only through the eyes, was dependent upon the presence of light, metaphorically conceived as the nourishing principle of life itself. But whereas neoplatonists had been concerned with love primarily as a means of leading the human soul beyond corporeality to a perception of absolute beauty, goodness, and even immortality, the Romantics, without denying the validity of a spiritual quest, were interested in the light of love chiefly as a way of coping with problems in earthly existence. These converse orientations are strikingly revealed by the sun imagery of each period. As a symbol of God's love for his creation, the sun had been well established since early Biblical times, and even those, like Shelley, who denied a personal God employed it as an emblem of cosmic energy or human imagination. Though in purely physical terms the sun not only draws earth's moisture toward itself but also extends itself as warmth toward earth, the neoplatonists had used the celestial body primarily to illustrate the attracting force of the divine while the Romantics concentrated upon those powers that descended to the world of man. This latter view is especially obvious in the outright distrust of some early nineteenth-century authors toward a light that leads mortals beyond their natural habitat. Certainly in Shelley's "Alastor" the search for something not of this earth results in extinction rather than achievement, and the central theme of Keats's *Endymion* seems to be fulfillment (albeit a mixture of mortal and divine) upon earth itself.

The divergence in perspective is further revealed by the association of beauty with love in the earlier period and of poetic imagination with love in the later one. Although both beauty and imagination were included in the idealism of each age, the emphasis differed. Dante, while believing that poetic inspiration emanates from above, was overwhelmingly concerned with the combination of love and beauty that draws man *upward* into divinity, while the Romantics seemed more aware of the love and imagination that comes *down* from heaven. Thus Wordsworth might well exhort the poet to fulfill his mundane goals:

> If thou indeed derive thy light from Heaven,
> Then, to the measure of that heaven-born light,
> Shine, Poet! in thy place, and be content.

Possibly the neoplatonists' preoccupation with beauty, which by its very nature attracts *to* itself, accurately reflects a pre-Renaissance medieval otherworldliness; post-Renaissance humanism, on the other hand, would logically exalt that inspiration which reaches *from* itself to mortals below. Therefore the Romantics, in contrast to those earlier authors who delineated love as an ascending ladder or a spiral into the empyrean, quite properly described their concept as "light *from* heaven."

But even such basic terminology bore differing implications to highly individualistic thinkers, so that the supernal light was portrayed as having a variety of influences upon human beings. One of the most fervid expressions of Romantic hopes concludes Coleridge's "Religious Musings," in which the effect of God's love for man is likened to the result of warm sunlight on ice. Implicit in this comparison is not only the customary assumption that human response expresses a desire for the good and the beautiful but also that joy is one of its inherent components. In addition to its warming effects, the divine light of love was generally thought a means of expanding intellectual powers, as Keats's "Ode to Psyche" admirably demonstrates. Indeed warming and illuminating love might be deemed the most exalted use of creative imagination. Accordingly, Shelley, in "Lines Written among the Euganean Hills," refers to the "love from Petrarch's urn" as "A quenchless lamp by which the heart/ Sees things unearthly." Moreover, love could be a way of transcending the confinements of earthly existence, of achieving a union with some higher entity, or of effecting a justice beyond mortal laws, as shown in Coleridge's "Rime of the Ancient Mariner," Shelley's "Epipsychidion" and "The Triumph of Life," Keats's *Endymion*, and a variety of spectral narratives.

Yet if love was truly a divine light in both the sensible and intelligible respects, it nevertheless entailed many problems to which the wisdom of the past offered no pat solutions. Assuming that the origin of such impetus was the Almighty Being, one might argue that adherence to its promptings represented a nobler obedience than submission to man-made law and therefore that the individual conscience would be the most valid criterion for moral judgment. Yet one might also contend that if spiritual illumination was not perfectly received in the human realm its guidance would not be infallible. Even if it shone unerringly on earth, it could be misunderstood by man's combined entity of body-and-soul. For while it might, as Byron suggests in *The Giaour*, lift "our low desire" above the earthly plane, it does not completely obliterate the animal in man. It might indeed become so weakened and distorted in the material world that its actual appearance is nothing more than a meteor-ray or will-o'-the-wisp. In this deceptive aspect it is impressively depicted by Shelley in "Lines Written in the Bay of Lerici." There the poet asserts that if he were a spirit drawn by starlight or an unthinking fish attracted to a fisherman's lantern (only to be speared), he might not worry about the effects of responding to the light of love. Unfortunately as a rational man he cannot "worship the delusive flame" without envisioning the dire consequences of such pleasure. Certainly Burns maintained that not only his susceptibility but the divine light itself had misled him, though Wordsworth, treating that assertion as blasphemy, retorted that if such impetus had truly come from heaven it could not possibly have led astray. Whatever the nature of the false inspiration — whether an influence of unheavenly origin or merely man's failure to comprehend the heavenly message — some Romantics felt that direct, unhindered apprehension of the true light would be possible only in the life beyond, a state of existence to which Shelley looked forward perhaps more than his contemporaries —

> some world far from ours,
> Where music and moonlight and feeling
> Are one. ("To Jane: 'The Keen Stars Were Twinkling' ")

In addition to these perplexing moral problems there was a more disturbing question of whether the light of love, like the imagination with which it was frequently identified, did actually emanate from an external, objective heaven or whether it was merely a projection of the inner eye. Could it indeed have been a "light that never was, on sea or land" — nothing more than a dream? A partial resolution to this problem, at least for some of the Romantics, apparently lay in their general belief that the

xviii

god of love inheres not in the object of desire but rather in the very act of loving — in the *response* to some inspiring light, however evanescent it may be. Hence one need not know its ultimate source to profit from its benefits to the human soul. Or could the light perhaps be merely evidence of the soul's pre-existent mode of apprehension, fading in intensity as man grows farther from his unborn state? Indeed the theme of the "visionary splendour" with which youth invests the world is variously treated in Wordsworth's "Ode: Intimations of Immortality" and "Evening Voluntaries," Coleridge's "Dejection: An Ode," Shelley's "Lines Written among the Euganean Hills," and the first canto of Byron's *Don Juan.* Though in some instances it might be argued that loss of the gleam would be compensated by a deeper, more empathic, feeling for humanity, most Romantic artists believed that the light of imaginative love was tantamount to the life force itself. As a result, there was much discussion concerning the states of human existence most conducive to reception of its impetus.

But whatever the problems or the disagreements, writers attuned to the spirit of Romanticism proclaimed love's dominion over all other considerations, and this one belief distinguished them sharply from many of their predecessors and from the more circumspect Victorians who followed. Though every Romantic author interpreted love according to his individual personality and social background, each one — whether a peasant like Burns, an aristocrat like Byron, or a man of conventional morality like Scott — acknowledged fealty to that common ideal. Their treatments of subjects as diverse as incest, ghostly liaisons, and honorable wedlock can all be categorized as Romantic because they basically exalted love to such an extent that sacrifices in its behalf seemed worthwhile and even apparent misdeeds perpetrated in its pursuit became venial. As Scott asserted in his *Lay of the Last Minstrel* (1805),

> Love rules the court, the camp, the grove,
> And men below, and saints above,
> And love is heaven, and heaven is love.

Though some theologians still attributed man's fall to Adam's extraordinary affection for Eve, the Romantics generally preferred to regard that emotion less as a threat to divine edict than as a means of restoring the lost paradise or as salvation itself. Depending upon results, it could therefore (like Shelley's West Wind) be either destroyer or rejuvenator.

But it was largely in the latter function that authors rebelling against a rationalistic world view preferred to consider love. The fact that they chose to identify the emotion with favorite speculations reveals the esteem in which it was ordinarily held. Hence, in addition to its customary identification with human attachments, it became associated with appreciation of nature, empathic understanding, humor, imagination, and the regeneration of corrupt society. In a time of diverse cosmographies and increasingly complex interpretations of existence, human affection gave needed stability, providing a creativity myth to which the age could attach itself. Though love, like other manifestations of organic life, was constantly developing, it provided a norm countering whatever centrifugal forces threatened to hurl man farther from centrality. Moreover, it was a beneficial antidote to the solipsism and self-consciousness that beset highly introspective natures, breaking down barriers and divisions. For while creative imagination promoted the expression of individuality, there was ever present the danger of fragmentation; and love served as a means of restoring man's contact with his own kind, with social institutions, and with the supernatural.

PART ONE

Comic Love

CHAPTER I

Burns and the Triumph
of Empathic Humor

Robert Burns's distinction as a love poet stems chiefly from his ability to perceive the comic aspects of what he considered a very serious emotion. The eighteenth-century adaptation of sentiment to comedy, as well as the Scottish vernacular tradition, afforded him ample precedent for this seemingly paradoxical combination. As random comments in his letters indicate, he was obviously interested in examining the comic spirit; yet he apparently elaborated no critical manifesto of his own to explain his practice. Perhaps because he was often regarded as an inspired but untaught genius who succeeded without conscious artistry, influential critics of the early nineteenth century usually looked not to him for illustrations of their comic theories but rather to Jean Paul Richter, who had obligingly translated his own precepts into concrete examples. Not until after many of the speculations about humor had crystallized into definite concepts could Burns's achievement be fully analyzed.[1] Just as his poetry had unwittingly sanctioned in advance many of the tenets enunciated in Wordsworth's preface to *Lyrical*

---

1. Stuart M. Tave's *The Amiable Humorist* (Chicago, 1960), which surveys comic theory of the eighteenth and early nineteenth centuries, clearly demonstrates what meager attention Romantic critics paid to Burns's humorous treatment of love.

Ballads (1800), so too his portrayals of comic love anticipated theories of subsequent analysts and, consequently, have become increasingly meaningful in the light of critical doctrines articulated after his practice.

As Romantic critics saw it, the dichotomy between humor and wit inherited from the eighteenth century constituted one of the basic cleavages between neoclassicism and their own aesthetic of natural sensibility. In his introduction to *Lectures on the English Comic Writers*, Hazlitt made the distinction explicit: "Humour is the describing the ludicrous as it is in itself; wit is the exposing it, by comparing or contrasting it with something else. Humour is, as it were, the growth of nature and accident; wit is the product of art and fancy." [2] Whereas wit, being contrived and generally derisive, was considered the province of the mind, humor, being natural and empathic, belonged essentially to the heart. Similarly De Quincey, when he attempted to popularize Richter's philosophical theories on the comic, carefully emphasized the distinction between wit as "a purely intellectual thing" and humor as a phenomenon that brought into play "the *moral* nature" involving the will, affections, and temperament. [3] Humor in Richter's creative works, according to De Quincey, was interwoven with pathos, his gentle satire characterized by smiles rather than by scornful laughter. Subsequently Carlyle, who had assimilated much of the comic psychology in Richter's *Vorschule der Aesthetik* (1804), demeaned the irony and caricature of neoclassical satirists to a position conspicuously lower than that of humor. "True humour," Carlyle explained in his second essay on Richter, "springs not more from the head than from the heart; it is not contempt, its essence is love; it issues not in laughter, but in still smiles, which lie far deeper." [4] Through a kinship with sensibility, therefore, the ultimate justification of humor resembled that for human love: it helped unite man with mankind.

Despite objections from purists who preferred their emotions and their genres unalloyed, the analogy of love and humor was generally endorsed by Romantic critics as a valid precept for life, as well as art. Even the delicate question of whether the heart was capable of sympathetic laughter was argued affirmatively by Lamb, who differentiated between "the petrifying sneer of a demon which excludes and kills Love" and "the cordial laughter of a man which implies and cherishes it." [5] By laughing *with* rather than *at* humanity, one might enjoy himself while heightening his benevolent proclivities. And if humor was produced by what was universally comic, laughter, especially from a man sufficiently perceptive to associate the ludicrous with traits in himself, could prove highly edifying. Keats, in the letter that evolves his principle of imaginative identification, selfless sympathy, and suspended judgment known as "negative capability," significantly progressed toward this doctrine from a statement praising the superiority of humor over wit.[6] As Keats realized, humor enabled an imaginative understanding whereby one was made to *feel* rather than (as in wit) to *start*. Furthermore, the artistic advantages of humor were seen to rest on valid psychological grounds. As both De Quincey and Carlyle pointed out in their respective analyses of Richter, humor prevented sensibility from deteriorating into maudlin sentimentality. However serious the emotion of love might be, a touch of the comic — what Bergson in his essay *Laughter* defined as "a momentary anesthesia of the heart" — contributed to a healthful perspective. The conjunction of active and passive, far from annihilating one another, restored a sane equilibrium appropriate to the Romantic goal of unified sensibilities. By its very nature life was seen to be full of incongruities, paradoxes, and frustrations imposed by mundane limitations. Yet if the dominant principle of life was (like that of its creator) love, then the force striving for unity with the infinite tended to transcend finite limitations. Hence the juxtaposition of finite and infinite, which Richter postulated as the true source of humor, contributed to the desired totality of existence.

The soundness of Romantic insight, striving for the union of reason, sentiment, intuition, and imagination, was later confirmed by professional psychologists. Sigmund Freud, who endorsed many of the Romantic theories on the comic derived from Richter, demonstrated that levity, however pleasurable, was an earnest matter, especially when it involved "broken" humor "that smiles through tears."[7] Subsequent psychologists have also explained the compatibility of love and humor in their own terms

2. "On Wit and Humour" (1818), *The Complete Works of William Hazlitt*, ed. P. P. Howe (London, 1930–34), VI, 15.

3. "John Paul Frederick Richter" (1821), *The Collected Writings of Thomas De Quincey*, ed. David Masson (Edinburgh, 1889–90), XI, 270.

4. "Jean Paul Friedrich Richter" (1827), *The Works of Thomas Carlyle*, ed. H. D. Traill (London, 1896–99), XXVI, 17.

5. "On the Genius and Character of Hogarth" (1811), *The Works of Charles and Mary Lamb*, ed. E. V. Lucas (London, 1903–1905), I, 86.

6. *The Letters of John Keats*, ed. Hyder E. Rollins (Cambridge, Mass., 1958), I, 193. Subsequent references to Keats's letters appear in the text.

7. *Jokes and Their Relation to the Unconscious* (1905), *The Standard Edition of the Complete Psychological Works of Sigmund Freud*, tr. and ed. James Strachey (London, 1953–64), VIII, 232.

without seriously disrupting Romantic concepts. While love is customarily associated now with the integrative or self-transcending tendency and the comic spirit with the self-assertive, human emotions are usually mixed. Love, in all except its hypothetically pure instances, is sufficiently ambivalent to include some of the self-assertive. Sexual love, particularly in regard to masculine behavior, contains enough of the aggressive to invite forms of the comic that are indeed far less sympathetic than humor. Nor does laughter provoked by such instances undermine the essential seriousness, for the emotions meet on common ground.

Yet exactly how much of prevalent theory on comic love Burns was consciously aware of is difficult to ascertain. It seems likely, however, that he may have been acquainted with one of the longest treatises on the comic spirit, that by the Scottish philosopher-poet James Beattie, whose poems and essays Burns greatly admired.[8] Continuing the traditions first popularized by Addison and Steele (and later by Sterne), Beattie, in his "Essay on Laughter and Ludicrous Composition" (1776), claimed that laughter arising from innocent mirth was not only therapeutically desirable but also indicative of a benevolent, rather than a spiteful, nature. Moreover, he predicted a genre of which Burns was to become the chief poetical exponent. "As romantic love in its natural regular procedure is now become so copious a source of joy and sorrow, hope and fear, triumph and disappointment," Beattie asserted, "we might reasonably conclude, that in its more whimsical forms and vagaries it could scarce fail to supply materials for laughter."[9] His views on the *vis comica* were essentially standard, even though his terminology differed somewhat from that of other aestheticians and his specific definitions perhaps did not indicate rigid classification.[10] *Wit* he described as the "unexpected discovery of resemblance between ideas supposed dissimilar" — a kind of *discordia concors* such as Dr. Johnson saw in metaphysical analogies. *Humor* Beattie identified with the "comic exhibition of singular characters, sentiments, and imagery." Yet he certainly divided the comic spirit into two categories according to the responses it evoked: the *ridiculous* arousing contempt or disapproval, and the *ludicrous* producing an uncomplicated, risible emotion. This latter reaction was brought about by the pleasant awareness of inconsistencies — often in an unusual mixture of similarity and contrariety. As the "Essay" further analyzed it, innocent laughter could be purely "animal" if occasioned by tickling or sudden gladness and "sentimental" when it proceeded from feeling or sentiment. Since theories such as these were already

6

formulated, Burns, who was especially sensitive to the incongruities of certain character traits in particular situations, had only to put the sentimental comic into practice.

Before fully understanding Burns's treatment of "romantic love," however, one must recognize that to him sexual attraction was the most compelling justification for existence. Complete gratification in love became virtually synonymous with the pursuit of happiness; and from this basic premise, which colored all he had to say about love, stemmed the related attitudes expressed throughout his poetry. Associated from the beginning with poetic inspiration, this "delicious Passion," as he explained to Dr. John Moore, was held "to be the first of human joys, our dearest pleasure here below." [11] His most celebrated affirmation of loyalty to the eternal feminine, "Green grow the Rashes," declares that lasses alone compensate for the anxieties of life.[12] Dividing humanity into those with hearts and those without, Burns vows his preference for the simple joys of making love, one of the few inalienable rights of the poor. The basic distinction between the "warly race" obsessed with respectability and those who respond to the gadflies of feeling appears in several other poems, especially the "Epistle" to William Logan (I, 300–302), which contains the poet's expression of sincere delight in womankind: "I like them dearly; / God bless them a'!" Obviously Burns does not assume that a man's love need be confined to one girl. In opposition to grave Calvinistic strictures condemning earthly joys, he cites scriptural (and therefore irrefutable) authority that Solomon, traditionally the wisest of men and devotee of infinite variety, "dearly lov'd the lasses." Carrying matters a step further in poems contributed to *The Merry Muses of Caledonia*, Burns is often very explicit, sometimes by means of clever metaphors, about the unsurpassed pleasures women afford sexually. Obversely, as lines from "To J.

8. In addition to several references to Beattie's poems, he alludes to the "Essay on Truth" in "The Vision" (ll. 171–74) and was presumably acquainted with the "Essay on Poetry and Music" (*The Letters of Robert Burns*, ed. J. DeLancey Ferguson [Oxford, 1931], II, 148). Since the "Essay on Laughter" was often printed with Beattie's other essays, Burns probably knew it.

9. *Essays* (London, 1779), p. 438.

10. *Essays*, pp. 301–305, 380–83.

11. *Letters*, I, 108.

12. *The Poems and Songs of Robert Burns*, ed. James Kinsley (Oxford, 1968), I, 59–60. All subsequent references to Burns's poetry cite volume and page of this edition.

S****" (I, 178–83) indicate, he characterizes the loss of physical love as the worst blight of senility, depriving man of his greatest joy.

Quite logically, a belief so devoutly affirmed had to be translated into practice, and many of Burns's poems celebrate the following of natural inclination — a precept he advocated most convincingly from the masculine viewpoint. Despite some admissions, as in the "Epistle to a Young Friend" (I, 248–51), that illicit affection hardened the heart and petrified the feelings, he usually assumed that the most ardent flames of love ought to be kindled immediately because they were too often of short duration. Hence he advised his brother William: ". . . try for intimacy as soon as you feel the first symptoms of the passion." [13] Somewhat like his bard in "Love and Liberty" (I, 206), Burns usually regarded it a mortal sin to thwart divinely implanted instinct. Being a man entailed fulfilling the obligations of manhood, and whoever shirked them was not entitled to the name. In an attempt to refine a coarse original of his song "The Taylor" (II, 872–73), Burns implies this argument as explanation for the central character's behavior. Whereas in the earlier version the tailor sadistically took advantage of a sleeping maiden, in Burns's humorous redaction he attains his goal through ingratiating charm. (This alteration itself indicates how the poet frequently softened the harsh original without radically changing its import.) The profession of Burns's tailor provides him with nothing more than an entrée; his real vocation is that of a lover who "kend the way to woo." In one choice line the poet laconically sums up all that is indelicate in the earlier account, adds what is needed to conclude the anecdote, and comments on the action: "The Taylor prov'd a man O."

A much richer psychological treatment of this theme appears in the song "Had I the wyte" (II, 842–43). A man obviously disturbed by his recent excursion into adultery tries to allay his conscience by repeated questioning whether he ought to be blamed for his actions. Part of the humor no doubt stems from the transposition of customary roles in love — of an aggressive Lady Booby plotting the seduction of a relatively passive Joseph Andrews. But the crowning achievement in the lyric is the speaker's unwitting revelation of his own naïveté and his unwillingness to admit that the married woman had actually manipulated him. Knowing that he would not wish his valor impugned, she had shrewdly called him "a coward loon" for his reluctance to enter her house. Then perceiving his vanity and susceptibility to pity, she complained of how cruelly her absent husband treated her and thereby threw all the blame for her own actions upon a tyrannical spouse. What indeed could a sympathetic young man do but comfort and console her? In retrospect he protests:

> Could I for shame refus'd her;
> And wad na Manhood been to blame,
> Had I unkindly us'd her. (II, 842)

After performing his duty, he reveals some uncertainty about true manly behavior by recounting that on the following morning he tried to drown his compunction in brandy, though he continues to solicit our comforting assurance that he was not the one to blame.

A somewhat different aspect of the problem is reflected in many of Burns's autobiographical poems that poignantly describe the suffering inflicted by conventional morality on natural deeds of love. The concept of vice as a virtue carried to excess was difficult for him to comprehend when the virtue was love and when others of his acquaintance seemingly enjoyed the pleasures without concomitant pains. Nevertheless, his overall attitude was remarkably consistent in that he not only followed masculine instinct but also assumed all the parental responsibilities that his encompassing affection and limited financial means could provide. The pathos tinged with humor in poems concerning his own difficulties with unplanned parenthood no doubt reveals his mixed reactions. Probably the best illustration occurs in "A Poet's Welcome to his love-begotten Daughter" (I, 99–100), which concedes his great delight upon first becoming an illegitimate father. Assuring his child by Elizabeth Paton that she is just as welcome as though she had been invited, he tenderly addresses her as "Sweet fruit o' monie a merry dint" (I, 100).

Not even the pains attendant on illegitimacy could diminish the swaggering bravado he assumes in a few of his poems celebrating propagation of bastards. One reason for such boasting on his part was undoubtedly the private masculine audience to whom such poems were initially addressed. Furthermore, his defiance of ecclesiastical authorities, who in some cases had been no better than he, for the penance and fine they imposed upon him could best be expressed with mocking raillery. Though in "A Poet's Welcome" he merely disclaims any objection to being called "fornicator," he boldly asserts his right to that distinction in "The Fornicator" (I, 101–

13. *Letters*, I, 332.

102). That Burns sincerely believed he had been made to suffer excessively is clear from his repeated comparison of himself to Biblical "men of God," who achieved ultimate salvation despite rather cavalier attitudes toward the seventh commandment. King David and King Solomon, both famous as poets and adulterers, provided him with choice illustrations of sexual energy as the true manifestation of vitality. In "Robert Burns' Answer" (I, 278–80), a devil-may-care poem regarding his own ill repute, the poet argues that even though he may give women's "wames a random pouse," the manly sport of fornication should not call down great abuse from men who admire King David as one of the "lang syne saunts." Burns then concludes with a fanciful tale, the true index of his indignation, about how he made fools of the Kirk Session that assessed punishment for his transgression. According to this account, the defendant candidly admitted he would never be any better unless he were gelded; and the minister, perhaps on the analogy that an offending eye ought to be plucked out, immediately endorsed amputation of whatever proved to be a "sp'ritual foe." But instead Burns facetiously recommended putting the offending part under the guidance of the lass — a suggestion that pleased the Session "warst ava" and ended the interview.

The autobiographical poem that even the most devoted followers of Burns sometimes find difficult to justify is the "Epistle to J. R******" (I, 61–63), with its elaborate metaphor of game-poaching. First must be remembered, however, the character of the individual for whose enjoyment it was originally intended. The opening lines of the "Epistle" characterize its recipient as "rough, rude, ready-witted R[ankine]," a man apparently well known for his rowdy festivities and exposés of hypocritical clergymen. Hence the principal anecdote was especially appropriate. Then too, the tradition of witty comparisons was so well established in Scottish vernacular poetry that Burns's analogy of poaching and promiscuous love-making would not have appeared so derogatory to the woman as it may seem today. As Burns put it,

> 'Twas ae night lately, in my fun,
> I gaed a rovin wi' the gun,
> An' brought a *Paitrick* to the *grun'*. (I, 62)

Indeed many of Burns's poems employ metaphors, such as ploughing, threshing, playing the fiddle, filling the bowl, and shooting wild birds, that were common in the Scottish tradition long before he used them. Thus in the poem addressed to Rankine the implied comparison of his affair with Elizabeth Paton, the servant girl who bore his first child, to shooting down a partridge that did not rightfully belong to him and consequently having to pay a guinea's fine in the Poacher-Court (Kirk Session) ought to be regarded as a clever and natural treatment of the subject. If it reveals a sportive flippancy toward the begetting of bastards, it is nevertheless distinct from mere locker-room braggadocio. By connecting two of the most primitive survival drives in man — hunting for food and gratifying the sexual impulse — it atavistically reveals a basic masculine desire to make a sportive pleasure of necessity.

Nevertheless, Burns's depiction of young girls who have unwisely yielded to the rapture of love shows highly sympathetic insight, sometimes mixed with restrained masculine humor, into their various plights. Portraying them without ridicule or sentimentality, he accepts their condition as an unfortunate though natural consequence of love. The "sleepy bit lassie" in "The Taylor fell thro' the bed" (II, 509) naïvely thought the tailor could do her no harm, and indeed he gave her such satisfaction that now she longs for his return. Slightly graver complications have ensued for the girl in "To the Weaver's gin ye go" (I, 382–83), who laments the loss of her happiness for granting more than her heart to a weaver lad. Though reluctant to tell what occurred, she now fears that information will soon become increasingly obvious to everyone. But the subtlest and perhaps most appealing characterization of such a girl appears in the first set of lyrics entitled "Duncan Gray" (I, 393). Whereas her friends can still enjoy themselves, she now has the cares of unintentional motherhood, which she with half-hearted jocularity blames on the bad girthing. While she and Duncan were riding a horse on Lammas night, she recalls, the girthing broke, and one fall followed another. Now she wistfully hopes that Duncan will keep his oath so that all (including the bad girthing) may be rectified. Also from the feminine point of view, "The rantin dog the Daddie o't" (I, 184) expresses the anxieties of an unwed, expectant mother who seeks assurance that Rob, the rollicking father of her child, will assume his paternal obligations. Quite understandably she finds it difficult to joke about her very serious plight, and adding to the embarrassment is her realization that she has taken in earnest what had only been poked in fun.

Burns's songs about courtship are also rich in portraits of charming young girls who, tempering good humor with common sense, know what they want and cleverly overcome obstacles to their goals. An outstanding example is the lass in the song "O whistle, and I'll come to ye, my lad" (II, 700–701). Since there seems to be parental objection to her lover, she gives him explicit instructions on how to reach her without letting anyone else know. And though she wants him to ignore her publicly, she nevertheless insists that he is not to court another, even in jest, for fear he may accidentally be enticed away. In "Last May a braw wooer" (II, 795–96) a girl less in control of the situation pretends to be virtually inaccessible and, to her dismay, almost loses the young man to a rival. With cunning, however, she proceeds to win him back and reveals her dissembling nature even in her public reasons for marrying him — not for her own sake but, ironically, just "to preserve the poor body in life." Especially winsome is the maiden in "I'm o'er young to Marry Yet" (I, 384), who pleads with her suitor that at her tender age and as her mother's only child she is psychologically unprepared for marriage. But unwilling to reject his proposal completely, she suggests that should he come again next summer she will be older and perhaps ready to reconsider.

Timidity in men, on the other hand, is a topic rarely mentioned by Burns. Significantly, in his gallery of lovers the traditionally humorous bashful young men are almost nonexistent. He did, however, compose to the tune of "The Bashful Lover" lyrics entitled "On a bank of Flowers" (II, 514–15), portraying a lad who is shy only at first. Having chanced upon lightly clad Nelly asleep among summer flowers, Willie begins by merely gazing and wishing; but when she awakes and flees in terror, he presumably overcomes his initial hesitancy and overtakes her in the woods.

The most despicable variety of courtship in Burns's view was that which hypocritically aimed at marriage for money, and he was particularly scornful of men offering themselves as marketable commodities. "There's a youth in this City" (II, 525–26) pokes fun at a handsome, elegantly attired young man in search of a wealthy girl to marry. Several prospects with commendable fortunes are eager to have him, but actually he loves none of them so much as himself. A thoroughly cynical attitude toward the transience of feminine beauty is satirized in the song, "Hey for a lass wi' a tocher" (II, 808–9), in which a man extols woman's wealth as her only enduring attraction. Without denying the witchcraft of youthful beauty, he brazenly expresses his preference for a lass with "acres o' charms." Of course, shallow-hearted girls may also prefer silver to love.

Meg o' the mill, in the second set of lyrics concerning her exploits (II, 689), foolishly jilts a desirable miller for a repulsive but rich laird. In all these instances, as in Burns's poems of social protest, wealth is deplored as a corrupting influence.

Comedy of a more playful sort is produced by refining the natural instinct of courtship into sophisticated skill — such as the fine art of seduction. In "Extempore — to Mr. Gavin Hamilton" (I, 236–37), a poem that strips the ornamental tinsel from many seemingly important matters and shows them as trivial, Burns relates how he applied the same technique to a female Whig. Her initial refusal to have faith in a poet, as well as his exalted reference to "Her whigship," arouses our antipathy toward a pretentious woman who deserves to be not only corrected but leveled. The poet's adroitness in the game of "love for love's sake" is so great that, despite her inevitable objections while they "grew lovingly big," he taught her "her terrors were naething." Burns concludes:

> Her whigship was wonderful pleased,
>   But charmingly tickled wi' ae thing;
> Her fingers I lovingly squeezed,
>   And kissed her and promised her — naething. (I, 237)

Whatever the consequences, seduction might be regarded as a challenging sport in which each of the two individuals, while abiding by the rules of the game, fulfills his prescribed part.

By transposing the customary roles of male and female, as Thurber has often done in our day, Burns provided another rich source of the comic, well exemplified in "Wha is that at my bower door" (II, 616–17). In the original song the woman is blatantly aggressive whereas the man is meekly compliant. In Burns's version, the woman, though less conniving, is still manipulator of the action and puts up only token resistance to letting her lover, Findlay, in. He, on the other hand, understands his obligations: he must argue until she deludes herself into thinking that, against her better judgment, his rhetoric has overwhelmed her. These pretenses are clear from the dialogue; the girl introduces in conditional clauses exactly what she ought to fear while Findlay counters with his assurance that each condition will be fulfilled. When he promises to abide by her last stipulation — never to tell what may transpire in her bower — there is no longer any need for him to remain outside.

Burns was also interested in burlesquing artificial conventions of court-ship in his second set of lyrics entitled "Duncan Gray" (II, 666–68). When he sent the words of this song to George Thomson, he observed that the melody "precludes sentiment" and that "the ludicrous is its ruling fea-ture." [14] Both Meg, with the proud disdain of a courtly lady, and Duncan, with his lachrymose despair verging on suicide, so overplay their roles that they achieve the comic of exaggeration. Excessive sentimentality in Duncan, however, produces its own reaction, for he banishes affectation by realizing the absurdity of dying for "a haughty hizzie." As he recovers his health, Meg, discovering how much his love had meant to her, grows ill pining for him. The fact that Duncan is "a lad o' grace," as well as a shrewd psychologist trained in Scottish common-sense philosophy, permits all to turn out well. Pitying Meg, who suffers as he himself once lan-guished, he demonstrates his true worth by magnanimously refusing to cause her death. The guarded manner in which he accepts her indicates he has learned a very practical lesson in amatory psychology: nothing is quite so attractive as casual indifference.

Perhaps because of the limited range of possibilities inherent in the sub-ject, Burns rarely approached the comical aspects of married love with the geniality and compassion required of true humor. In writing of domestic situations, he easily turned from humor to satire, and it should not be sur-prising that the preponderance of marriage poems are, by their very na-ture, sharply succinct and often epigrammatic. This antipathy toward the marital state, revealed with varying degrees of aggressiveness in the ma-jority of his poems treating comic love, is exactly what one should expect. According to Freud's analysis, no institution in our society has been more carefully guarded by accepted morality or more vulnerable to attack than the connubial relationship.[15] The prevalence of cynical jokes deriding wed-lock as bedlock illustrates the unconscious antagonism which men in partic-ular feel toward rigid suppression of sexual liberty. Since this hostility can be temporarily freed from the unconscious by means of some clever wit-ticism — a "pleasure premium," that enables us to laugh at what we revere — tendentious wit aimed at marriage momentarily overcomes what-ever inhibitive power exists and permits us to enjoy a release of aggres-sion, often quite contrary to what our sober thoughts might recommend. Burns's practice would indeed tend to support Freud's theory. Regarding marriage as a mixed blessing, he was not able, as he admits in "Yestreen I had a pint o' wine" (II, 555–56), to resign himself wholeheartedly to its restraints. Yet his ability to identify imaginatively with either opponent in marital warfare not only relieved him of acerbity but permitted him, usually with the verbal economy of an excellent raconteur, to turn even the worst situation into a good joke.

One group of his poems about marriage emphasizes the change which a husband feels has occurred in his wife since their wedding. Stanza vi of "Extempore — to Mr. Gavin Hamilton" (I, 236) cogently points out how during courtship the lover sparkles and glows when "Approaching his bonie bit gay thing," but after the irrevocable ceremony he learns he has acquired a dressed-up "naething." The unfortunate man in "O ay my wife she dang me" (II, 881–82) has suffered considerably; yet there is something admirably winning about his resignation to fate. Though the peace and rest he anticipated in marriage were never realized, at least he has the consolation of knowing that, after enduring "pains o' hell" on earth, he is assured of bliss above. The husband in the justly admired "Whistle o'er the lave o't" (I, 434–35) has also had his hopes shattered, but through an amazing humor born of torment he seems to be chuckling while cataloguing his woes. All that he had associated with Maggie before the wedding has now changed to its antithesis, and but for fear Maggie would find out, he would even name the one he wishes were in her grave. Implying far more than he expresses, he refrains from elaborating on each unpleasantness and turns it into jest by whistling about what cannot be altered. No doubt the evasive and suggestive quality that makes him a fascinating conversationalist also renders him a most exasperating husband to a shrew.

A considerable number of marriage poems are concerned less with mutability than with exposing and ridiculing an intolerable wife. In so doing, they also reveal the curious relationship between the shortcomings of one spouse and the weaknesses of the other. For example, in "The Henpeck'd Husband" (II, 909) Burns expresses the belief that a vixen is partially the fault of a spineless, fearful husband who deserves reproach rather than pity. The anomalous situation would never occur if the husband of such a woman wisely subdued her by breaking either her spirit or her heart. The efficacy of such action is demonstrated in "My Wife's a wanton, wee thing" (II, 512), in which the man expresses doubt concerning his licentious wife's ability to behave unless she is controlled as a

14. *Letters*, II, 135.
15. *Jokes*, p. 110.

child ought to be ruled — namely, by the rod. Perhaps the only suffering husband who genuinely elicits our pity, however, is the one in "Kelly-burnbraes" (II, 644–46). There the unfortunate man yields his termagant wife to the devil, who thereupon discovers her to be more than a match for him and his demons. Upon returning the shrew to earth, the devil admits that he had never been truly in hell until he acquired a wife.

Among several poems that disparage the husband without particularly ennobling the wife, some make light of the essentially serious affliction of impotence in advanced age. The young woman in "What can a young lassie" (II, 607–8) temporarily evokes our sympathy with complaints about her peevish, jealous old husband until she reveals her plan to torment him to death and then use his "auld brass" to buy herself a "new pan." The subject receives an almost poignant treatment in "The deuk's dang o'er my daddie" (II, 652–53), where acrid hostility between the lusty wife and her incapable spouse is mixed with remembrance of happier bygone days and nights. Two of Burns's songs deal with an equally old marital jest, cuckoldry, but they do so in a manner characteristic of his humor. The women of "O an ye were dead Gudeman" (II, 835) and "We'll hide the Couper" (II, 848–49) are openly and defiantly committing adultery with their lovers while their husbands do nothing but resign themselves to their proverbial horns. Though some compassion is naturally directed toward the poor, helpless cuckolds, the comic pleasure derived from these two lyrics stems less from a debasement of the husbands than from our fascination with the hussies' brazen determination to satisfy their desires.

Burns could hardly write of love without relating it humorously to another of his chief delights, John Barleycorn, which he recognized as a true, though unscrupulous, liberator of psychic energy. In some instances alcohol could demean its imbiber to such a ludicrous state that he became excellent material for mordantly satirical, aggressive comedy. Especially when associated with Calvinistic moral attitudes, as in "Holy Willie's Prayer" (I, 74–78), tippling served to accentuate what Burns considered the irreconcilability of canon law with man's instinctive nature. Willie's anthropomorphic concept of God — capriciously unjust, vindictive, and incapable of love — reveals the speaker himself. Since his sexual drive is wholly identified with proscribed pleasure, what Burns would have called human love can never be anything but lust in Willie Fisher, who ironically justifies his own promiscuity by pleading drunkenness. Also in "The Holy Fair" (I, 128–37) a perversion of what ought to be the celebration

16

of divine love in a communion service is allied with alcohol and lechery. Superstition and hypocrisy in the preaching tent combined with careless fun in an adjacent tavern justify the poet's attack on the Scottish Kirk — a corruption of faith that ideally should be characterized by good deeds, sincerity, and love. Hence he comments ironically on the man who, by letting his hand wander over the bosom of his lass during a sermon, makes a mockery of both religion and human love. As the scene moves to the tavern, he portrays a predominant mood of lechery whereby liquor alters Venus Uranus into a lusty pandemic lass. Thus what began with a hard-hearted religion leads, through the stimulation of drink, to a parody of love — "houghmagandie."

With less satire and far greater humor, Burns treats the bibulous freeing of emotion more sympathetically in "Tam o' Shanter" (II, 557–64). Just as good Scotch drink presumably released Burns's thoughts and feelings for poetical composition, so too it heightens Tam's amiability toward both Souter Johnie and the landlady, causing him to postpone his return to a hostile, sullen wife. Unfortunately it later contributes to his admiration for an attractive witch dancing lustily in a sark so short that it barely covers, and as a result Tam is momentarily deprived of rational control. Quite unconsciously he roars out the ingenuous praise that almost undoes him. With mock-serious didacticism, Burns in the conclusion warns that the path leading from alcohol to lecherous contemplation often culminates in disaster. The negative moral lesson is, of course, a variant of the admonition in a classic naughty story pertinent to mice and ardent men. Because Tam loses his head to drink and a "cutty sark," his mare is bereft of her tail.

An entirely different attitude toward the combination of love and alcohol is found in "Love and Liberty" (I, 195–209), often published as "The Jolly Beggars." Its characters, who have a simple, intuitively acute perception of man's nature, possess no inhibitions whatever and accept the basic instincts without any concern for what is ordinarily called ethical standards. What might in polite society be condemned as obscene is from their point of view perfectly normal. Indeed the comedy of this cantata, which is universally considered Burns's masterpiece, verges on what Freud analyzed as the naïvely comical — the effect often produced in adult listeners by the spontaneous, forthright comments of children.[16] The poet's

16. *Jokes*, pp. 182–88.

sympathy with (and at times even undisguised envy of) a segment of humanity usually thought beneath contempt is just as sincere as the beggars' irrepressible and appealing candor. Had these uninhibited outcasts been deliberately attacking institutions of the society they rejected, then some of their satirical jibes might be considered tendentious wit: the reader would have to assume that through enticement of comic pleasure they were trying to elicit his hostility against principles which he had been conditioned to respect unquestioningly, despite an unconscious dislike.[17] There are indeed occasional touches of such wit in their oblique comments on marriage, respectability, legality, and religion, particularly in the Merry Andrew's song and the final chorus; yet these bits of aggression are casually tossed off at inhabitants of a world having little contact with theirs. The supremely winning quality of the beggars is their belief in both love and liberty not in the negative sense of revolt against restraint but rather as positive virtues. The old soldier and his doxy, both of whom enjoy their present indulgence in love and drink rather than the exploits of their former military careers; the professional Merry Andrew who admits to being a fool; the female pickpocket whose Highland lover died on the gallows for defiance of Lowland laws; the small fiddler who proposes cohabitation with the pickpocket; the bold tinker who offers himself to the same "unblushing fair"; the bard who, resigning himself to the loss of one mistress because he has two others left, sings in praise of free love and freely flowing drink — all reveal in an unsophisticated way their refusal to be duped by the hypocritical cant of society.

There is something wonderfully refreshing, as Burns himself acknowledged in his commonplace book, about associating with such people.[18] Though their actual deeds may be no better than those of respectable friends, the beggars' mental attitude is more appealing because of its unpretentious honesty. They spontaneously express by both precept and example what all of us know intuitively but have been taught to renounce. The occasional intrusion of artificial diction on their vernacular, to which many critics have objected, subtly reminds us of conventional society's attempt to veneer their basic propensities; yet the beggars remain essentially loyal to all that is natural in humanity. They have indeed achieved the "happy state" described in one of Burns's favorite quotations: ". . . when souls each other draw, / When love is liberty, and nature law" (Pope's "Eloïsa to Abelard," ll. 91–92).[19] Especially when we compare the beggars' adherence to their own code of behavior with the contrasting failure of society to abide by its ethical standards, we realize the supreme humor with which the poet conceived his work.

There were inevitably nineteenth-century critics who let Burns's personal frailties and artistic improprieties prejudice their estimates of his achievement. Yet among the most objectively perceptive, his extraordinary ability to fuse the seemingly heterogeneous elements of love and comedy by means of uniquely incisive humor did not go wholly unnoticed. Lamb, who was quick to recognize in Burns some qualities he himself possessed, observed "a jocular pathos, which makes one feel in laughter." [20] After reading a collection of Burns's unpublished letters, Byron remarked: "What an antithetical mind! — tenderness, roughness — delicacy, coarseness — sentiment, sensuality — soaring and grovelling, dirt and deity — all mixed up in that one compound of inspired clay!" [21] Carlyle, equally aware of these paradoxes, especially stressed "the tenderness, the playful pathos" and perceived that the principle of love which characterized Burns's poetry "occasionally manifests itself in the shape of Humour." [22] Aside from the drollery associated with caricature, Carlyle claimed for Burns "in his sunny moods, a full buoyant flood of mirth" related to his ability to be a "brother and often playmate to all Nature." To emphasize this extraordinary ability Carlyle especially cited those poems expressing a fellow feeling with animals, presumably because mice, mares, and sheep would seem the most difficult creatures with whom a love poet could imaginatively identify himself. And while some genteel critics regarded his subject matter as crudely unpoetical, Matthew Arnold thought Burns had provided a genuine criticism of life, ironic though it was.[23] Despite a revulsion from "Scotch drink, Scotch religion, and Scotch manners," Arnold stressed the "overwhelming sense of the pathos of things" and singled out for illustration of particular merit those works

17. *Jokes*, pp. 90–119.
18. *Robert Burns's Commonplace Book 1783–1785*, ed. James C. Ewing and D. Cook (Glasgow, 1938), pp. 7–8.
19. See *Letters*, I, 8; II, 271. Cf. also Pope's *Essay on Man*, III, 207–8.
20. Letter of 20 March 1799 to Southey, *The Letters of Charles and Mary Lamb*, ed. E. V. Lucas (London, 1935), I, 152.
21. Journal entry for 13 December 1813, *The Works of Lord Byron: Letters and Journals*, ed. Rowland E. Prothero (London, 1898–1901), II, 376–77 — hereafter cited as *LJ*.
22. "Burns" (1828), *Works*, XXVI, 283.
23. "The Study of Poetry" (1880), *The Works of Matthew Arnold* (London, 1903–1904), IV, 32–40.

he especially admired. Strangely enough, all that he selected dealt humorously with love. If such poems lacked the requisite high seriousness that excluded their author from the Victorian Valhalla of poetical heroism, it was because Burns (like Chaucer, with whom Arnold repeatedly compared him) believed that many serious observations on life could be uttered more effectively in jest than in grave solemnity.

CHAPTER II

From Wit to Irony
in Byronic Comedy

W HEN MODERN CRITICS following in the wake of T. S. Eliot belabor the Scottishness of Byron's poetry, they frequently reiterate what was obvious to many nineteenth-century commentators. But whereas Eliot saw in him even a physical resemblance to Sir Walter Scott, his only popular rival, Byron himself acknowledged that (among many less palatable comparisons) feuilletonists had often likened him, both poetically and personally, to Burns.[1] Quite significantly, moreover, that similarity was given unqualified endorsement by Sir Walter Scott in a manuscript note printed by E. H. Coleridge: "Burns, in depth of poetical feeling, in strong shrewd sense to balance and regulate this, in the *tact* to make his poetry tell by connecting it with the stream of public thought and the sentiment of the age, in *commanded* wildness of fancy and profligacy or recklessness as to moral and *occasionally* as to religious matters, was much more like Lord Byron than any other person to whom Lord B. says he had been compared."[2] In Scott's opinion the supposed difference between

1. See Byron's entry of 15 October 1821 in "Detached Thoughts," *LJ*, V, 407–8. For Eliot's essay on Byron (1937), see *On Poetry and Poets* (1967), pp. 223–39.
2. *LJ*, II, 376*n*. On 27 January 1822 Byron wrote Sir Walter: "I was bred a canny Scot till ten years old" (*LJ*, VI, 5).

peasant and peer did not exist when, in their moments of true greatness, they acted as poets. Similar views were expressed in one of the outstanding literary journals, the *London Magazine*, soon after Byron's body had been returned to England for burial. In an essay entitled "Robert Burns and Lord Byron," Allan Cunningham, who knew both men personally, drew several illuminating parallels between them and judiciously balanced the two poets as contrasting but essentially kindred products of his native land.[3] Whether the similarities between the two men are attributable to Scottish ancestry or to like environments (most of Byron's first ten years having been humbly spent in Aberdeen) may remain debatable. Yet they were undeniably the only Romantic poets who could smile and even jest at love without demeaning its extraordinary importance.

Probably more explanatory of their comparable attitudes than accidents of blood or background is the fact that both men, being handsome and having relatively low resistance to sexual temptations, actually experienced the intense physical passions described in their poems. A profound understanding of love they regarded as the only basis for accurate representation of it in their literary productions; and since faithful delineation meant more to them than polished craftsmanship, they in all likelihood would have rejected Yeats's dictum that man's intellect must choose between "Perfection of the life, or of the work." Moreover, both Burns and Byron realistically acknowledged the inexorable shortcomings of earthly affection without invalidating its intrinsic merit. For them love was eternal, not because it defied alteration but rather because of its infinite adaptability to new objects of attachment: the essence remained though successive affairs embodying it were shattered. The only reprehensible violation of their amatory code, whether induced by hypocrisy or vanity, consisted of being false to one's genuine emotions, for eros could not survive the fragile passion cementing two people. Consequently both poets accepted with good humor the instinctive propensities of man much more readily than the idealistic schemes for overhauling him, and they inevitably regarded whatever violated "the natural" as an endless vein of comedy. Both tacitly assumed that any valid study of affection had to begin with an acceptance of humanity in the raw, irrespective of ethos. But instead of ridiculing man, as earlier traditions of raillery had done, for not living up to his ideals, they directed their scorn toward whatever attempted to remake him into what he was not. The butt of their jokes therefore became not the individual unable to conform but those people or institutions refusing to concede the truth about human existence. The hostility toward artificial restraint which these poets expressed was equal to their tolerance of unaffected mankind.

Despite their use of similar ingredients, Burns's approach differed from Byron's notably in shifted emphases and different settings. Burns's comedy, according to contemporary terminology, was largely that of humor; Byron's was by virtue of its aggressiveness essentially wit. Instead of developing the comic as a natural outgrowth of character, as Burns had often evolved it, Byron achieved some of his finest accomplishments by portraying an individual against a particular milieu in which manners, morals, and situations provided the ludicrous materials. Much of this divergence, however, may also have stemmed from their different backgrounds. Whereas Burns's comical treatment of love sprang largely from the vernacular poetry of Scotland, Byron's came primarily from the more sophisticated neoclassical tradition of England. The influence of Pope was predominant in Byron's early satires, though it diminished as he grew older — fortunately so, since he lacked the frame of absolute moral standards essential to a clear-cut distinction between what *is* and what *ought to be*. In the most mature Byronic irony (and particularly that treating love) the *vis comica* arose chiefly from the discrepancy between reality and what is pretended about it. No doubt Fielding, with his emphasis upon affectation as the only true source of the ridiculous, and Sterne, with his sympathetic understanding of human foibles, contributed to this development, for both were perennial favorites of Byron. Furthermore, the drama of sensibility, as well as Shakespeare's comedies, demonstrated that mirth and gravity might be successfully interlaced. This hybrid genre had indeed accepted both laughter and tears as valid means of sensitizing the heart, and while eschewing bawdry, it justified its existence by adding the leaven of comic artificiality to the sour dough of morality. *The Rivals*, from which Byron never tired of quoting, showed that seemingly antipodal attitudes toward love could be placed side by side without obliterating one another. Moreover, the unusual popularity of the English pantomime, which could transform stories as tragic as those of Dr. Faustus and Don Juan into diverting afterpieces for the London stage, indicated that theatrical audiences favored the amalgamation of satire and

3. 10 (August 1824), 117–122. Cf. *Don Juan*, X, 16–19. See also Leslie A. Marchand, *Byron: A Biography* (New York, 1957), III, 1168.

sentiment. With increasing maturity Byron proved that humor need not be the only romantic adaptation of the comic spirit: even irony in the temperate climate of sensibility might be softened by humanitarian sympathies.

Impervious though Byron generally was to critical theory, his personal library contained (as evidenced by the 1816 sale catalogue) two books that might, if he studied them, have given him insight into the psychology of laughter.[4] From the first of these, Lord Kames's *Elements of Criticism* (1805), he could have gleaned little for his particular use except perhaps the distinction between the ludicrous (the playful), the risible (the mirthful), and the ridiculous (the mirthful which is also contemptible). His subsequent attempt, noted in the Ravenna journal of "Detached Thoughts" (1821), to recollect what Kames had written about the power to "call up agreeable ideas" suggests at least a hazy remembrance of that work.[5] The other book, Richard Payne Knight's *Analytical Inquiry into the Principles of Taste* (1808), is much more likely to have made an impression because Byron was personally acquainted with its author. With the bold conviction that he was indeed an arbiter of infallible taste, Knight had in his last major division, entitled "Of the Passions," devoted an entire chapter to close scrutiny "Of the Ridiculous," which the young Byron might have found both congenial and practical. Though Knight had initially defined laughter very much in the Hobbesian tradition as "an expression of joy and exultation" arising primarily from a kind of triumphant malignity, he also made concessions to the age of sentiment by admitting that there existed a modicum of "sympathy in joy, as well as in sorrow — in laughter, as well as in tears." Comedy he thought most successful when it united incongruities that degraded man's natural character. Furthermore, in keeping with the fashionable contemporary view, he declared that "the usual and principal action of all comedy" was love. Though he conceived both wit and humor to be dependent upon ingenious recognition of similarity in the essentially dissimilar, *wit* as he defined it was displayed in images and ideas, *humor* primarily in manners. What he asserted about the "mock heroic" reflected not only the idolatry of Pope surviving in conservative literary circles but also a thoroughly unromantic explanation of the comic spirit; for in his opinion that popular neoclassical genre was ludicrous chiefly because it deflated whatever was exalted.[6]

Byron, however, was constitutionally opposed to overschematized systems (as evidenced most clearly by his ridicule of Hunt's) [7] and bothered little about the whys and wherefores of aesthetic response. Since his own life demonstrated the compatibility of love and the comic spirit, he chose from the beginning to model his art directly upon personal experience. And though his first volume of poetry, *Fugitive Pieces* (1806), contained many graceful compliments to those who had received his friendship and youthful love, it also reflected a sentimentally callow preoccupation with affections so transient as to invite occasionally flippant treatment. In a way that curiously foreshadows virtually all his satires on human emotions, one of his juvenilia reveals an aggressive tendency less toward passion at its zenith than toward the artificial conventions threatening its dissolution. The poem "To a Lady Who Presented to the Author a Lock of Hair Braided with His Own, and Appointed a Night in December to Meet Him in the Garden" is presumably addressed to the same girl whose extraordinary beauty he previously extolled in the lines "To Mary, on Receiving Her Picture." Though he had been content to adopt the inherited traditions of society verse in his earlier tribute to her, the progress of their love affair had so altered his perspective that he saw his originally idealized inamorata as material for an exciting roll in the hay. The inconvenience to which this "courtly" lady wished to subject him, simply because she had high-flown notions of amatory behavior, invited his trimming ridicule. He argued that, since their affections were "fix'd," they need not indulge in the usual claptrap of sighing, whining, and pretending jealousy "Merely to make [their] love romantic." Lydia Languish's silly weeping, to which he compared hers, was after all calculated to be ludicrously affected. And though an Italian garden might be an appropriate trysting place for lovers like Romeo and Juliet, an English garden in December was frigid enough to stifle ardor. Why should they not meet in a warmer season or inside? In the first edition Byron recommended: "Oh! let me in your chamber greet you" and subsequently in that original version: "There if my passion fail to please, / Next night I'll

4. See William H. Marshall, "The Catalogue for the Sale of Byron's Books," *The Library Chronicle*, 34 (1968), 24–50. The two items are #214 and #215.

5. See *LJ*, I, 123; V, 459. Another copy of Kames's work was in Byron's library in Pisa when Leigh Hunt arrived in 1822 (*Lord Byron and Some of His Contemporaries* [Philadelphia, 1828], p. 45).

6. *Analytical Inquiry into the Principles of Taste* (London, 1808), p. 414.

7. *LJ*, IV, 237.

be content to freeze." [8] It was indelicate sentiments such as these to which his mentor, the Rev. J. T. Becher, objected sufficiently to urge suppression of Byron's first collection. Pallid though such indiscretions now seem, they show their young author not only an enemy of literary affectation but from the start a hard-nosed realist determined to cut through obfuscations and delve to the bottom of things.

Not until the poet, in the fashion of neoclassical satirists, had developed a ludicrous situation in *The Waltz* (1813) did he create a comedy of manners suitable for giving the lie to social pretenses. Yet that work lacks both the commitment to an ethical norm required of successful satire and the detachment essential to irony. It fails ultimately because there is no set of values to which the author is attached and from which vantage point a volley of righteous artillery might be issued. Certainly Augustan satirists would have condemned Byron's shifting attitude; for through his persona, he seemed to endure, then pity, and ultimately embrace what he initially disliked. In so doing, Byron revealed that he was more naturalist than satirist, and his spokesman proves to be a latent opportunist who assails the waltz only until he himself discovers its possibilities. Hence the reader, deprived of any positive stance, must accept the decline and fall of virtually everyone in three-quarter time. Even if the poem's goal was fundamentally aesthetic rather than ethical, the poet would have to be taxed with tonal inconsistency. Beyond Byron's concession that it was "in the old style of *English Bards, and Scotch Reviewers*" [9] (as though he had outgrown hit-and-run couplets), *The Waltz* lacks the epigrammatic wit and mordant satire distinguishing his earlier work and in addition fails to develop the coherent, sustained situation expected in a more mature composition.

Probably the poem's only successful ingredient is the personage who introduces himself through the prefatory epistle. This fascinating character, whom Byron employed to express his ironic view, has excellent potential for satirizing love in Regency society. He is a type well established in both the novel and the drama — a booby squire whose very name, Horace Hornem, immediately suggests cuckoldry. He explains in the prose letter that after fifteen years of marital bliss on the family estate he was persuaded to take his family to London for a social season largely because his daughters had reached "a marriageable (or, as they call it, *marketable*) age." No doubt the reader is initially meant to sympathize with the pleasantly simple man, who explains that his not-so-country wife

26

does not permit him to ride inside the barouche, that place being reserved for her gallant. Consequently we share his dismay at first seeing his wife, formerly adept at the sedate minuet, being whirled around by a strange partner at the Countess of Waltzaway's ball. The country gentleman did not then understand what even a city child knew—that the excuse for this unbridled intimacy was called "valtzing." The revolving dance permitting couples to embrace familiarly had during his absence from town become the rage. Whatever his initial aversion may have been, he soon learned after trying it himself how easily an insular prejudice against a foreign import can be overcome by its pleasure, and that, if the waltz is not intoxicating delight in itself, at least it may serve as prelude to something beyond. By his own admission, he has succumbed to the fashionable vogue and is discovering its hitherto unfathomed opportunities, having four times overturned his wife's maid while practicing. In acknowledgment of his debt, he has addressed to the waltz, unlawfully begotten daughter of Terpsichore, an "apostrophic hymn," which is the sketchy poem that follows his prose account.

With these highly piquant ingredients for unmannerly comedy, Byron's failure to develop a unifying story or a consistent moral stance for his satiric paean is disappointing. The best a reader can do is enjoy Hornem's lascivious observations and Byron's clever phrases. As the author points out through his persona, the muse Terpsichore, "too long misdeemed a maid," must, if she is indeed mother of the waltz, have lost her former chaste modesty. Certainly the daughter has none, for in plain sight of all this personified dance offers her bosom "and bids us take the rest." The squire, in the fashion of a confirmed libertine, then pays his devoirs to the seductive lady as one of several German imports such as Rhenish wines, defaulted debts, bowel-rousing literature, and "royal blood." He praises her as an inebriator of the heart, an aphrodisiac to the body, and the key to eugenic improvement. Her chicanery in the ballroom provides the same opportunities for the *beau monde* that the tavern near Mauchline parish church affords Burns's Ayrshire hedonists in "The Holy Fair." The voluptuous dance has broken down inhibiting barriers between the sexes and

---

8. See the textual notes in Ernest Hartley Coleridge's edition of *The Works of Lord Byron: Poetry* (London, 1898–1903), I, 37–38. With the exception of *Don Juan*, all subsequent citations of Byron's poetry are from this edition, hereafter referred to as *Poetry*.

9. *LJ*, II, 176.

becomes an excellent means of achieving desired ends — whether advantageous marriage or promiscuity. Patronized by the Prince as though she were an uncouth German princess, the waltz has become the very symbol of Regency womanhood. Then Byron, temporarily stepping from behind his spokesman's mask, preaches against both the amoral (who are cheapening what they expect to enjoy) and the moral (who are inadvertently prostituting what they hold most dear) for abetting public intimacy. Only in the final stanza, in a vain attempt to wrest unity out of chaos, does the poet as country squire return to adulation of the waltz as a means of assuring one's own lineal descendants in the heirs of friends.

When Byron succeeded in shedding the cant that had encrusted his own publicly espoused ethics (particularly after the collapse of his marriage and sanctimonious attitudes of erstwhile friends toward his disgrace), he was ready for an ironic approach to life — one that might incorporate the double standard. He became increasingly fascinated with juxtaposing two contrary perspectives without making one prevail over the other, since the comic aspect, deriving chiefly from the discrepancy between the two, brought out the inherent pitfalls of each. Though his satiric barbs were reserved for truly deserving follies, his over-all *Weltansicht* grew more sympathetic and mellow in a country tolerating his own peccadillos. The gossipy letters he wrote John Murray and other morally liberal friends about sexual license in Italy no doubt prompted his publisher to request "a good Venetian tale describing manners." [10] In response Byron complied with *Beppo: A Venetian Story* (1818), depicting from his dual perspective some of the interesting sociological features of Adriatic mores. Neither condemning nor condoning the dissolute standards of a city long reputed to be the wickedest in Christendom, he chose rather to accept for rhetorical purposes the established norms of Venice as background for incisive commentary on universal human nature.

The idea that considerations of love took precedence over all others in the lives of Italian women intrigued Byron, who had readily availed himself of the opportunities such ethics afforded. As he wrote Tom Moore on 25 March 1817: "The perversion, not only of action, but of reasoning, is singular in the women. It is not that they do not consider the thing itself as wrong, and very wrong, but *love* (the *sentiment* of love) is not merely an excuse for it, but makes it an *actual virtue*." [11] Byron's research as a comparative sociologist further convinced him that man is not by inclination monogamous and that the Italians, to prevent misogamy, had wisely allowed for occasional aberrations into innocent adultery. As Byron explained the accepted rules to Murray, "a woman is virtuous (according to the code) who limits herself to her husband and one lover; those who have two, three, or more, are a little *wild*; but it is only those who are indiscriminately diffuse, and form a low connection . . . who are considered as overstepping the modesty of marriage." [12] What Byron considered particularly healthy about this arrangement, in strong contrast to English furtiveness, was the absolute candor with which these relations were publicly countenanced. Having himself formed a passionate connection with Signora Marianna Segati, he was amazed at "the frank undisguised way in which every body avows everything in this part of the world." [13] Thus subterfuge and hypocrisy, through which unregularized attachments have traditionally been undermined, had in Venice been eliminated, to the obvious improvement of societal happiness.

As a comparatively detached narrator in *Beppo*, Byron dropped the false prudishness of *The Waltz* and showed that human nature throughout the world differed only in the superficial variations imposed by custom or niceties of terminology. It was primarily the ability to distance himself from mundane profligacy that allowed both an objective overview and seemingly impartial commentary. In the relatively carefree, chatty manner learned from Frere's *Whistlecraft* and its Italian precursors, he accepted the world on its own terms, pretending all the while to be a front-row spectator at life's drama but not a member of the cast. The ludicrous aspects of his sketch he constantly enriched by subtly hinting at the discrepancy between pretension and reality. For this purpose the *ottava rima* stanza was ideally suited since, within the compass of only eight lines, it permitted an exaggerated elaboration of the romanticized façade to be placed beside the disarming, often disillusioning, truth. In this mode of ironic comedy Byron became the undisputed master, usually by overdistending the fragile bubble for six lines and then deflating the frail illusion with a piercing couplet. He realized, as Freud was later to maintain, that man derives great pleasure from seeing others unmasked since there is something delightfully comical in the exposure of sham. [14] And all of

---

10. Samuel Smiles, *A Publisher and His Friends* (London, 1891), I, 372.
11. *LJ*, IV, 81.
12. *LJ*, IV, 40.
13. *LJ*, IV, 41.
14. See *Jokes*, pp. 201–2.

Beppo is a *ridotto* or masquerade in which, one by one, the masks are removed.

The scene opens with Byron's mock-serious elucidation that in Roman Catholic countries inhabitants enjoy their *divertissements* to excess before the abstinence of Lent, knowing they can buy repentance thereafter with self-denial. Consequently the Venetian carnival, a "farewell to carnal dishes" before resignation to "ill-dressed fishes," shows how a surfeit of indulgence leads to ascetic renunciation or how the worst sinner may be converted to abstemious sainthood. With pretended naïveté, however, the poet explains this phenomenon as a shallow *ingenu* of the polite world might be expected to understand it — as a parting drink with friends — though he clearly understands the deeper psychological implications. Especially during this season the extraordinarily attractive Italian women know how to incite love, beginning with glances that culminate in what prudes call "adulterous beds." But such puritanism has no real meaning in the context of this setting. Though Venetian wives are just as eager to maintain the appearance of honor as they were in Shakespeare's time simply by hiding dishonorable deeds, modern husbands, quite unlike Othello, would never "suffocate a wife no more than twenty, / Because she had a 'Cavalier Servente'" (17:7–8). A contemporary Italian husband confronted with Othello's problem would have solved it easily by taking another wife "or *another's*." Much of the poem's carnival atmosphere depends upon a tolerance of this casual laxness toward marital infidelity or at least an offhand suspension of judgment. Such revels, Byron appears to say, could happen only during the pre-Lenten festivities of Venice, where even the symbolic gondola, a floating love nest free from prying eyes, permits no end of concealed pleasure when its blinds are drawn. Thus the narrator establishes so firmly the mood for lascivious delight that when he resorts to occasional mock-heroic didacticism, the reader knows precisely how to interpret his tongue-in-cheek exaggerations.

This long preamble might have been superfluous had the central character's own hectic life just before her husband's return not been the illuminating parallel to the carnival. Like her native city, Laura is of a "certain age" and amazingly resistant to temporal ravages. Fortunately, too, she is married (not to the sea but to a merchant named Beppo), for in Christian countries minor indiscretions of wives are viewed more leniently than those of single ladies. While her husband was still in evidence, friends deemed her "a woman of the strictest principle,/ So much as to be thought almost invincible" (26:7–8). Only veiled hints about the couple's true, but unexpressed, sentiments at his last departure suggest that their devotion is not what they pretend publicly, for the narrator in recalling the almost too pathetic farewell (in which both had a presentiment that he would never return) suggests that all partings ought to be equally sad — but rarely are. Thus while Laura knelt upon the shore, Beppo left his "Adriatic Ariadne" (28:7–8), and this allusion to Theseus' unjustified desertion of his beloved aligns all our sympathy with the forsaken wife. Indeed Laura studiously acts like a mourning widow disconsolate over her loss — until she takes a lover or, as the narrator unsentimentally calls him, "a vice-husband." Of course, she dares not admit to accepting the successor for personal gratification but rationalizes that some "daring housebreaker or sprite" could possibly harm her if she did not take on a man "*chiefly to protect her.*" As a human watchdog, he is therefore established in her home "in all the rights of wrong." [15] The coxcomb count whom she selects for the domestic vacancy is in every sense a man "of great liberality" (where pleasure, rather than money, is concerned) and naturally is meant to perform his office only until Beppo shall return. Though popular opinion is against him, he pleases Laura by satisfactorily fulfilling his functions. [16]

Upon this liaison Byron focuses in order to analyze comically the institution of *cavalier servente*, essentially a carnival of adultery within prescribed bounds. Venetian frankness about the desire for sexual variety — a subject that Shelley, Browning, and Dickens dared to treat only under the protective veil of ambiguity — received Byron's enthusiastic endorsement. The convenient arrangement made by Laura and the count has lasted six years without serious estrangement (as such liaisons sometimes endure), though they naturally have experienced the inevitable petty differences of cohabitation. Their bond is held by chains too slight to be worth breaking, and in such a state they are "As happy as unlawful love could make them" (54:2). Laura, whose name (as Andrew Rutherford asserted) may have been ironically selected to suggest the quite different

---

15. For Venetian anecdotes involving cicisbeism and infidelity, see *LJ*, IV, 26–28.

16. That Byron himself grew somewhat weary of servitude to the Countess Guiccioli can be seen in his letter of 3 October 1819 to Hobhouse (*LJ*, IV, 357).

woman idolized by Petrarch,[17] is superbly suited to the relationship because she is a sophisticated married woman who "knows the world," pleases by being absolutely natural, and therefore among connoisseurs of amatory sport is preferred to immature young girls. The count's qualifications for his job are impeccable:

> His heart was one of those which most enamour us,
> Wax to receive, and marble to retain:
> He was a lover of the good old school,
> Who still become more constant as they cool. (34:5–8)

Though moderately ridiculous in some minor details — something is radically amiss with a man deemed a hero by his own valet — he performs even his menial duties without whimper; as supernumerary slave or kept gentleman he obeys unquestioningly every word his mistress utters. So well established is this institutionalized relation in tramontane countries, the narrator informs us, that "no one notices or cares a pin."

The truth is, of course, that despite a difference in public attitudes toward such affairs, the custom is equally common in England, though no dignifying term for it exists; and the poet ironically moralizes: "But Heaven preserve Old England from such courses!/ Or what becomes of damage and divorces?" (37:7–8). In the permissive atmosphere of Venice no such legal blights can result, although Laura's envious female friends think it

> quite amazing
> That, at her time of life, so many were
> Admirers still, — but "Men are so debased,
> Those brazen Creatures always suit their taste." (67:5–8)

The return of Beppo disguised as a philogynous Turk provides opportunity for contrast between Turkish enslavement of women and their so-called emancipation in England — to the unequivocal detriment of the latter. Though the practice of having "Four wives by law, and concubines 'ad libitum'" seems barbaric, the poet shows the superiority of naturally simple women in the harem to the liberated but obnoxious English bluestockings with their affected presumptions. To the narrator the harem woman represents the unlost golden age of innocent youth ("old Saturn's reign of sugar-candy"), to which he drinks not in the appropriate beverages of "Milk and Water" but in brandy, which will effect the closest approximation to paradise now possible. The liberal-minded Beppo, whose fabulous oriental experiences have further broadened his view, does not completely destroy the Venetian lovers' Eden, though obviously his reappearance does spell the end of a cozy domestic arrangement. In his quietly masterful way, he proves to be extraordinarily tolerant, and despite Laura's peevishness at his unexpected arrival, he and the count remain permanent friends. Thus recognition of basic physical necessity results not only in comic exposure of those who pretend that such requisites do not exist but also an implied praise of a society wisely providing loopholes where such apertures are beneficial. Like the anecdote of Colonel Fitzgerald's twenty-five-year devotion to another man's wife and his ultimate recompense, it is a "moral tale" because virtue (in Byron's though not in Richardson's sense) has been rewarded.[18]

The supreme achievement of Romantic love in the comic vein is, of course, interspersed throughout *Don Juan*. The full characterization of a narrator, however inconsistently he may step in and out of his own story, creates an additional dimension that enriches Byronic humor, for it allows the poet to be objective and subjective by turns, to show cloaked reasons contrasting with unconsciously valid ones, and to depict not only the façade but also what lies behind it. Beneath his own pretended flippancy about all values esteemed by civilization runs an undercurrent of seriousness, and the discrepancy between the tone of the narrator and what he conveys is another source of comic strength. Despite occasional savagery, the work is partly in the tradition of Romantic humor because it unites those seemingly antithetical elements contributing to empathic understanding. Rejection of supposedly incompatible contraries in an artistic production was, according to Byron, a narrow-minded negation of real life, which demanded reconciliation of opposites as the prerequisite of survival. In response to the strictures of Murray's friend Cohen, who was

17. *Byron: A Critical Study* (Edinburgh and London, 1965), p. 119n. That the unattainable Laura of Petrarch was generally accepted as the Romantic ideal of untarnishable love is seen in references to her in Rousseau's *Nouvelle Héloïse*, Godwin's *St. Leon*, and Mrs. Radcliffe's *Mysteries of Udolpho*. Byron's famous attempt to deflate her image appears in the couplet: "Think you, if Laura had been Petrarch's wife,/ He would have written sonnets all his life?" (*Don Juan*, III, 8:7–8).
18. See *LJ*, IV, 27.

jarred by the sudden oscillations between "fun and gravity" in *Don Juan,*
Byron replied:

> His metaphor is, that "we are never scorched and drenched at the
> same time." . . . Did he never play at Cricket, or walk a mile in hot
> weather? Did he never spill a dish of tea over his testicles in handing
> a cup to his charmer, to the great shame of his nankeen breeches? Did
> he never swim in the sea at Noonday with the Sun in his eyes and on
> his head, which all the foam of Ocean could not cool? [19]

What distinguished it from other "epics," Byron asserted, was its faithfulness to reality such as only a cosmopolite could depict. Hence he demanded
of his friend Douglas Kinnaird:

> It may be profligate but is it not *life*, is it not *the thing*? Could any
> man have written it who has not lived in the world? — and tooled
> in a post-chaise? — in a hackney coach? — in a gondola? — against
> a wall? — in a court carriage? — in a vis à vis? — on a table? —
> and under it? . . . I had such projects for the Don, but Cant is
> [so] much stronger than C*** now-a-days, that the benefit of ex-
> perience in a man who had well weighed the worth of both mono-
> syllables, must be lost to despairing posterity.[20]

Byron's earliest reference to *Don Juan* describes it as "ludicrous (*à la
Beppo*)"; soon afterwards he explained that his intention was "to be a
little quietly facetious upon every thing" and later that the work was
"never intended to be serious" but merely "a playful satire." [21] Yet English reviewers, reflecting the growing trend toward propriety, condemned
its lasciviousness and blasphemy of all that should have been held sacred.
Though lewd verse (such as the "most correct" Alexander Pope wrote for
his intimate coterie) had never ceased to be read in England, poetry
aspiring to artistic recognition was generally expected to adhere to an exalted moral tone. However pallid Byron's improprieties may seem to modern readers nurtured by drugstore paperbacks, one has only to read the
first reviews of *Don Juan* to understand contemporary revulsion from its
amorality. We may recall Richard Woodhouse's spinsterish fear that his
friend Keats had affected "the 'Don Juan' style of mingling up sentiment
& sneering," as well as the embarrassingly frank depiction of love, in "The
Eve of St. Agnes." [22] As he informed Keats's publisher John Taylor,

Woodhouse had already warned the poet that Porphyro's fulfillment of "all the acts of a bonâ fide husband, while [Madeline] fancies she is only playing the part of a Wife in a dream" would "render the poem unfit for ladies, & indeed scarcely to be mentioned to them among the 'things that are.'" Byron might have explained the feminine aversion to such matters, as indeed he accounted for Teresa Guiccioli's detestation of his masterpiece, by asserting: ". . . it arises from the wish of all women to exalt the *sentiment* of the passions, and to keep up the illusion which is their empire. Now *Don Juan* strips off this illusion, and laughs at that and most other things. I never knew a woman who did *not* protect *Rousseau*, nor one who did not dislike de Grammont, Gil Blas, and all the *comedy* of the passions, when brought out naturally." [23] It must have given him incalculable delight to hear from the publisher Galignani that by 1823 *Don Juan* was selling twice as well as any other of his works — especially among women.[24] Defending the ethical import of his poem chiefly on the grounds that true morality cannot thrive under the shadow of self-deception, he staked his counters on the judgment of posterity.

But his main objection was not to women who asserted its offensiveness (Lady Caroline Lamb, Augusta Leigh, and Lady Byron professed absolute horror) but to prurient men who, while savoring every spicy tidbit, objected to its publication. And none drew his venom any more than Murray's professional advisers — that "cursed puritanical committee" or "back-shop synod," as he contemptuously called them.[25] With Browning, he might have replied, "*de te, fabula*," but instead he responded by protesting (perhaps too much) that it was "the most moral of poems." [26] Nor are these assertions contradictory when one recalls his dictum that "There is no sterner moralist than pleasure" (*Don Juan*, III, 65:8). The outline

---

19. Letter of 12 August 1819 to Murray (*LJ*, IV, 341). Omissions in Prothero's text are supplied from Marchand's MS. transcription (*Byron*, II, 807).

20. Letter of 26 October 1819, *Byron: A Self-Portrait*, ed. Peter Quennell (London, 1950), II, 491. Omissions in Quennell's text are supplied from Marchand's MS. transcription (*Byron*, II, 823–24).

21. Letters of 10 July, 19 September 1818, and 12 August 1819, *LJ*, IV, 245, 260, 343.

22. *The Letters of John Keats*, II, 163.

23. Letter of 6 July 1821 to Murray, *LJ*, V, 321.

24. See letter of 9 April 1823 to John Hunt, *LJ*, VI, 192.

25. See *LJ*, IV, 279; V, 32–33.

26. Letter of 1 February 1819 to Murray, *LJ*, IV, 279.

of the work designed for Murray's benefit reveals that the episodes were planned to lead his central character down an amatory "primrose path" to "the everlasting bonfire":

> I meant to have made him a *Cavalier Servente* in Italy, and a cause for a divorce in England, and a Sentimental "Werther-faced man" in Germany, so as to show the different ridicules of the society in each of those countries, and to have displayed him gradually *gâté* and *blasé* as he grew older, as is natural. But I had not quite fixed whether to make him end in Hell, or in an unhappy marriage, not knowing which would be the severest. The Spanish tradition says Hell: but it is probably only an Allegory of the other state.[27]

Morality prevailed because poetic justice would, one way or another, ultimately be done. Though the work incorporated enough "siege, battle, and adventure" to give it epic stature and excitement, the tentative plan, as well as the actual accomplishment, shows how much it was intended to be a comedy of love.

But as even the biographically oriented critics have had to concede, not all of *Don Juan* is modeled upon Byron's escapades or the irrefutable activities of acquaintances. And though Byron's reading has been carefully examined, especially by Elizabeth French Boyd, in order to analyze the ingredients of his comic epic, attempts to connect that work with an evolving tradition of Don Juan literature have ultimately ended in failure. Despite Byron's assertion in the opening stanza that his "hero" is to be associated with the pantomime figure of that name (I, 1:6–8), scholarly efforts to identify a specific *dramatis persona* have merely lengthened footnotes without casting new light upon his immediate ancestry. Literary and operatic antecedents that might have begotten Byron's most famous character have been meticulously scrutinized, but most of them have proved so dissimilar to Juan that, unless he is dismissed as a biological mutation, the poor fellow's paternity remains very much in doubt. Hence scholars have ordinarily concluded that Byron was determined either to present a startlingly original treatment or, if he had more than a superficial acquaintance with the old Spanish legend, to be utterly disrespectful of tradition.[28] What they have overlooked is the development during 1817 of a comic but lovable Don Juan figure in minor productions of the London stage, and some of the extraordinary delineations may have provided the self-exiled poet with suggestions for his handling of the legendary

Spaniard. One of these theatrical depictions, a Harlequin Don Juan, was probably the immediate progenitor of Byron's character.

In addition to Charles Anthony Delpini's operatic pantomime entitled *Don Juan; or, the Libertine Destroyed: A Tragic Pantomimical Entertainment in Two Acts*, which Byron might have seen or even read while still in England, there were at least three anonymous Don Juan pantomimes that had been licensed and performed in London during this period.[29] One of these significantly included, as embellishment to the serious plot, some of the characters derived from the *commedia dell'arte*. In particular, the enlarged role of Scaramouch, Don Juan's servant, embodied much of the comedy assigned to the traditional Italian clowns of that name just as their boisterous German counterpart, Hanswurst, was often cast as the Don's attendant in German redactions of the story. Byron's friend Joseph Grimaldi became the most famous of all English pantomime clowns and, largely as a result of his Italian heritage, elaborated the "harlequinade" portion of the pantomime chiefly to display his own virtuosity. He played Scaramouch in one such version of *Don Juan*, described as "the tragic pantomimic ballet," that opened at the new Covent Garden Theatre on 20 November 1809.[30] The adaptation that Jane Austen saw at the Lyceum on 14 September 1813, during one of her visits to London, must have been in the same tradition of including a memorable clown as the Don's servant; for after writing her sister that in the last of "three musical things" Juan had been "left in hell at half past eleven," she noted that the work had both a "scaramouch and a ghost."[31]

This juxtaposition of the ludicrous and the serious in theatrical presen-

27. *LJ*, V, 242–43. Herein Byron also suggested the possibility of Juan's being guillotined during the Reign of Terror.

28. See E. H. Coleridge's introduction in *Poetry*, VI, xvi; Elizabeth French Boyd, *Byron's Don Juan* (New York, 1958), pp. 35–39; Leo Weinstein, *The Metamorphoses of Don Juan*, Stanford Studies in Language and Literature, No. 18 (Stanford, 1959), pp. 79–82; and *The Theater of Don Juan: A Collection of Plays and Views, 1630–1963*, ed. Oscar Mandel (Lincoln, Nebraska, 1963), pp. 11, 21, 447–48. G. B. Shaw, in his "Epistle Dedicatory" to *Man and Superman*, swept Byron's character aside as "only a vagabond libertine" and declared Mozart's to be "the last of the true Don Juans."

29. Allardyce Nicoll, *A History of English Drama, 1660–1900* (Cambridge, 1952–59), III, 325.

30. *Memoirs of Joseph Grimaldi*, ed. "Boz" (Charles Dickens) and rev. Charles Whitehead (London, 1846), II, 73, 81–84, 106–7.

31. *Jane Austen's Letters*, ed. R. W. Chapman (London, 1952), pp. 321, 338.

tations initially characterized Italian treatments of the legend, and Mozart's version fell very definitely within this tradition, for its librettist, Lorenzo da Ponte, had no qualms about adding occasional elements from the *commedia dell'arte*, particularly in the second act of *Don Giovanni*. Furthermore, as musicologists have repeatedly observed, Mozart himself acknowledged this conjunction of tragedy and comedy not only in his musical score but also in his designation of the opera as a *dramma giocoso*. Thus the Don Juan legend, as it evolved pantomimically and operatically, was not all sobriety but often alternated with outright buffoonery. As in Marlowe's *Dr. Faustus* (the pantomimic adaptation of which became extraordinarily popular on the London stage), comic and tragic scenes, far from canceling out one another, dramatically brought each other into bold relief. In fact, the comic subplot often provided sly commentary as a distorted reflection of the tragic development. Yet prior to Byron's departure from England in April 1816, there had apparently been no attempt to fuse the two plots.

In his day, as indeed for more than a century afterwards, the undisputed center for pantomime in London was the Drury Lane Theatre, on whose Sub-Committee of Management Byron served during his last year in England. Theatrical notices show that, from the first, adaptations of the Don Juan legend were particularly associated with that company, though of course numerous other pantomimes were performed there during Byron's intimate acquaintance with its productions. Its Christmas pantomime, incorporating the traditional harlequinade characters in an extravagant spectacle, was annually an outstanding event. In one of these, *Harlequin and Fancy; or, the Poet's Last Shilling*, Byron himself performed. As he noted years later in his journal, he and his friend Douglas Kinnaird had put on masques and joined the "hoi polloi" in the masquerade scene of Drury Lane's Christmas pantomime for 1815 in order "to see the effect of a theatre from the Stage."[32] What especially fascinated Byron about their participation as supernumerary dancers was that both of them had taken part in the original masquerade given in 1814 by "'us Youth' of Watier's Club to Wellington and Co.," of which the Drury Lane enactment was only theatrical mimesis. This pantomime, which gave Byron a first-hand acquaintance with the relation of stage illusion to reality, was written by his old friend and Drury Lane associate Thomas Dibdin as a light encore complementing the substantial drama of the evening, Lillo's *George Barnwell*, which was customarily performed on December 26 before drunken, holiday-spirited audiences as a moral lesson to the dissipated. Like Christmas pantomimes in England even to this day, it incorporated speaking, singing, dancing, burlesque, satire, allusions to contemporary events, and sentiment — all strung upon the slender framework of a preliminary "opening" and an elaborate "harlequinade."[33]

But generally the pantomime, despite its growing popularity among theater-goers of all ages, tended to be looked down upon by intellectuals as the small beer of theatrical beverages.[34] Indeed many sophisticated reviewers completely ignored such productions, and Leigh Hunt was obviously endangering his critical reputation when he defended his "great predilection" for them in two articles in the *Examiner*, 5 and 26 January 1817 (pp. 7, 57). Although comedy had virtually ceased to be written, pantomime, he asserted, "flourishes as much as ever, and makes all parties comfortable; it enchants the little holiday folks; it draws ten-fold applauding thunder from the gods; it makes giggle all those who can afford to be made giggle." Furthermore, he claimed that pantomime, infused as it was with "animal spirit," had become "the best medium of dramatic satire." His analysis of how the principal characters of the harlequinade developed on the English stage provides one of the best contemporary accounts and is also a reliable index to the prevailing interest in comic love. Whereas in Italian productions Harlequin had been merely a "servant, messenger, or other person in low life," through English elevation he became "always a lover who has eloped with his mistress, and this gives him a tastier and pleasanter air with us, while it not only leaves him all his activity, but gives him every possible reason for it. Activity indeed at least shares his passion with love. He is the perpetual motion personified. . . . Who does not wish such a fellow success with his mistress, and see moreover that he must gain it?" Columbine, whose name signifies "little dove," remained approximately what she had been on the Italian stage — a sprightly servant; according to Hunt's execrable diction, she was a "fit companion for that vivacious fugitive, and an epitome of all that is trim and chaceable."

32. *LJ*, V, 444. Byron acknowledged that he had been compared to both Harlequin and the Clown (*LJ*, V, 408).

33. See *European Magazine*, 69 (1816), 51–52, 92, 149.

34. Some of this condescension is reflected in a perceptive comment written by Lady Caroline Lamb. Fearing that *Don Juan* would irreparably harm Byron's reputation as a serious poet, she asserted that Edmund Kean could not impair his own reputation more if he played the role of Harlequin (*LJ*, IV, 366*n*).

Pantaloon, the dull old gentleman cast as her father and unsuccessful protector, was inevitably found less entertaining than the Clown, Scaramouch, who by aiding Harlequin and frustrating Pantaloon tended to steal the comic show. Grimaldi, through his extraordinary talents, had not only established himself as the unrivaled Clown but had also enlarged that role. In Hunt's estimate then, the Harlequin pantomime had successfully entrenched itself in English hearts by its three outstanding features — bustle, variety, and sudden change.

Nicoll's lists of pantomimes performed during this period show that Hunt was far from alone in his admiration, and theatrical notices in the *European Magazine* demonstrate that Don Juan pantomimes were quite popular on the London stage even before 1817, when the extraordinary vogue of Mozart's *Don Giovanni* injected new life into the old legend. Having attended both of the first two London performances of *Don Giovanni* at the King's Theatre on 12 and 15 April, Hazlitt wrote an unusually long review for the *Examiner* of 20 April (pp. 252–54).[35] Though unconvinced that the opera's plot merited its popular comparison with Shakespeare, he readily conceded that its music was delightful. His view of Mozart's contribution, in keeping with the contemporary notion that the pleasant melodies generally lacked tragic depth, is curiously reminiscent of Hunt's analysis of the English harlequinade and suggests how Mozart's treatment could be assimilated into pantomimic productions: "The personal character of the composer's mind, a light, airy, voluptuous spirit, is infused into every line of it; the intoxication of pleasure, the sunshine of hope, the dancing of the animal spirits; the bustle of action, the sinkings of tenderness and pity, are there, but nothing else."

The immense popularity of Mozart's work inevitably spawned not only new productions of the old pantomimes but some unusual burlesques. Following Cumberland's *Wheel of Fortune*, Covent Garden on 20 May 1817 presented a new afterpiece entitled *The Libertine*, which Isaac Pocock had based on Shadwell's dramatic treatment of the Don Juan story and augmented with Italian arias and background music directly from Mozart's opera. According to Hazlitt's review in the *Examiner* for 25 May (pp. 331–32), it was a complete failure, from which only Mozart's incomparable music emerged triumphant. What was extraordinary about this adaptation and of particular interest to the study of Byron is that Charles Kemble, who played the title role in Pocock's musical drama, took unprecedented liberties with the interpretation of Juan's character. He went through his usual exploits of seduction, according to Hazlitt's account, not with exulting wickedness but, rather, "evident marks of reluctance and contrition." Therefore it seemed highly unjust to the reviewer that a man so well meaning and so obviously the victim of female circumstance should be "forced into acts of villainy against his will." Moreover, that diabolical fiends with flaming torches should claim him "as their lawful prize" appeared a gross violation of poetic justice. What did favorably impress Hazlitt was "an exquisite device of the Managers, superadded to the original story" — namely, "a splendid car brought to receive him by the Devil, in the likeness of a great dragon, writhing round and round upon a wheel of fire." The whole production, very much in the harlequinade tradition, was undoubtedly a cross between a burlesque frolic and an operatic extravaganza.

According to the theatrical reviewer of the *European Magazine* for May, Covent Garden's revival of *The Libertine*, as well as "immense houses" drawn by Mozart's *Don Giovanni*, prompted the Royal Circus and Surrey Theatre to announce an unusual work described as "A New Comic, Heroic, Operatic, Tragic, Pantomimic, Burlesque Burletta Spectacular Parody, under the title of *Don Giovanni; or, a Spectre on Horseback*" (LXXI, 441–42). The popularity of this mongrel performance, at a theatre particularly famous for its comic burlettas and melodramatic romances under the direction of Thomas Dibdin, invited further debasement after its first appearance on 26 May. As the reviewer for the *European Magazine* described the situation in October, "The success of *Don Giovanni* has induced the performers to take it severally for their benefits — and the principal characters have been changed almost with every evening's entertainment" (LXXII, 357–358). Virtually all performers in the cast, including the two leading women, had at one time or another impersonated "the amorous spark," so that Dibdin's burlesque was indeed burlesqued. Yet the greatest novelty was apparently a transvestite performance in which Mrs. Brooks (ordinarily the Donna Anna) played Don Giovanni and an actor named Fitzwilliam (customarily the Leporello) assumed the role of Donna Anna. The effect of this inversion, according to the properly restrained reviewer, was that his "risible faculties were excited to the utmost." Beyond such parody, little remained to be done to the traditional legend short of total dismemberment. One of the final steps

35. Hazlitt claimed this unsigned review and the one of Pocock's *Libertine*. See *The Complete Works of William Hazlitt*, V, 362–66, 370–72.

toward disintegration was William T. Moncrieff's burletta *Giovanni in London; or, the Libertine Reclaimed*, which opened at the Olympic Theatre on 26 December 1817. This operatic extravaganza reduced the legend to a domestic cockney farce with transvestite overtones, ultimately redeeming the philanderer through marital reformation.

Once Don Juan was accepted as a comic character, natural progression led to a harlequinade treatment in a Christmas pantomime — *Harlequin's Vision; or, the Feast of the Statue*, first performed on 26 December 1817 at Drury Lane. In the *Examiner* for 11 January 1818, Hunt left no doubt as to his intense dislike of this production (pp. 25–26). Though praising the grandiose stage effects of the storm at sea, in which the Clown was violently tossed about and narrowly escaped Jonah's fate, he attributed the pantomime's general failure largely to "fastening itself upon the story and *not* the music of an attractive opera, which story has been exhausted at all ends of the town." The absorption of the Don Juan characters into the harlequinade mold produced what he termed "a tragic-comic non-descript." Again by strange reversal of traditional roles, Don Juan became the victim of female desire, for Proserpine, determined that the attractive man's soul would serve her in hell, arranged to have him go through a series of wicked actions in order to gratify her Infernal Majesty. Hunt could not help admitting that he was somewhat shocked by such immorality. Reflections upon the actions might be useful, as well as beneficial, if one could only determine whether or not the pantomimist were "joking." But the tone, which baffled the reviewer, was obviously one of ambivalent irony rather than straightforward satire, and if the author intended merely a parody of Don Juan, Hunt pronounced it "not a happy one" — a sentiment also shared by the anonymous reviewer of *Blackwood's* for January 1818 (II, 430).[36] Even so, this production is notable in the evolution of the legend for amalgamating the characters of Don Juan and Harlequin in the pantomime's major action.

Though Byron was living in Venice when the miraculous transformations were being made in Don Juan's theatrical personality, he more than likely, as a result of diligent efforts to keep up with events in England, knew what was being performed on the London stage, especially at Drury Lane. His correspondence with Murray alone during 1817 and 1818 prior to beginning work on *Don Juan* demonstrates how eager he was for shipments of books and periodicals, and the fact that topics of burning interest in England found their way into the narrator's "asides" in *Don Juan* is irrefutable proof that such shipments reached him in Venice. Furthermore, his reading of the *Examiner* and *Blackwood's Edinburgh Magazine* can be documented beyond question in his correspondence. Though the extent of his knowledge about a comical but lovable Don Juan prior to his own may be uncertain, the mere suggestion that the legend could be assimilated into the English harlequin pantomime was all he needed since he already possessed intimate acquaintance with that highly stylized genre. Adapted to popular taste of the day, the Don Juan legend had ceased to be the tragedy of a skeptical sensualist and had become the comedy of a sentimental lover.

However much Byron drew from other literary forms, it must have occurred to him that the techniques of the harlequinade would be very useful to the kind of informal long poem he wished to write. The very essence of both was deft improvisation within an extraordinarily flexible structure. When Murray asked him for a plan of the work, he responded that there was no over-all design for "Donny Johnny"; instead he defended the buffoonery, as well as the license of such writing, and in a verbal echo of Hunt's defense of harlequin pantomimes retorted: "Do you suppose that I could have any intention but to giggle and make giggle?" [37] Like elaborate Christmas pantomimes, *Don Juan* permitted its author to mingle satire and sentiment, moral lessons and indecencies, and while displaying the virtuosity of his "hero" in farcical frolics to be moderately irreverent about anything that came to mind.[38] It enabled the poet to interweave seemingly irrelevant comments on subjects of topical interest much as they were mirrored in harlequinades and also to shift his central character in various guises through a series of cleverly constructed episodes. In each role, however, Juan remained a variation of the English Harlequin, who endeared himself to the audience while winning some attractive Columbine. Despite an obnoxious Pantaloon in the form of husband, father, or environmental obstacle, he succeeded as a lover not only through his own ingenuity but also through either the inadvertent or deliberate aid of various Scaramouches. Since the pattern of *Don Juan* owes

36. This pantomime, originally licensed as *The Feast of the Statue; or, Harlequin Libertine* (Nicoll, IV, 460), was also reviewed in the *Champion* for 4 January 1818 (by John Keats), the *Theatrical Inquisitor* for January 1818 (XII, 51), and the *European Magazine* for January 1818 (LXXIII, 55–56).

37. *LJ*, IV, 343.

38. For pertinent comments by Byron on his *Don Juan*, see *LJ*, IV, 260, 279, 342; VI, 155–56.

much to that of an amorphous subliterary genre so modest that many of its productions never found their way into print, there is notable irony in Byron's calling it "an epic," especially since it was designed to be true not to the heroic tradition but to an unheroic age.

Defying epic convention, Byron's persona starts his narration at the beginning, so that he may account for the products of unhappy misalliance, which, if not viewed with some geniality, might indeed become the object of pity. Two couples united without affection provide excellent comic material for the poet's undermining wit and, moreover, determine the kind of initiation young Juan will have in the ways of love. His own parents compose one of these nominal unions. His mother, Donna Inez, lacking even a rudimentary understanding of human nature, is a fraudulent intellectual convinced of her infallible self-righteousness. As the narrator asserts in one of many sly innuendoes that reveal erroneous popular belief pitted against submerged truth, her virtues are "equall'd by her wit alone" (I, 10:4).[39] As "Morality's prim personification" without any "female errors," she has all the attributes of an excellent old maid in bluestocking coteries. Indeed her flaunted perfection so bores her already alienated husband, Don Jose, that "like a lineal son of Eve" he goes "plucking various fruit without her leave" (I, 18:7–8). Society, that evil-tongued monster, delights in spreading rumors about his infidelity, and naturally the gossips side with Inez, especially when she sanctimoniously refuses to utter a word — even though to do so might allay vicious scandal. Like all egomaniacs, she is so antagonized by her husband's neglect (not to mention the damage done to her self-image) that she hostilely stirs up quarrels with him. Yet behind her pious exterior lie motivations far from admirable. Rumor has it that, despite her frigid demeanor, she had previously forgotten "her very prudent carriage" with Don Alfonso. Hence, even at the risk of endangering her son, she maliciously encourages Juan's affair with Alfonso's young wife in order to discredit the successor in her old lover's affections.

Whereas Byron's depiction of Inez is dominated by the deep-seated resentment he obviously felt toward Lady Byron, whose fortress of pharisaical rectitude he had found impregnable, his humorous sympathy with Jose (in some respects a projection of himself as maligned husband) becomes equally marked. There is something casually endearing about so phlegmatic and imperturbable a man, who tolerantly allows his wife whatever diversions she enjoys. But his nonchalance has only provoked her tantrums, additionally violent since he is not a fighter and since extra-marital affairs have put him in the wrong. Nevertheless, our compassion for him is limited by his moderately ludicrous, unheroic behavior. An Hidalgo of purest Gothic blood, he has the characteristics of a tired aristocrat: he was "born bilious" (I, 35:5–8). In keeping with his disposition, he takes the coward's way out when threatened by divorce and accompanying disgrace; he dies, thoughtlessly spoiling the fun of scandalmongers who anticipated "a charming cause."

The other loveless marriage is that of Donna Julia and Don Alfonso, a January-and-May relationship since she is twenty-three and he fifty. Despite cohabitation and a reasonable forbearance of each other's foibles, no real union exists: they are neither *one* nor *two*. Julia's old husband is naturally jealous, and his age obviously rankles her, as becomes apparent under the stress of the "levee" in her boudoir. Even so, she has hitherto been perfectly faithful despite common knowledge that "Ladies even of the most uneasy virtue/ Prefer a spouse whose age is short of thirty" (I, 62:7–8). She is perceptive enough, upon becoming aware of Juan's approaching manhood, to understand intuitively the reason for her reserve toward him. But as the product of corrupt civilization she too resorts to dissemblance, for "love is taught hypocrisy from youth" (I, 72:8). Her halfhearted determination to repress forbidden passion causes her to weave a network of defense in which she ultimately ensnares herself. Initially she implores the Virgin for strength, swearing never to see Juan again; but when he fails to appear during her visit with his mother, she is sorely disappointed that her prayers have been answered and does not pray again. There is further satire on self-deception in her resolution to overcome all inclination toward sin by facing it squarely. Possibly, she thinks, a Platonic or spiritual relationship — "love within its proper limits" — will prevent her feelings from descending to the plane of carnality. Ultimately all this reliance upon mind where only heart is concerned proves to be the most dangerous subterfuge of all, since human love, as Byron's narrator repeatedly asserts, is unavoidably physical.

Because of his mother's phobia of anything that even "hints continuation of the species," Juan has experienced an unwholesomely cloistered rearing that makes him the fuse for this sexual powder keg. The un-

---

39. All citations of *Don Juan* are from *Byron's "Don Juan": A Variorum Edition*, ed. Truman Guy Steffan and Willis W. Pratt (Austin, Texas, 1957).

healthy damming up of his libido has merely increased the pressure within him to overwhelm his inhibitions, and the manly arts of war in which he is trained ("to scale a fortress — or a nunnery") are in fact only misdirected expressions of male instinct. Hence Juan at sixteen is unable to comprehend why he becomes shy around Julia. And his adolescent fancies, during which he soulfully communes with nature in a Wordsworthian fog of amatory melancholy, divert him from possible self-knowledge. Though both Inez and Julia understand his lovesickness, they for different motives deliberately avoid enlightening him. Only the opportunity is lacking for Juan to translate his mystifying feelings into action, and that occasion presents itself on a summer evening when Juan and Julia follow natural inclination so gradually that the progression seems inevitable. Julia's stupid reliance on her own innocence and his inexperience permits Byron to satirize the reputedly feminine trust in pure affection. At the very moment her heart yields her body, reason forces the incongruous protest — "I will ne'er consent." With misleading obtuseness that further contributes to the irony, the narrator comically blames not the lovers but Plato's pimping philosophy for having paved the way to sin. Then in a shrewd burlesque of all mankind, he turns moralist just as his own respectability is on the verge of being impugned. Like the most tantalizing of gossips, he declares: "I can't go on;/ I'm almost sorry that I e'er begun" (I, 115:7-8).

What Byron's technique of comic unmasking reveals, as many of his more metaphysical contemporaries were unwilling to concede, is the frailty of spirit where flesh is concerned and therefore the predominance of sex in passionate love. The result of naïve self-deception, particularly among the emotionally deprived, leads to an attachment based on physical gratification, and in Juan there is more callow sentiment than seriousness. In order to continue the liaison, Julia must resort (as we see in the boudoir scene) to self-degrading deceit and false accusations, which ultimately result in the loss of her self-respect. Yet her flamboyant victory over a deceived husband, whose *posse comitatus* consists of other husbands determined that no woman transgress with impunity lest her example corrupt their wives, is one of the greatest bedroom farces in English literature, surpassing even those of Fielding and the Restoration stage. Part of its achievement is the complete realignment in our sympathies and antipathies, contrary to what rationality would endorse. For in spite of our morals, we laugh at an inverted set of values.[40] In this riotous comedy of situation we relish the degradation of Alfonso, who, though obviously in the right, appears foolish by trying publicly to prove himself a cuckold. Meanwhile Julia, guilty beyond question, wins our favor with her ingenuity, which is impelled by a love so intense that it obliterates all other considerations. In a stained-glass posture of wronged innocence, she claims extraordinary virtue while heaping disgraceful insults upon her husband. Equally effective as histrionic technique is her prudent silence before Alfonso after the disappointed intruders have left. Accepting a forced apology from her vanquished spouse, she temporarily exults in victory and threatens (like Aristophanic women) to expel him from that evanescent Eden Byron frequently identified with sexual delight. But with the unexpected discovery of Juan's shoes, the tide of marital battle shifts instantly. After a scuffle Juan (like Joseph fleeing from Potiphar's wife) escapes stark naked; but there the similarity ends. The accidental exposure at this point is a triumph of anticlimax. From the hedonist's viewpoint, Juan is still properly attired for his favorite sport; to the moralist, however, sin has been divested of its glamor and sent forth shivering into the night.

Between the Julian and the Turkish cantos ludicrous elements touching on affection provide only a biased view, since they are directed primarily against the sentimentality for which Romantic love is most famous. Juan's melancholy lovesickness, heightened by a nostalgic departure from Spain, is ingloriously regurgitated in a nauseous attack of *mal de mer*. Interspersed between saccharine addresses to an absent Julia, his violent retching in the midst of a storm successfully purges all lingering ardor and produces an ironic juxtaposition that dramatizes love's dependence upon physical well-being. Ultimately even the farewell letter of Julia meets an ignominious end: it is torn up by starving men on the lifeboat in order to determine who will be eaten by the luckier passengers. Hence the last tangible memento (a poignant threnody on the injustice women must bear), instead of keeping her memory alive in his heart, becomes the means of selecting a victim for cannibalistic sacrifice. This biting irony partly functions as a check upon lugubrious sentiment; moreover, it serves to free Juan from irrevocable attachment, so that he is ready for a new

40. Upon reading proof of this scene, Hobhouse wrote Byron: ". . . think what you would say of it, if written by another." Byron replied that since his work was only comical it could have no serious effect: "Now Lust is a serious passion, and cannot be excited by the ludicrous." See *Poetry*, VI, 62*n*.

liaison. What might seem to be either superficial or immature affection therefore provides the narrator with one of his cleverest assaults on the absurdity of "Platonic" love. According to his mock argument, he paradoxically hates inconstancy but justifies it aesthetically as the universal appreciation of beauty wherever it exists. His "spiritualized" progression, rather than proceeding from admiration of an individual to perception of the ideal, is an appetitive quest leading in the opposite direction. The archetype must be sought in a multiplicity of earthly replicas, none of whom is completely satisfactory in herself.

There is further deflation of sentimentality in the narrator's comments on the Haidée episode, though herein the idyllic dream is affirmed with equal conviction. In his practical manner he asserts that health and idleness are oil and gunpowder to "passion's flame" (II, 169–70). Romantic notions notwithstanding, Venus cannot flourish without the sustaining aid of Ceres and Bacchus, for "the best feelings must have victual" (II, 145:1). The mundane commentator's praise of eggs and oysters as amatory food indicates the kind of love he most readily comprehends. He also betrays a repressed envy of the lovers on this Cycladean isle by remarks denigrating their paradisal bliss. The shared affection of Juan and Haidée he considers nothing more than intoxication of the senses, though admittedly the "best of life" is an escape from reality afforded momentarily by inebriation (II, 179:2). He further avers that, since mutability is the law of nature (II, 214), passion cannot possibly endure unless moderately challenging obstacles are placed in its path, as in the fortunate case of a *cavalier servente*. Love that progresses into the stage of matrimony suffers the fate of wine that sours into vinegar (III, 5). Thus the cynical narrator in Byron's employ functions very much like Shakespeare's Mercutio and Juliet's nurse as ballast against the oversweetness of unreflective affection, providing not only comic relief from the ultimately tragic outcome of the Haidée episode but normalizing our feelings. Love is shown to be at once the supreme joy of life and "the very god of evil" (II, 205:7). The comprehensive truth conveyed by such irony lies not in a resolution or alternation of antithetic reactions but in the simultaneous apprehension of both realities.

Events leading Juan into the Sultan's harem skirt around topics potentially more explosive than any other in the entire work; for apart from transposing the male and female roles to burlesque a trite seduction scene, Byron jested about the forbidden subject of homosexuality.[41] Though his contemporaries were willing to grant pagans like Sappho, Anacreon, and Catullus — all blacklisted from Juan's classical education (I, 42) — the right to treat that passion openly and seriously, they preferred not to countenance its existence in their morally enlightened society. Byron could make his daring observations only through agile maneuvers. By denouncing all serious amatory writing (V, 1–2), by treating sexual deviation as material for low comedy, and by transporting his scene to the concupiscent atmosphere of a Turkish palace, he was enabled to touch lightly upon love directed toward the wrong end. The first mild hint of sexual transformation is provided by the eunuch Baba ("a black old neutral personage/ Of the third sex"), who buys Juan in the slave market of Constantinople. With manly bravado, Juan at first refuses to assume the feminine attire of an odalisque, fearing that his fate in such dress would indeed be worse than death. Only Baba's warning, drawn from sad experience, that he may be deprived of all gender unless he complies, convinces Juan that deceptive clothing is preferable to castration. As he embarks on an extraordinary career as a transvestite, irreverently termed "Christian nun," he swears to defend his "honor" manfully. Yet when his English acquaintance, in parting, tauntingly advises the femininely clad slave to protect his name and not to recapitulate Eve's fall, Juan continues the jest with all the conviction of a female impersonator, saying: "the Sultan's self shan't carry me,/ Unless his highness promises to marry me" (V, 84:7–8).

To Juan's astonishment, he becomes the property not of the Sultan but of his favorite wife, Gulbeyaz. This imperious Sultana, accustomed to acquiring anything she wants (like the selfish male who assumes the world was created for his private delectation) thinks the question "Christian, canst thou love?" ample hint of her desire. But Juan, in one of the cleverest burlesques of a sentimental virgin defending her honor, eloquently argues that since only the free can love he will not relinquish his virtue to an aggressive seducer. Recollection of Haidée at this crucial moment causes him to weep. This unexpected thwarting of what Gulbeyaz deems "nature's general law" causes her to rage like a thunderstorm (during which she threatens to cut off more than his acquaintance), but her anger ultimately resolves itself in a shower of tears. Ironically, how-

41. In the "Thyrza" poems Byron dared to celebrate his love for John Edleston only by referring to him as a woman.

ever, her lachrymose behavior so moves the "hero" that it dissolves his weak resolution not to "sin — except to his own wish" (V, 141:6). Humbled by her seeming contrition, he is ready to atone in the only acceptable manner when the Sultan's arrival prevents his succumbing to the rapacious Sultana. On the other hand, as the giggling attendants realize, the Sultan's notice of the new slave's beauty threatens Juan with an even more horrendous fate.

The harem situation into which Juan is shunted for the night titillates the sensual imagination with its infinite variety of sexual experience. For protective covering, the narrator is virtually compelled to retreat defensively into a pretended naïveté shielding him from obscenity. He frankly wonders how Turks can cope with their polygamous arrangement: "Most wise men with *one* moderate woman wed,/ Will scarcely find philosophy for more" (VI, 12:5–6). He prepares us for the seraglio frolic by warning that the oda is a "labyrinth of love" containing "a thousand bosoms there/ Beating for love as the caged birds for air" (VI, 28:7; 26:7–8). The odalisques, having only the Sultan as outlet for this repressed desire, are passion-starved — a condition produced not so much by sincere devotion to their lord as by padlocked chastity. Inevitably their pent-up emotions spill over on one another, as evidenced by excessive kissing and fondling. Though no one suspects that the new arrival, Juanna, is other than she appears to be, they are drawn to her by inexplicable magnetism so great that several vie for the privilege of sharing their couches with her. The voluptuous Dudu, to whom Juanna is ultimately awarded, then leads her to bed, bestows "a chaste kiss," and even offers to undress her, though the last favor is modestly declined. During the night the epicene bedfellow evidently proves truer to nature than to costume, for Dudu wakens the harem with a piercing scream. She had dreamt of seeking an inaccessible golden apple, but after it fell and she attempted to bite it, "A bee flew out and stung her to the heart" (VI, 77:7). As she buries her head in her bedmate's breast, a blushing neck reveals that (even without Freud's aid) she has arrived at a thorough comprehension of her erotic dream.

Juan's narrow escape from the smoldering desires of Constantinople to the Russian court at St. Petersburg is bridged by the horrifying realism of war, itself a heinous variety of lust. But whereas death translates faithful Moslems from belligerent passion into a lechers' paradise of black-eyed houris, the vagaries of survival propel Juan into an earthly imitation of that voluptuous heaven. For comical effects in the escapade at Catherine's court, Byron again relied upon an inversion of customary roles in amatory relations. Instead of having women vie for the honor of being royal mistress while men speculate on the fortunes of attractive faces, as at Versailles under Louis XIV, the poet has Juan compete with a standing army of studs for the favor of an empress. Whereas Russian women slyly comment on masculine features most likely to please, great Catherine's reigning favorite, one of many six-foot fellows aspiring to that "high official situation," scowls, knowing her occasional inclination toward fair-faced boys. The very sight of Juan, looking like Cupid in an artillery lieutenant's uniform, is enough to take Catherine's heart without his even firing a shot. Carrying this transposition to its pregnant extremity, the narrator jests about how the lover who satisfies this "Quean of Queens" may be personally affected: "If once beyond her boudoir's precincts in ye went,/ Your 'Fortune' was in a fair way 'to swell/ A Man'" (IX, 63:5–7).

To the wishful male animal there has always been something intrinsically humorous about a woman of insatiable desire. Though she is in some respects the female counterpart of the legendary Don Juan, a woman bent upon endless seduction is seldom the villainous cause of tragedy that a man in that role usually is. Rather, she becomes the embodiment of ribald comedy; and Byron, at the expense of an adequately developed situation, fills much of this episode with risqué *double-entendre* about the none-too-private life of an empress who was not only overamorous but (by the time Juan arrived) overweight and overage. The gentlemanly narrator evaluates her as satisfactory for "those who like things rosy, ripe, and succulent," though she tends to use "her favourites too well" (IX, 62–63). Unlike that celebrated teaser, the half-chaste, stingy Elizabeth of England, Catherine is lavishly generous with all she can offer. Understandably, Juan finds basking in royal favor quite agreeable, despite the strenuous duty, since at seventeen he is young enough "To come off handsomely in that regard" (X, 22–23). Furthermore, he has reached that stage of life when all women — thanks to that great leveler, sex — provide equal pleasure, and there is no pretense that his present liaison is anything but sensual. The situation therefore offers the narrator an opportunity to make some of his most cynical observations. Love, he concludes, is basically vanity, and all euphemistic terms applied to it (Platonic, divine, sentimental, and canonical) are mere delusions when compared with the one sound description — "*Marriage in Disguise*" (IX, 73–76).

The depiction of the London society in which Juan subsequently moves caricatures, primarily through the agency of the "marriage mart," both false love and contrived matrimony. Except for a few comical situations and occasional witty touches, the episode is basically a return to the moralizing satire of *The Waltz*. Among the "thousand happy few" of the Establishment, where all success is measured by money, love too must have its price. Young ladies, like Smithfield mares — their assets emphasized, their flaws concealed — are trotted out before prospective buyers and sold to the highest bidder. As Juan discovers, everyone has some ulterior aim; hence he is well received in this company because, as Catherine's emissary and an apparently wealthy bachelor, he is a potential husband for single ladies, as well as excitement for those already bored with their wedded state. Initially London girls fail to impress him any more than does fashionable love ("half commercial, half pedantic"). Eventually he realizes that, in spite of some vain coquettes who take sadistic delight in breaking men's hearts, British women generally, though slower to warm, are more earnest when they do experience genuine love than those of other nationalities. Unfortunately, young wives who become seriously involved in extramarital relations often provoke divorce or damage suits, though the shrewder, more deceptive ones manage to enjoy their pleasures without scandal. Byron's most caustic assessment of English morality therefore reproaches his countrymen for countenancing sin as long as it is concealed and hypocritically victimizing as scapegoats those whose transgressions have been exposed.

The Amundevilles' house party furnishes components for one of the most dangerous entanglements with which Juan must cope, though, because the incident remains unfinished, we can only speculate on its ultimate resolution. There can be no doubt, however, from what the narrator tells us at the outset, that Juan was meant to wreak unintentional havoc in the marriage of his host and hostess. Lady Adeline, described as "The fair most fatal Juan ever met," apparently was to have been his major involvement in this section. Married to an aspiring politician, she dutifully performs all necessary obligations as wife and hostess. Indeed her fidelity to a husband with whom she fancies herself in love has never wavered; and since she is self-assured and universally admired, she has no desire to resort to coquetry. Her only defect is a vacant heart, and the poet warns that inner collapse of her staunch spirit will be "like an Earthquake's ruin" (XIV, 85:8). Though a thoroughbred who maintains a "calm

Patrician polish" by adhering to the Horatian dictum of *nil admirari*, she nevertheless hides a quintessence like that glassful of liquid champagne remaining when all the rest of the bottle is frozen.

Lord Henry is also a caricature of the English aristocrat — suavely aloof and imperturbable, yet at times capable of fiery action. We are told that he "in each circumstance of love or war/ Had still preserved his perpendicular" (XIV, 71:7–8). Yet, despite his virtues and handsome exterior, he lacks that certain *esprit* or (as Byron calls it) "soul" generally thought necessary to satisfy the feminine heart. Hence their union, blessed by not only an heir but also that unimpassioned *amour anglais* about which Continentals have often jested, is "Serene, and noble, — conjugal, but cold" (XIV, 86:8). The narrator, with his characteristic retreat that piques our curiosity without satisfying it, quizzically wonders at this point whether anyone really knows how women should be approached. At any rate, Lord Henry, like many of his compatriots, is so deeply engrossed in parliamentary affairs that he gives little thought to love.

Though at first the ambiance of Norman Abbey suggests gaiety and comic self-deception, Juan soon becomes embroiled in a serious intrigue involving three women, each extraordinarily fascinating in her own way. The Duchess of Fitz-Fulke, who has had considerable experience in love, immediately starts flirting with the handsome stranger. Her brazen aggressiveness is abetted by the absence of her husband, whose aristocratic attitude toward marriage makes theirs a union "Which never meets, and therefore can't fall out" (XIV, 45:8); and even her current *amour*, Lord Augustus, is decadently resigned to her promiscuity. The other house guests, divisible into the *Bores* and the *Bored*, are absolutely delighted with fresh gossip to alleviate dreary conversation. Only Adeline is genuinely disturbed — and for the wrong reasons. Little realizing the full implications of her own "intense interest" in Juan, she feels obliged both to prevent a *contretemps* with Lord Augustus and to save the "inexperienced" foreigner from an *éclat* or even court proceedings, whereby wealthy poachers on love's estate are punished. Furthermore, she knows that the Duchess is just the sort to bewitch and torture a man. With unimpugnable motives, Adeline therefore urges her husband to warn Juan of imminent danger; but Henry, stuffily facetious, refuses to interfere in anyone's business except the king's. Her alternative solution is marriage, which she recommends to Juan. Yet she is annoyed by his subsequent infatuation with Aurora Raby, whose ethereal innocence and passive indifference contribute to a spiritual kinship between them.

The lascivious Duchess, whose charms have nothing to do with captivating his soul, takes the initiative in an accelerating crescendo. Upon learning of the Abbey's resident spectre, the Black Friar, she decides to impersonate him in order to frighten Juan. In this escapade Byron achieves one of his cleverest burlesques of literary conventions by deliberately upsetting the usual rationale of Gothic romances. Tales of horror ordinarily focused upon some chaste heroine terrified almost out of her wits by threats of death or worse, yet somehow, through frozen vigor and prim innocence, successful in her escape with everything still intact. Fear generated by these hair-raising stories was, according to their apologists, intended to heighten sensibility, whether to beauty, compassion, or love. But as Byron inverts this dubious logic, putting aesthetic moralists at an impasse, the scaring of Juan makes him easy prey for the female apparition: the "hero" is trapped into ravishment.[42] The second time the "ghost" stalks her victim, Juan, clad only in his nightgown, determines to overcome his fear boldly. He disrobes the phantom and finds none other than "her frolic Grace." The narrator coyly refuses to divulge what they did in the "tender moonlight situation,/ Such as enables Man to show his strength/ Moral or physical" (XVII, 12:2–4), but from their disheveled looks at breakfast the Duchess seems to have staked out her claim to his body. Though both are obviously debilitated, Juan's face retains the deceptive appearance of immaculate naïveté which highly becomes a professional virgin.

In the interim, Adeline, by demonstrating her versatile cordiality toward local gentry politically useful to her husband and afterwards admitting the expedience of her actions, has lost favor with Juan. She obviously must make a bold play to recapture him from her two rivals. As an extraordinary combination of body and soul, of the sensual and the sentimental, she might well have succeeded wholly where Aurora and the Duchess achieve only half measure. Yet her fascination with Juan violates a cardinal tenet of her glittering but shallow society: where love is accepted only as a means of achieving ambitious aims or as the diversion of a moment, she threatens to take it seriously. Exactly what course she would have pursued to destroy inadvertently her own position in the "microcosm on stilts" Byron unfortunately did not live to write.

Perhaps the final cantos display Bryon's humor and irony better than other portions of *Don Juan* because the paradoxical attitude required by his comic view corresponded with his ambivalent feelings toward English society and love within it. Just as he could not forget the glorious years when he had been idolized by the social, intellectual, and political lions of England, he could not forgive the iconoclastic hypocrisy that ostracized him simply because a public scandal had made him a pariah. Proud though he was of belonging to an elite which for centuries had arrogated to itself all that money and power could lure, he was unable to eradicate the Presbyterian conscience of his Scottish youth or close his mind to the pettiness of that self-centered coterie misnamed the "Great World." His extraordinary humor therefore was born of intense suffering and like all good comedy never strayed far from the potentially tragic. As he himself declared, "And if I laugh at any mortal thing,/ 'Tis that I may not weep" (IV, 4:1-2). What many of his contemporaries took as scorn was an inherent tendency to jest about subjects that none had dared to scrutinize objectively. Proleptically challenging the world's censure, he vowed:

> But now I'm going to be immoral; now
> I mean to show things really as they are,
> Not as they ought to be: for I avow,
> That till we see what's what in fact, we're far
> From much improvement . . . . (XII, 40:1-5)

In this vein he judged *Don Quixote* the saddest of all tales "Because it makes us smile" (XIII, 9:2). According to his interpretation, Cervantes, far from debasing the knight's admirable pursuits, had sympathetically portrayed the ludicrous aspects of devotion to goals unattainable in this imperfect world. Similarly, Byron's irony strove to reconcile his skeptical rejection of all knowledge with impractical idealism. Though his method did not always succeed like the oyster's in converting gritty irritation into pearl, laughter, even at what he loved, was part of his survival mechanism — a stoical acceptance of life's unalterable realities.

42. After Teresa Guiccioli left her husband, Byron on 29 October 1819 wrote Hoppner: "I should like to know *who* has been carried off — except poor dear *me*. I have been more ravished myself than any body since the Trojan war" (*LJ*, IV, 370).

PART TWO

Marital Love

CHAPTER III

The Necessity of Marriage:
Burns and Wordsworth

THOUGH THE LATER Romantic poets became notorious for their flagrant assaults on the institution of marriage, one cannot overlook the fact that some of their distinguished contemporaries — less stridently, perhaps, but with equal certitude — advocated matrimonial love. If they did not celebrate, in the Victorian manner of Coventry Patmore, a spiritually ordained wedlock described in mystical metaphors, they also did not represent it as the framework of social and financial stability essential to Jane Austen's world. Nor were they obsessed, in the twentieth-century fashion, with sexual satisfaction as the cornerstone of the nuptial structure. Their praise embodied a much more comprehensive approach, which because of its sobriety has often gone unnoticed. Significantly, the notable exponents of a balanced physical and spiritual union blessed by heavenly, as well as human, law were men who, having experienced love both within and without marriage, concluded that the former state was preferable. Though their final choice by no means precluded the possibility of unsanctified love, their attitude reflected the sore disappointments and heartaches of unblessed passion as ample justification for steering their emotionally tossed barks into the safer haven of matrimony. Their portrayal of marital love, far from being associated with hypocrisy, must therefore be regarded as a studied judgment arrived at not through either mere conformity to custom or accession to convenience.

Burns sanctions marriage primarily in the spirit of a gourmet who, having sampled many rich foods, praises one for staple diet without denying the appetizing qualities of others for occasional delectation. His readiness to dispense advice on the subject even while conceding his own inability to heed it consistently, as the concluding lines of "Epistle to a Young Friend" admit, indicates not insincerity but rather greater honesty than most men display concerning their vacillating sentiments. Even if the onus of sin and the anxieties of concealment can be glossed over, the most important objection to illicit indulgence is that it inevitably "petrifies" one's most sensitive feelings. However much the thrill of novel excitement quickens the delicate mechanism that enables a man to be not only a gratifying lover but also a successful poet, it later gives way to a remorse that destroys either the condemned emotions or human sensibility itself. In either case the effect is stultifying. Therefore the poet warns against reliance solely on human prompting; especially when a man is "tempest-driven," he ought to rely upon "A correspondence fix'd wi' Heav'n" (I, 250).

Ironically, Burns also realized that divine guidance might be misunderstood by fallible man and that love — emblazoned in his firmament by the imagery of light, fire, and warmth — might be misdirected, especially in someone constitutionally overreceptive to it. Marriage, he knew, worked great hardships on him simply because of his inherent predisposition toward the biological urge. In an early poem, "A Prayer, in the Prospect of Death," he rationalizes his own frailty primarily on the grounds of instinctual responsiveness to emotion:

> Thou know'st that Thou hast formed me,
>   With Passions wild and strong;
> And list'ning to their witching voice
>   Has often led me wrong. (I, 20)

Even bolder in shifting partial responsibility from the sinner to the creator is a variation of this idea in "The Vision," where Burns asserts, through the voice of his local muse, Coila, that sensitivity to divine impulse (which enables him to be an inspired bard of the human heart) carries with it an endogenous flaw. Too often he has been swept by youthful ardor into the maelstroms of untrustworthy passion, though Coila credits herself with teaching him, in such instances, to "soothe [his] flame" by pouring forth the excess into song. Admittedly, "Fancy's *meteor-ray*" has sometimes misled him into "Pleasure's devious way," but for these aberrations his sympathetic muse offers the ultimate in consolation by declaring that even this false illumination emanated originally from God: ". . . the *light* that led astray,/ Was *light* from Heaven" (I, 112).

His epistolary comments on marriage are difficult to fit into any pattern because some of his observations were addressed to rollicking male friends accustomed to making light of matrimony as a pragmatic solution to the problems of bed and board. Furthermore, his highly ambivalent attitudes on the subject varied considerably from time to time. That his feelings, especially during salad days, were not always idealistic can be seen in his letter of 13 September 1784 to John Tennant: "Who would not be in raptures with a woman that will make him 300£ richer[?] — And then to have a woman to lye with when one pleases, without running any risk of the cursed expence of bastards and all the other concomitants of that species of Smuggling — These are solid views of matrimony."[1] His particular experience with Jean Armour occasioned a wide gamut of reactions to the matrimonial state. In April 1786, after Jean's father had forced destruction of the written pledge that would have acknowledged her as his wife, Burns wrote a mock-heroic lament to John Arnot as though he were a bereaved widower recently deprived of his greatest blessing (I, 27–28). By 12 June 1786 he wrote an even more sentimental account of his dilemma to David Brice, charging reproachfully of Jean: ". . . she has made me completely miserable. — Never man lov'd, or rather ador'd, a woman more than I did her. . . . I have tryed often to forget her . . . but all in vain" (I, 31). His remarks to John Beugo on 9 September 1788, after the union with Jean had been publicly avowed, are a return to a slightly cynical approval of connubial benefits. He advised his friend that marriage would "be a very great improvement on the Dish of Life. . . . I like the idea of an honest country Rake of my acquaintance, who, like myself, married lately. — Speaking to me of his late step, 'L—d, man,' says he, 'a body's baith cheaper and better sair't'" (I, 252).

On the other hand, a few of his poetical comments express genuine happiness in matrimony. Though the slightly postured "Epistle to Davie, a

---

1. *Letters*, I, 20. Subsequent references to Burns's letters appear in the text.

Brother Poet" employs conventional rhetoric to reassure its author that indigent poets have joys the rich cannot experience, much of the euphoria is obviously sincere. Davie Sillar is apparently well pleased with Meg, his "dearest part," as Burns declares himself to be with his own wife. Some of this delight, which appears more conspicuously in the song "I hae a wife o' my ain," is essentially the joy of ownership, some the product of "tender feelings." Just the mention of Jean's name is enough to set him on fire, and recollection of her in moments of distress brings solace. Hence he implores God to make her His "most peculiar care." The poet's emotions, whether for Jean or Davie, enable him to endure "the tenebrific scene" and revive his spavined Pegasus. Though Burns may have been tailoring his thoughts to Sillar's measurements, there is no doubt that in his mind the pure affection of marital love and masculine friendship were comparable.

Although some of his confessions of infidelity remind one of a drunkard inveighing against alcohol while swilling down another drink, there is strong indication that he honestly loved Jean despite an insatiable longing for variety. The fact that he always returned to her after repeated divagations suggests, however, that his loyalty needed to be reaffirmed by testing it against sporadic attachments. Certainly in poems that do not strive after calculated public effect he alludes to her as the outstanding amatory experience of his life. From the first she was apparently "the jewel . . . o' them a'" among the belles of Mauchline (I, 57). The song "I love my Jean" is too forthright to be just a graceful compliment, even though, according to Burns's possibly facetious note, it was composed during the honeymoon (III, 1277); it must be interpreted as a tribute to an absent wife whose presence is evoked by association with every beautiful aspect of nature:

> There's not a bony flower, that springs
>   By fountain, shaw, or green;
> There's not a bony bird that sings
>   But minds me o' my Jean. — (I, 422)

Nor is it surprising that for a concrete analogy of the abstract concept of Eve, whom he depicts with extraordinary good humor in the Kilmarnock manuscript of his "Address to the Deil," he should choose his own wife, the appealing innocent "Wi' guileless heart" (I, 171n).

All that can be ascertained about Jean — including her willingness to rear one of her husband's natural children by the barmaid Anne Park and her stoical resignation to the poet's aberrant ways with the alleged comment "Oor Rab should hae had twa wives" — indicates that she was even more compassionate than humanity's first progenitress, who never had to cope with such problems. That Jean was an extremely tolerant wife can be seen in Burns's partial association of her with the unsophisticated but canny muse who consecrates him in "The Vision." The likening of Coila's exposed leg to that of Jean, though unabashedly earthy, reveals his affectionate intimacy with both. Since Coila taught him to translate passion cathartically into poetry, she is indeed the imaginative equivalent of his wife, providing both sympathy and stability. No greater encomium could have been paid to either woman by a dedicated poet who was also very much a lover. If his wife in her simple way could not stimulate his intellect as any of Mnemosyne's daughters might, she could, though "hamely in attire," nourish his heart. For a rustic bard requiring unbroken contact with wholesome earth, that was infinitely more desirable.

In contrast to the association of Jean with an artistic muse are thoughts contained in a letter of November 1794 to George Thomson, editor of *Select Scotish Airs*, who preferred songs more circumspect than a few the poet had sent him. Although "Conjugal love" was, by Burns's admission, an emotion he felt deeply and venerated highly, it did not "make such a figure in Poesy as that other species of the Passion — 'Where Love is liberty & Nature law'" (II, 271). Like a musical instrument, nuptial affection could within restricted tonal range produce sweet melodies, but its gamut was so "scanty & confined," especially when compared to the other sort, that its poetic utility was limited. As he had explained in the previous letter to Thomson, he himself drew inspiration not from the "sober, gin-horse routine of existence" but from the Helicon of stunning feminine beauty (II, 265). In fact, it was in the "enthusiasm of the Passion" that he became "a very Poet" (II, 271).

Though this pronouncement may be borne out by the mass of delightful poems about unfettered love, certainly one of his finest songs was produced in honor of marital felicity under the most binding restraints of nature. What in the bawdy original had been a wife's cruel jest ridiculing her husband's impotence became, in Burns's redaction of "John Anderson my Jo" (II, 528–529), a moving acknowledgment of lifelong constancy. Though the feminine speaker recalls John's youthful appearance and casually observes the alteration, she does so with no regret or recrimination for the change in a man who has remained her sweetheart. Her blessing of his present condition suggests acceptance of inevitable circumstance as the key to contentment. Thoughts of their demise, which might be disquieting in another context, seem perfectly normal. Having "clamb the hill the gither," so too must they "totter down." The devotion which gave them happiness in life appears stronger than death itself, for they will remain together, sleeping at the foot of the hill.

Burns's most idealistic portrayal of domestic tranquility is "The Cotter's Saturday Night." Though its sentimental platitudes offend modern readers, one cannot forget that in the late eighteenth century (when Mackenzie's *Man of Feeling* was still wept over) and even in the Victorian era, Burns's picture of familial bliss was unassailable. Despite some artificiality in pose and diction, it received Romantic endorsement for praising "The *lowly train* in life's sequester'd scene" and celebrating "native feelings strong, the guileless ways" (I, 146). Whereas Gray's "Elegy" (from which Burns quotes for his poem's epigraph) had merely defended the simple poor against patronage of the ambitious, Burns proclaims the superiority of humble life blessed by innocent tenderness. In the first stanza he states that the lawyer Robert Aiken, to whom the poem is dedicated, would have been "far happier" in a cottage, even though his friend's true worth might then not have been publicly recognized. Thus the earlier measure of man in terms of worldly distinction (Gray's "mute inglorious Milton" or "Cromwell guiltless of his country's blood") is superseded by a standard of happiness within man himself—an individual kingdom of God.

The cotter's situation is symbolic of the contented man's lot. Though weary from plowing, he is satisfied with his week's labor and returns home in pleasant anticipation of Sunday rest. Even more heartening to him are the ecstatic greetings of his young bairns and thrifty wife, whose complete devotion enables him to suspend temporarily all responsibilities and worries. The arrival of his elder children, gainfully employed on neighboring farms, completes the family circle, and amidst this tightly knit group the parents naturally project their earthly aspirations into their offspring. Though the cotter is overgenerous with moral preachments, the genuineness of his piety is undeniable whether he reads from the Bible or leads the family in prayer. In a sociologically valid conclusion, Burns asserts that the stability of this particular household and many others like it renders the Scots enduringly stalwart. Wherever the family is strong in its own rectitude and closely allied with God — one has only to consider Wordsworth's "Michael" to realize the catastrophic effects of its disintegration — it insures not only private happiness but also public respect.

Through Jenny, the only child to be named and characterized in the poem, the continuity essential to domestic, as well as national, welfare is assured. For primarily in the unbroken succession of the family does marital love assert its superiority over ecstatic passion. However much critics may carp at Burns's overzealous advocacy of bourgeois morality (particularly the solicitations about Jenny's honor), one must concede that for maximum happiness he knew feminine virtue to be desirable. The antithetical results for the ruined maid — a stock character upon whom sentimentalists of the day lavished tearful sympathy — are poignantly recorded by Burns in "To a Mountain-Daisy," where the deflowered plant is compared to the maiden betrayed by guileless trust. Therefore, the "Love sparkling in [Jenny's] e'e" causes the mother understandable fear. She is relieved to discover that Jenny's heart is disposed not toward a "wild, worthless *Rake*" but toward a shy young man of commendable intentions. The poet himself is so carried away that he concludes with a glowing apostrophe to the love of Jenny and her swain, who through marriage will perpetuate this atmosphere of domestic bliss.

When William and Dorothy Wordsworth stood at Burns's grave in 1803, they recited stanzas from "A Bard's Epitaph," in which the "poor Inhabitant below" had imprudently conceded that "thoughtless follies laid him low,/ And stain'd his name" (I, 247).[2] Public self-castigation of that sort, which had lightened the burden of remorse for the living man, unfortunately invited defamation of character after death. Thus when Wordsworth wrote his poem "At the Grave of Burns" (III, 65–67),[3] acknowledging his incalculable debt to the older poet, he could not help contrasting the innocent child who had died just three weeks before the Wordsworths' arrival in Dumfries and the distinguished father who lay be-

2. In his *Letter to a Friend of Robert Burns* (1816) Wordsworth cited these lines, lamenting that they unintentionally conceded the worst slander of biographers. See *The Prose Works of William Wordsworth*, ed. Alexander B. Grosart (London, 1876), II, 15.

3. Quotations from Wordsworth's poems refer to *The Poetical Works of William Wordsworth*, ed. and rev. Ernest de Selincourt and Helen Darbishire (Oxford, 1952–59). Citations of *The Prelude* are from the 2nd edition by Ernest de Selincourt, rev. Helen Darbishire (Oxford, 1959).

side him. Whereas the son's existence among the blessed was beyond question, Wordsworth asks "pitying grace" from Him who had often checked the deceased poet in life's "devious race." Yet by evening Wordsworth's apprehensions were put to rest because he seemed to hear Seraphim chanting a hymn of "love that casts out fear." Similarly in "Thoughts: Suggested the Day Following" (III, 67–69) he implores the Divinity not only in behalf of the errant poet but of all humanity, to whom such frailties are, after all, not uncommon. Lest the poet's sons be tempted to yield to similar proclivities, however, he warns them (rather heavy-handedly, perhaps, since Wordsworth had little justification for hurling stones where such transgressions were concerned) to reject seductive lays and never "deem that 'light which leads astray/ Is light from Heaven.'"[4]

Though such consolations may resemble those Job received from his friends, Wordsworth did rise unequivocally to the defense of Burns when the latter's posthumous reputation was at its nadir. Seeking to restore the Scottish poet's image to its rightful luster after the tarnishing wrought by Dr. James Currie's *Life* (1800), Wordsworth wrote his *Letter to a Friend of Robert Burns* (1816), censuring the puritanical biographer with superficiality and indiscretion. Unquestionably many allegations about Burns's moral lapses could be verified in particular instances. But Currie's presentation, he thought, lacked objectivity and also failed to analyze the poet's own feelings and motivations. Equally compelling in the argument of this *Letter* was Wordsworth's determination to criticize the limited perceptions of his old enemy Francis Jeffrey. For if the first biographer had made Burns a spineless weakling, the most influential critic of the time had turned him into a calculating schemer. In reviewing Cromek's *Reliques of Robert Burns*, Jeffrey had sullied the dead poet by impugning his integrity, claiming that Burns's opposition to conventional decency was a ruse for justifying sin and pretending that the finer sensibilities of genius were not bound by customary morality.[5]

Wordsworth's most impressive rejoinder was astutely drawn from Burns's own denunciation of the rigidly righteous in "Address to the Unco Guid" (I, 52–54), which stresses the limitations not only of man's knowledge but of his ability to judge others. The external observer cannot perceive "The moving *Why*" behind another's act or the subsequent remorse, nor can he know which temptations have actually been resisted. As Wordsworth analyzed the moral problem, one privilege of poetic genius was to taste pleasure wherever possible, despite the later necessity of bewailing any error. He conceded that Burns "would have proved a still greater poet if, by strength of reason, he could have controlled the propensities which his sensibility engendered; but he would have been a poet of a different class."[6] Furthermore, Wordsworth was sure that Burns could not have portrayed human emotions as poignantly had he not preached "from the text of his own errors." This perceptive insight into Burns's psychological nature also reveals much about Wordsworth, who may have been projecting his self-reproach by declaring that the Scottish poet "was conscious of sufficient cause to dread his own passions."[7]

Certainly that ideas underlies "Vaudracour and Julia" (II, 59–67).[8] The story, which so outgrew its original proportions in early drafts of *The Prelude* (Book IX) that by 1820 it deserved separate publication, is a revealing account of lovers whose suffering initially stems from their defiance of the marital code. But the tragedy is less a consequence of passion than of youthful weakness before obstacles raised against their unregularized union. Since their private vows seem enough "for a life of love,/ For endless constancy, and placid truth" (ll. 32–33), it is principally the opposition of a society bent on enforcing class and religious distinctions that shatters their hopes. Contributing further to destruction is Vaudracour's ineffectuality in finding a viable solution for himself and the pregnant Julia, since all his attempts prove futile until finally he is compelled to renounce his beloved in order to save his own life. Though his execution would have gained her nothing, the alternative is one that a conscientious man cannot live with: after Julia's confinement to a convent and the death of their infant son, Vaudracour gradually lapses into insanity.

Severed from its original matrix, this narrative is scarcely more defensible than Matthew Arnold pronounced it. As an illustration of how tyranny enforced by the *ancien régime* could blight domestic happiness (as the introductory lines to its briefest form in the 1850 *Prelude* suggest), it is at best diffuse; and what makes it even more unsatisfactory is that the lovers seem to have suffered to no purpose. Nevertheless, the episode is entitled to careful analysis for its philosophical and psychological im-

4. "To the Sons of Burns" (III, 69–71), ll. 39–41.
5. See *Edinburgh Review*, 13 (January 1809), 249–76.
6. *Prose Works*, II, 15.
7. *Prose Works*, II, 15.
8. The 1820 text is employed here because it heightens many of the features suggested in the earlier versions.

portance in Wordsworthian studies. It bears a close relationship to the theoretical love of mankind associated with French revolutionary ideals, for such abstractions, Wordsworth realized, need specific basis in the love of individuals — that contact with flesh-and-blood reality which he recommended in the preface to *Lyrical Ballads* (1800) as the anchor for valid metaphysics. Without an exemplum, the protestations of freedom, love, and other moral values, for which Michel Beaupuy was the most convincing spokesman, would be merely insubstantial theory. What charged the entire atmosphere (and Wordsworth along with it) was the assumption that these goals were about to be transformed into actuality through valorous deeds or, as the poet phrased it, that nature was "standing on the brink/ Of some great trial" (IX, A404-5). Beaupuy himself had converted these principles into action, and Wordsworth drew a parallel between the French patriot's sincere affection for humanity and the love which "in his idler day" he paid to woman (IX, A312-27). Furthermore, Beaupuy had assumed that universal brotherhood could be established only through abrogation of restrictions depriving man of his birthright and that, translating this ideal to the personal sphere, emotional freedom could be insured only by social independence of the individual. In the context of such ideas "Vaudracour and Julia" becomes a pertinent commentary on the catastrophic results of all oppression.

The lovers' tragedy also points significantly in another direction, for it alludes obliquely to the basic problems involved in Wordsworth's affair with Annette Vallon. Like myth, the tale adumbrates essential truths through intentional fabrication, and it must therefore be seen as the reflection of crucial experiences contributing to the poet's emotional development. Despite a dearth of factual evidence, it seems probable that Wordsworth and his French beloved did plan to marry but were prevented from doing so by various circumstances. Like the characters in the story, they apparently entrusted their "cause/ To nature for a happy end of all" (ll. 62–63); yet even before the birth of their child, they were separated. Wordsworth's severe mental anguish after these events corresponds partially with Vaudracour's suffering, which the poet presents with sympathetic understanding; and something of his own self-reproach is apparent through his castigation of Vaudracour's weakness. Presumably he felt that a strong man would have defied parental and social obstructions in such a way as to effect a happy resolution or, like Beaupuy, might have died a hero's death fighting for his ideals. A prudent man, foreseeing possible difficulties, would likely have avoided the perils altogether. But it was the unfortunate combination in Vaudracour's character of improvidence and vacillation that created a predicament allowing no solution.

The tragic story provided an objective correlative for Wordsworth's own debilitating remorse, knowledge of which is necessary to a complete understanding of his distraught condition after his return to England. When his guardian uncles cut off funds and thereby forced him to leave France in late 1792, the most likely prospect of supporting Annette and their child was through ordination in the Anglican Church. Hence departure for England before the birth of Caroline — which seemed perhaps a flight from obligation — might actually have provided a favorable solution. But since Annette had been reared in a devoutly Roman Catholic family, a religious cleavage may have proved more of a barrier to marriage than differences in political ideology. Upon the outbreak of war between England and France in early 1793, both international and familial obstacles beyond Wordsworth's control trapped him in an insoluble dilemma. As he reconsidered the events from a distance of some twelve years, he darkened the poetical conclusion with sombre catastrophes that, by contrast, made his own situation bearable. After all, he and Annette had presumably done their utmost to salvage lives impaired by a love they were incapable of guiding successfully. Their passion, however all-consuming at the moment, had not developed with the gradual, steady growth that bound Vaudracour and Julia; and when better circumstances made marriage possible, the love requisite for nuptial union no longer existed. Matrimony, as Wordsworth wisely perceived, needed firmer ties than atonement for injuries previously inflicted, and a wedding urged primarily by concern for an illegitimate child could not be justified. The immediate effect of separation from Annette had, nevertheless, been disastrous for a man tortured by the discrepancy between his former self-image and the inferences he was forced to draw from his ensuing behavior. However much regret salved his conscience, he knew that in a moment of crisis he had failed to be the poet-hero he envisioned. Like Vaudracour he had set in motion consequences he was powerless to avoid.

Yet it was typical of Wordsworth to turn that defeat into ultimate victory. Like the boy of Winander, whose momentary disappointment leads to profound understanding, or like the spokesman of the Intimations "Ode," who grieves not for what is lost but rejoices in what remains, he profited from his disillusionment. His French love affair had provided more practical schooling for the human heart — without which a poet's mind could never grow — than any other combination of events. The severe crisis of conscience not only humbled him but increased his comprehension of both human frailty and the seemingly inconsequential aspects of daily life. On the other hand, the experience probably contributed to the Roman austerity that strangers often noticed in his demeanor. Human affection, he had discovered, was a very dangerous emotion; as the beginning of "Vaudracour and Julia" warns, it "sports more desperately with minds/ Than ever fortune hath been known to do" (ll. 6–7).[9] His reference to a mistress of France I as a woman "bound to him/ In chains of mutual passion" (*Prelude*, IX, A486–87) shows metaphorically that he considered even monarchial lust to be enslaving. Sexual passion could therefore not be trusted, though its deplorable consequences no doubt merited humanity's tears. For Wordsworth true love, like Bergson's divinity, had to be enduring.

His subsequent phobia of eroticism led to a deliberate absence of that species of poetry from his work, and in several instances he explained his attitude. His Pastor in *The Excursion* argues with moralistic bias that enough suffering exists already in "requited passion," as well as "hopeless love," so that a poet should not encourage further amatory distress (VII, 367–73). He uttered a similar view to his friend Aubrey de Vere, who recorded that the avoidance of love poetry "was by no means because the theme did not interest him, but because, treated as it commonly has been, it tends rather to disturb and lower the reader's moral and imaginative being than to elevate it. He feared to handle it amiss."[10] But it was not only that he felt a certain repugnance toward sensual poetry (such as Moore and Byron wrote); he actually doubted that, because of diffidence and limited empathy, he could do it justice. His refusal to describe the physical pleasures of Vaudracour and Julia is justified not on the grounds of ethical priggishness but on the belief that such depiction was not his forte:

> I pass the raptures of the pair; — such theme
> Is, by innumerable poets, touched
> In more delightful verse than skill of mine
> Could fashion. (ll. 87–90)

There was, moreover, a well-established tradition among sentimental writers who sought a response not of quickened pulses but of tears, and a sidelong glance at the once popular topic of the "ruined maiden" may explain how this inheritance from the age of sensibility persisted. Though Goldsmith and Goethe are still famous for their sympathetic delineations of fallen womanhood, the *locus classicus* for that subject during the Romantic age was Henry Mackenzie's *Man of Feeling* (1771), the fountainhead of weeping for undeserved suffering.[11] Its most elaborately developed episode reveals how an innocent girl, Emily Atkins, sank unwittingly into abject degradation. To a friend, she recalls her infatuation with a young gentleman who feigned honorable intentions; but instead he placed her in a house of doubtful repute, liberation from which depended upon becoming his mistress. Marriage, he argued, would utterly stifle love, which could last only so long as freedom was preserved. Rejecting his offer, she faced pregnancy, imprisonment, and prostitution. Though ultimately Emily's father rescues her, he ironically bewails her loss of honor more than possible death. But Harley, the spokesman of true sensibility, beseeches Mr. Atkins to look beyond the world's shallow judgment and show compassion for someone cruelly injured by unwise love.

The theme of the deserted woman particularly attracted Wordsworth — whether through remorse for his treatment of Annette, or the prevalence of a tradition with which he felt highly compatible, or a combination of both. Philosophically committed to love stabilized by marriage, he treated the subject most effectively from its negative aspect by concentrating on the deplorable aftereffects of a dissolved union. One of his richest psychological studies is "The Thorn" (II, 240–48), a poem made additionally horrifying by its eerie setting. Though the situation of a half-crazed mother who murders her illegitimate infant was so commonplace that man's sensitivity had become inured to it, Wordsworth tried to infuse into the occurrence (as did Goethe, in the character of Gretchen) such striking, imaginative novelty that the reader might be moved to sympathetic response. If his garrulous spokesman is ill-adapted to this primary intent,

9. That Annette herself experienced a similar revulsion can be seen in a letter she wrote to Dorothy Wordsworth on 20 March 1793 detailing her advice to the infant Caroline: "Conserve la [ces jours heureux de l'innocence] longtemps, ma Caroline, si tu veux être heureuse; sois toujours sourde aux cris des passions." See Émile Legouis, *William Wordsworth and Annette Vallon* (London, 1922), p. 130.

10. *Prose Works*, III, 491.

11. Its popularity was such that nine editions were called for by 1800, thirty-nine by 1824.

as Coleridge suggested in the *Biographia Literaria* (Chapter XVII), he is nevertheless an appropriate choragus mouthing humanity's indifference. Unlike the single-minded narrator of a typical dramatic monologue, he lacks both a decided viewpoint and discerning insight. He serves rather as a collator of public opinion, ingesting a weird mixture of fact, hearsay, and fantastic superstition with as little discrimination as a vacuum sweeper and then disgorging it with equal detachment.

Though many tantalizing details of the narrator's story cannot be ascertained, it is verifiable beyond question that high on a mountain ridge grows a thorn tree near a pond and a moss-covered mound. With seemingly deliberate malice the colorful mosses clasp tenaciously round its trunk as if to strangle it or drag it into the earth. To this desolate spot for some twenty years has come a mad woman to renew, as well as relieve, her anguish. In youth she had given herself wholeheartedly to a lover whom she expected to marry but who jilted her on their wedding day. The devastating psychological effect, described in a simplistic but superb metaphor, was a "cruel, cruel fire" that "almost turn'd her brain to tinder." That she was wildly distraught and pregnant six months later was unquestionable, but what became of her child no one knows. Without any evidence whatever, some claim "she hanged her baby on the tree" while others assert "she drowned it in the pond." Yet all concur that the infant's bones must lie beneath the mound. Those who self-righteously demand that Martha Ray should be brought to justice have tried to exhume the body as evidence — only to be thwarted by an inexplicable shifting of the ground which preserves the elusive secret. Weird cries emanating from the spot have convinced others of her affinity with the supernatural, so that fanciful theories have been attached to the entire situation. Indeed, like the clinging moss and the boisterous winds threatening the thorn, all the folk in the vicinity have heaped added burdens on a sensitive soul in need of understanding. Alienated from society and without any means of re-establishing contact, she lives in utter hopelessness.

But Wordsworth's most pathetic example of tribulations caused by abandonment is Margaret's "silent suffering" in "The Ruined Cottage." In its original form, as well as the subsequent elaboration in Book I of *The Excursion*, the tale is justified as a means of heightening sensibility among readers who find "In mournful thoughts . . ./ A power to virtue friendly." [12] The tragedy is much more than a series of calamities; its most poignant aspect, painful as well as inspiring, involves Margaret's intense happiness in marriage, which contains the seeds of misery she must endure when deprived of her husband. That those capable of the most fervent and loyal affection appear to be singled out for exquisite torture was an idea that very much intrigued Wordsworth: ". . . the good die first,/ And they whose hearts are dry as summer dust/ Burn to the socket" (I, 500–502). (His poem beginning " 'Tis said that some have died for love" also suggests that Wordsworth feared the god Eros as an exacting accountant who demanded "grievous pain" in recompense for raptures previously granted.) A more theological implication is that the capacity for human affection is also the measure of an ability to love God; and Margaret becomes an example of one who comprehends "The unbounded might of prayer," learning that "consolation springs,/ From sources deeper far than deepest pain" (I, 936–38).

Wordsworth's own married life was sufficiently gratifying to evoke poetic celebration of wedded love in its more positive aspects. His most beautiful poetic tribute to his wife (II, 213–14), whom he had known since early childhood not only as a family and school acquaintance but also as one of Dorothy's intimate friends, is very much what one would expect after two ostensibly happy years of marriage. The poet describes his impressions of Mary in three stages of progressive development — frequently using light imagery that boldly strikes the mind's eye. The first stanza catches the effervescent gaiety of youth, for "When first she gleamed upon [his] sight," she possessed all the fascination of a sprite skilled in amatory witchcraft. Her physical attributes were those associated with the most appealing times of the day and the year. Yet she obviously seemed more ethereal than substantial, more evanescent than permanent. Like all sheer delights, she was as fragile as "a moment's ornament," a phantom whose motivations were undiscernible, whose captivating effects were ineluctable. Maturing into womanhood, she acquired, without obliterating her spiritual quality, the necessary household virtues in which seemingly antithetic elements were balanced with perfect equanimity. In her he saw the potentialities of a complete life combining "transient sorrows, simple wiles,/ Praise, blame, love, kisses, tears, and smiles."

---

12. "The Ruined Cottage," ll. 483–84; *The Excursion*, I, 632–34. For "The Ruined Cottage" see editorial notes to *The Excursion* in *Poetical Works*, V, 379–404. For an earlier version of this poem, see Jonathan Wordsworth's *The Music of Humanity* (London, 1969).

Looking upon her "with eye serene" after marriage, he claimed to understand her significance as the vital force ("The very pulse of the machine") making their home a viable enterprise. She was a thinking mortal who, somewhat like exceptional plumbing, made the work of everyday life not just possible but pleasant. If Wordsworth commended her rationality, temperate nature, endurance, and skill, certainly he did so without the least air of condescension. These were model attributes in a wife, however blind impractical lovers might be to the requirements of domestic partnership. Furthermore, the use of three strong verbs in conjunction — "To warn, to comfort, and command" — vivified her as more than just a docile helpmate. She obviously retained the fire and determination characterizing her youth. Nor had she lost the heavenly splendor in which she first appeared, but the poet's more intimate knowledge of her virtues disclosed not a supernatural being of questionable motives but one of "angelic light."

After twenty-two years of marriage, Wordsworth tactlessly addressed the following lines to his wife:

> Let other bards of angels sing,
> Bright suns without a spot;
> But thou art no such perfect thing:
> Rejoice that thou art not!
> Heed not tho' none should call thee fair;
> So, Mary, let it be
> If nought in loveliness compare
> With what thou art to me. (II, 35)

Even though Mary was admittedly no beauty at fifty-four, most readers would probably wish that her husband had left the obvious unsaid, however much he adhered poetically to the truth of nature. As though to mitigate his frankness, he wrote "Yes! thou art fair" to follow the above poem in the 1845 edition (II, 35). Yet this palinode is almost more excruciating than what it strove to retract, for the poet claims that in Mary he has often loved his fancy's own creation — that his imagination has bestowed upon her the charm which less perceptive individuals might not detect.

It is obvious that Wordsworth's love for his wife, which had developed steadily over many years, was something quite different from his flaming passion for Annette. His unwavering affection for Mary, though not so exciting, provided a firmer basis upon which to build a lasting relationship.

Yet Wordsworth could not conscientiously marry until in the summer of 1802 he had once more seen Annette and provided an equitable settlement for Caroline. Meanwhile the close association with his highly emotional sister Dorothy, though not completely satisfactory in itself, was undoubtedly stimulating. His dependence upon her after 1792 is conspicuously acknowledged in poems like "The Sparrow's Nest" (I, 227), where he asserts:

> She gave me eyes, she gave me ears;
> And humble cares, and delicate fears;
> A heart, the fountain of sweet tears;
>   And love, and thought, and joy. (ll. 17-20)

Dorothy's journals reveal that his intended marriage was indeed a traumatic threat to the extraordinary rapport that had existed between them, one that had recreated the essence of domestic life which they had not known since becoming orphans. Dorothy's fears, however, seem never to have been realized in the sister-in-law who had long been her close friend, for the three of them established a home together. When Thomas De Quincey first visited Dove Cottage in 1807, as recorded in the valuable essay written on Wordsworth in 1839, he met the women who satisfied the diverse souls within the poet's breast.[18] Though De Quincey's observations might have been even more revealing had they not been colored by Wordsworth's poetry and by a patent determination to balance Dorothy against Mary, his candid remarks are helpful in explaining the successful domesticity of this unusual *ménage à trois*.

Mrs. Wordsworth, whose appearance struck De Quincey as downright plain, nevertheless exercised "all the practical fascination of beauty, through the more compensatory charms of sweetness all but angelic, of simplicity the most entire, womanly self-respect and purity of heart." Though her intellect was in his opinion "not of an active order," she in a perceptive, taciturn way drew genial pleasure from her own thoughts. In his judgment she was ideally suited, with her "sunny benignity" and "radiant graciousness," to maintain the comforts of daily life. The lines in *The Prelude* (XI, A199-223) which describe an unnamed acquaintance are closely in accord with De Quincey's assessment of Mary: "She welcom'd what was given, and craved no more./ Whatever scene was present

13. See *The Collected Writings of Thomas De Quincey*, II, 236-38, 293-302.

to her eyes,/ That was the best." This willingness to accept whatever befell might not have made her an exciting mistress, but it certainly rendered her a most admirable wife.

The other woman in the establishment formed a strange complement to Mary. De Quincey, who very much esteemed Dorothy, saw the poet's spinster sister as an ardently impulsive yet very natural and sensible creature who shared "her illustrious brother's peculiarity of mind" and had for many years devoted herself to everything he loved. The essayist recognized her as someone with a dedicated mission — "to wait upon [Wordsworth] as the tenderest and most faithful of domestics; to love him as a sister; to sympathize with him as a confidante; to counsel him; to cheer him and sustain him by the natural expression of her feelings." [14] But despite her sensitivity of spirit, he thought her physically ungraceful and asexual. Since, to the best of verifiable knowledge, the poet's wife and sister each had her clearly marked domain, neither seems to have impinged upon the other. Whatever detractors may have said about Wordsworth's egotism and pomposity, one must remember that for over four decades he retained in one household the devoted affection of two remarkable women.

As Wordsworth in advancing years relied less upon intuitive and imaginative faculties previously held to be man's superior guides, he placed increasing emphasis upon duty, rational control, and resignation to divine providence as better means of achieving earthly happiness. Though in "Laodamia" (II, 267–72), as most critics have observed, he was preoccupied with restraint on passion, he also concerned himself with the problems of attaining a successful equilibrium within the bonds of matrimony. As in other conversational poems where antithetic viewpoints are presented by speakers differing in age or temperament, neither receives the poet's complete endorsement. Each polarity in "Laodamia" has undeniable merit, but the ideal which Wordsworth strove to express is a balanced synthesis of the two positions. Protesilaus admonishes his overzealous wife

> . . . to control
> Rebellious passion: for the Gods approve
> The depth, and not the tumult, of the soul;
> A fervent, not ungovernable love. (ll. 73–76)

In the original 1815 version the last line of this quotation read: "The fervor — not the impotence of love," implying that unrestrained passion would lead to what it least desired — its own debilitation.[15] Both versions stress amorous intensity, which (Protesilaus avers on his return from the spirit world) is divinely endorsed. Similarly the description of Laodamia as a suppliant states (ll. 7–8) that "fervent love" endows her with faith. However, Wordsworth also emphasizes that the essential complement to this gift, by which it becomes adaptable to mundane limitations, is the guidance of reason.

It was this ambivalence toward passion, a force capable of both good and evil, that put Wordsworth in judicial hot water. Quite unlike Dante, who apparently had no trouble fitting the dead into their rightful niches, Wordsworth could not make up his mind which punishment in Hades would be suitable for Protesilaus's wife. The original conclusion (1815–20) asks that forgiveness be granted because of her profound love. As a guiltless shade, Laodamia, ". . . in reason's spite, yet without crime," is "in a trance of passion thus removed" (ll. 159–60). Therefore she is initially consigned to the Elysian fields of eternal spring. But the 1827 revision banishes her to "a grosser clime" for transgressions "in Reason's spite." In the 1845 redaction, despite reference to "a wilful crime," a phrase added in 1832, she is doomed to "wear out her appointed time" *outside* the fields of "unfading flowers," separated from the "happy Ghosts." Though there was obviously much in Laodamia that evoked the poet's admiration, he seemed unsure that her virtues were sufficiently commendable to erase her "stain."

Most likely, Protesilaus is her harshest judge. He himself has indisputably earned the blessed state of Greek Hades for having died heroically. When he returns for their three-hour interview, his analysis of love exudes the smugness of deliberate martyrdom, despite its admirable stoicism and respect for piety. In an extremely preachy manner he attempts to convince his bereaved wife that passion has been instilled into humanity to annihilate selfhood and that one ought to direct natural yearning toward some exalted objective. While other Greek warriors preparing to fight the Trojans sought vain delights as the rationale of existence and while Laodamia's best pastime was weeping, he had turned his mind toward virtuous aspirations. By contemplating the supreme sacrifice for a noble goal, he had managed, according to his own account, to transcend self. But since

14. II, 296.
15. For the extensive textual revisions Wordsworth made in successive editions of this poem, see *Poetical Works*, II, 267n–272n.

his undisciplined memory often reverted to the joys shared with Laodamia, the prospect of losing her was not always compensated by hopes of Greek victory. Only through "lofty thought" embodied in valiant action could he overcome such weakness. Hence the attachment he now recommends is ". . . such love as Spirits feel/ In worlds whose course is equable and pure" (ll. 97–98). What he propounds is an affection such as ordinary mortals cannot know, though they may aspire to it through practice of "fearless virtue." His sermon falls on unreceptive ears, and it is scarcely ended when he must depart for Hades, leaving an ardent young wife dead from grief.

Laodamia's rejection of such love, at least while she is constituted of both body and spirit, is understandable. Her devotion to Protesilaus, shown by intense suffering and fervent supplication, has obviously aroused the pity of even the stern gods, and for this reason she is granted the rare boon of conversing with her husband's shade. Ironically, that concession bears with it the ingredients of subsequent destruction because within Laodamia's own nature is an unquenchable desire for more than destiny has allotted. When Mercury brings Protesilaus to her, commanding: "Accept the gift, behold him face to face," she does not receive it on Olympian terms but rather on her own, and she tries vainly to embrace the insubstantial visitant. Indeed her husband's appearance is so lifelike that she, refusing to believe him a spectre, invites him to her couch. But this is far more than was intended; a frowning Jove makes Protesilaus resemble the ghost he really is. Even so, Laodamia persists that others have triumphed over death and that love is the most potent force in the universe. Unfortunately a temperament such as hers, though "strong in love," is "all too weak/ In reason" (ll. 139–40). It is not just passion but rather her insubordinate refusal to accept what the gods have decreed (not only for her but for all mortals) that constitutes her "wilful" or rebellious crime. Unable to resign herself to the physical loss of her husband, she is, in the final version, forced to be separated from him in spirit. Wordsworth, emphasizing in natural symbols his cardinal doctrine of love, concludes by focusing on two trees growing from Protesilaus's tomb. Their withering beyond a certain height repeats the principle that impulses toward aspirational growth must be tempered by calm restraint. To ignore this wisdom is to inflict distress upon the human condition; to accept it as Mary Wordsworth obviously did was to achieve happiness.

One of the poet's final literary excursions into the subject of marital devotion resulted from reading Kenelm Henry Digby's *Broad Stone of Honour* (1822), which, to elucidate the ancient Greek belief that affection was "a source of wisdom and virtue," had quoted passages from Protesilaus's admonition to his wife in Wordsworth's poem.[16] In a chapter explaining how the ideals of chivalry (partly by elevating the status of womanhood) had altered the relations between the sexes, Digby illustrated with an authenticated story Plutarch's contention that love might be defined as "a remedy provided by the gods for the safety and preservation of youth." His exemplum concerns a Moslem princess's attraction to an imprisoned crusader and how both are saved by keeping their affections absolutely unblemished. No doubt love controlled as the purest friendship was enough to interest Wordsworth, but in addition there was the suggestion of a domestic trio that caught his fancy.

His ballad "The Armenian Lady's Love" (II, 96–101) enabled the poet to extol the inviolable sanctity of marriage under the conditions of medieval chivalry, at least as Romantic idealists tended to view them. Each of the three characters, by devotion to honor as prescribed in this ethical code, manages to subdue any base motives threatening to undermine a marital union. The imprisoned crusader, rather than yield opportunistically to the Moslem princess whose love would liberate him, explains his irrevocable ties with utmost tact:

> Wedded love with loyal Christians,
>   Lady, is a mystery rare;
> Body, heart, and soul in union,
>   Make one being of a pair. (ll. 61–64)

Devout belief so admirably affirmed wins her to Christianity, even though their escape together might threaten to reduce the princess to a handmaiden. So firm is their mutual adherence to Christian chivalry (the essence of which the Schlegels and Madame de Staël had postulated as the crucial difference between the "classic" and "romantic" spirits) that, however great their admiration for one another, there is no temptation to yield to sensuality. Nor does the crusader's countess, ever grateful for her husband's return, begrudge the sincere homage rendered the Armenian lady. As a full-fledged member of the family, she is reverenced "like a tutelary spirit" and, "like a sister, loved" (ll. 147–48). Even after their

16. London, 1876, V, 96–97.

deaths, as "Mute memento of that union," the husband lies sculptured on his tomb "As between two wedded Wives." But whereas Digby's reference to the crusader's tomb "placed between the figures of his two wives" implies that after the death of his countess he married the princess, Wordsworth's addition of the word "As" rules out the possibility of such a progression. What the poet evidently wished to show was that through adherence to a strict ethical code a triangular design for living might be achieved successfully. And though disenchanted realists may carp at the ballad's rosy picture of the Middle Ages, who dares assert that the poem's most incredible phenomenon, its domestic arrangement, could never have existed?

CHAPTER IV

The Idealization of Marriage: Coleridge and Scott

Whereas men like Burns and Wordsworth assessed marriage as the preferred choice among amatory arrangements, other contemporaries idealized it as potentially the most rewarding of human experiences. Though Coleridge elaborated profusely on the functions of love, he nowhere epitomized his basic concepts more clearly than in his epistolary analysis of Anton Wall's fairy tale *Amatonda*, which Henry Crabb Robinson had translated into English.[1] He found it praiseworthy not only for its "just and fair Moral" but also for its edifying account of "virtuous *Love*." This last phrase was, in his terminology, somewhat redundant, for while goodness alone could not bestow happiness unless combined with love, valid affection could not exist at all without virtue. Reciprocal love, he contended, was "like two correspondent concave mirrors, having a common focus," each reflecting and magnifying the other in "endless reduplication." As the optical image demonstrated, amorous intensity, far from being a retrenchment into a confining microcosm, involved a process of expansion. This emotion (as distinguished from friendship) wholly

1. See letter of 12 March 1811 to Robinson, *Collected Letters of Samuel Taylor Coleridge*, ed. Earl Leslie Griggs (Oxford, 1956–59), III, 302–7. Subsequent references to letters in this edition appear in the text.

united subject and object so that the two became inseparable. Toward such a state the beneficent hero of *Amatonda* progressed, moving from the contentment of cheerful industry to marriage; and this irrevocable attachment was assured of permanence by "long and deep Affection suddenly, in one moment, flash-transmutted into *Love*."

From an interpretation of married love in *Amatonda* arose Coleridge's provocative comments on a former neighbor's domestic arrangement — remarks which must have been particularly fascinating to Robinson, who was later responsible for the jest about Wordsworth's inordinate happiness with *three wives*.[2] Now that the close friendship of Wordsworth with Sara Hutchinson is known to have compounded Coleridge's envy of a man already beloved by two such estimable women as Dorothy and Mary, we can understand the sense of worldly injustice underscoring these caustic observations.[3] According to Coleridge's analysis, written after the rupture of their once intimate relationship, his erstwhile friend was totally oblivious to the deeper varieties of love: marriage was for him merely a convenient arrangement for the fulfillment of needs — a euphoric lubricant in a pulsating machine. According to this rather jaundiced perspective, Wordsworth was declared to be naturally incapable of love, which he seemed to regard as "a compound of Lust with Esteem & Friendship, confined to one Object, first by accidents of Association, and permanently, by the force of Habit & a sense of Duty" (III, 305). While such an attitude might "make a good Husband," Coleridge insisted that it did not indicate love, which in his view was itself no compound though able to unite with other emotions. These were remarkable pronouncements indeed from a man whose marriage had been egregiously unsuccessful and whose other affairs of the heart — with Mary Evans and Sara Hutchinson — had produced far more misery than happiness. Yet those failures in no way diminished his faith in cherished ideals or his hope of finding them realized outside a fairy tale. It was typical of him to analyze abstract love magnificently, regardless of whether or not his postulates crumbled when put to the test. However numerous his virtues were, practical application of theory was never said to be among them.

His insatiable yearning for some woman who might fulfill his concept of partnership is also suggested in the letter to Robinson, who was a close friend of Dorothy Wordsworth's confidante Mrs. Clarkson. Underlying the postscriptural assertion that if Catherine Clarkson had only been his sister he too might have been "a great man" is the tacit assumption that

Wordsworth owed much of his success to a sister's understanding. In a pathetic refrain of self-pity, Coleridge added: "I have never had any one, in whose Heart and House I could be an Inmate, who loved me enough to take pride & joy in the efforts of my power, being at the same time so by me beloved as to have an influence over my mind" (III, 307). Though Dorothy Wordsworth could with justification assert that Coleridge was devoted more to "a fanciful dream" than to any particular woman,[4] his hunger for a compatible soulmate was so avid that he would not relinquish hope of finding one. "My nature," he conceded in an 1803 notebook entry, "requires another Nature for its support . . . . Intensely similar, yet not the same; or . . . the same indeed, but dissimilar, as the same Breath sent with the same force, the same pauses, & with the same melody pre-imaged in the mind, into the Flute and the Clarion shall be the same Soul diversely incarnate."[5]

Yet Coleridge did not conceive of this ideal companion as pure spirit devoid of physical desire; indeed he complained that his wife was "uncommonly *cold* in her feelings of animal Love."[6] By a succession of natural and mathematical analogies he demonstrated that carnality in the material realm was the equivalent of the spiritual desire to perfect itself through union, for the body "in her homely way" tried "to interpret all the movements of the Soul" (III, 305). He later expressed the idea poetically in a quatrain entitled "Desire."[7] Even the spirit, he explained to Robinson, must have a particular sex, for without a "corresponding and adapted Difference," no genuine consummation could be achieved. Whereas lust might be expressed mathematically as the addition of one plus one, love was the multiplication of one by one. Lust he thought incapable of being the prelude to love, though he did concede that at times the two emotions might overlap. Even so, in his ethical system sexual

2. See Charles and Mary Lamb, *Letters*, II, 199.
3. For an enigmatic interlude that turned jealousy into a virtual obsession, see *The Notebooks of Samuel Taylor Coleridge*, ed. Kathleen Coburn (New York, 1957–61), II, 2975 & *n*, 3148 & *n*.
4. Letter of 12 April 1810 to Mrs. Clarkson, *The Letters of William and Dorothy Wordsworth: The Middle Years* (Oxford, 1937), I, 367.
5. *Notebooks*, I, 1679.
6. *Notebooks*, I, 979.
7. *The Complete Poetical Works of Samuel Taylor Coleridge*, ed. E. H. Coleridge (Oxford, 1957), I, 485. All subsequent citations of Coleridge's poetry, unless otherwise specified, are from this edition and are included parenthetically in the text.

intercourse was justifiable only when it contributed to the unity of two people; its immediate goal was not procreation. Absolutely essential to his morality was the purity of affection, and during his anguished relations with Sara Hutchinson he recorded that if "temporary Desire" should ever assume dominion over his spiritual attachment, he would regard himself as too fallen to deserve her respect. But it was not always easy to suppress bodily fire, which he likened to a volcano on the ocean floor that betrayed on rare occasions slight hint of the turbulence below.[8]

That a man so desperate for affection should be denied it seemed one of the tragic ironies of his life, not only to him but to many of his friends. Thomas Allsop, who knew the elderly sage of Highgate during the last sixteen years of the latter's domestication with the Gillmans, attested:

> The whole craving of his moral being was for love. Who is not affected . . . when he hears him exclaim—
>
> > *"To be* beloved *is* all *I need,*
> > *And whom I* love, *I* love *indeed."*
>
> "Why was I made for love, and love denied to me?"[9]

This mournful tone actually dominates many of Coleridge's reveries, and, as evidenced in his adaptation of a sonnet by Fulke Greville entitled "Farewell to Love," there is ordinarily a concomitant sense of injustice at having been betrayed by that vision to which he had dedicated, even sacrificed, his entire being. As he had learned, a unilateral affection, in which one sought while the other merely delighted in being sought, was utterly destructive. Only a constant interchange, as the poem "To Asra" affirms, was capable of bestowing a "Happy Life," the heaven Coleridge associated with reciprocal feeling. Granted his lofty ethics, the only satisfactory bond of which he could conceive was one blessed by matrimony and sustained by conventional morality. Yet it was his determination to fix the ideal in the actual combined with a corresponding refusal to accept mundane imperfections that entrapped him in an insoluble impasse.[10] Unable to shun marital responsibilities even after disintegration of his marriage to Sara Fricker, he was not only deprived of the love he craved at home but frustrated in seeking it elsewhere. His hopeless love for Sara Hutchinson not only tantalized him with thoughts of what might have been had he chosen the right woman but also accentuated the widening breach between him and his wife. Whereas either Burns or Byron would have resolved such troubles by diversionary tactics, measures that they might have employed were not open to a man like Coleridge, who tended to weaken before the mounting challenge. Since it was characteristic of him (just as he thought it typical of Hamlet) to be more concerned with thought than action, no real steps were taken until the deplorable impasse had corroded and dissolved.

Examination of Coleridge's vision, the failure of which ultimately caused inner spiritual decay, may help to explain why it held him captive for so long. It certainly casts light on the pattern of many Coleridgean endeavors that began in exultant expectations and ended in maddening disappointment. From the first, his identification of marriage with a return to Eden presupposed the ability of postlapsarian mortals to achieve more than sporadic glimpses of the lost paradise. An early poem, "Lines: On an Autumnal Evening" (I, 51–54), displays extraordinary desires for a love so idyllic that it could hardly be realized permanently outside the pastoral ode. "Domestic Peace" (I, 71–72) specifically details the conditions under which connubial bliss might flourish — not in palatial pomp or rebellious hatred but in an unpretentious, usually rural, environment ("a cottag'd vale") under the protective aegis of religion and unblemished honor. These stimulating hopes indeed seemed to be on the verge of fruition when he wrote "Pantisocracy" (I, 68–69) extolling the scheme that precipitated him into the regrettable marriage. Contrary to disparagers' claims that the Pantisocrats envisioned a communality of wives, the society these idealists originally planned to establish on the banks of the Susquehanna definitely postulated the sanctity of Christian marriage. Coleridge's sonnet clearly emphasizes that in Pennsylvania too he seeks "the cottag'd dell/ Where Virtue calm with careless step may stray" (ll. 5–6).

Though such aspirations were never to be collectively realized in America or even in Wales, they were given individual opportunities for achievement in southwestern England. Poems written in the fever of premarital expectations show Coleridge on the heights of Pisgah looking

8. *Notebooks*, II, 2984.
9. *Letters, Conversations, and Recollections of S. T. Coleridge* (London, 1836), I, 112.
10. In a work that Mary Shelley claimed was addressed to Coleridge ("Oh! there are spirits of the air"), Shelley upbraided the unnamed recipient of that poem for attaching love to the inconstants of this false earth.

forward to the promised homeland. "To the Nightingale" (I, 93–94) moves from praise of the celebrated bird to an even greater adulation of his betrothed Sara,

> . . . best beloved of human kind!
> When breathing the pure soul of tenderness,
> She thrills me with the Husband's promis'd name! (ll. 24–26)

Equally ecstatic in contemplation of their union is the poem "Lines in the Manner of Spenser" (I, 94–96), where the engaged couple discourse about "pure and spotless" affection sprung from heaven. The serenity of such lovers, as recounted in "The Hour When We Shall Meet Again" (I, 96), seems to derive from mere proximity to one another. Coleridge's use in that poem of the verb *cradle* ("My gentle Love, caressing and carest,/ With heaving heart shall cradle me to rest") reveals his own strong desire to be cared for and sheltered — a wish that he subsequently expressed by the image of the mother dove's wings. That his craving to be loved was not altogether infantile, however, is shown in "Lines: Written at Shurton Bars" (I, 96–100), which reveals an eagerness to protect his betrothed in times of distress. In this poem separation, proverbially the best of amatory stimulants, has allowed Coleridge one of his first opportunities to spiritual-ize love: his soul comforts the absent Sara just as hers consoles him. He even imagines how, when they are married and living in their own home, a storm may frighten her into the security of his arms.

The dream of paradisal happiness seemed even stronger when Coleridge and his "pensive Sara" inspected the cottage at Clevedon where they were to live after marriage. Impressions of that visit, commemorated in "The Eolian Harp" (I, 100–102), authenticate the poet's feeling of complete har-mony with his beloved and their environment; that sentiment in turn prompts neoplatonic speculations about the unity of all life in the uni-verse. The exquisite tranquility of the scene ("the world *so* hush'd"), the delightful stimuli to all senses, and the promise of fulfilled love amply justify his transcendental flight. How could anyone fail to love in a world so constituted? The simple wind harp, that popular metaphor for the poet responsive to natural inspiration, is even tactfully compared to

> . . . some coy maid half yielding to her lover,
> It pours such sweet upbraiding, as must needs
> Tempt to repeat the wrong! (ll. 15–17)

The analogy of love to a musical phenomenon thus becomes an associational bridge to the concept that all nature might be compared to the Eolian harp, for each string vibrates in its own fashion to the spirit animating the universe. In fact, the possibility that responses to human love are measures of receptivity to the divine soul is one that especially satisfies Coleridge. His affianced, however, shows an early symptom of uxorial behavior in admonishing him for unorthodox reflections, and he, with an overzealous desire to please, immediately debases his thought — and himself — as unregenerate. Consequently the poem ends with somewhat ominous portents of their future marital strife. For though he blesses the "Incomprehensible" (who is really Sara's God rather than his), along with his "Peace," "this Cot," and his "heart-honour'd Maid," her victory over him has been pyrrhic and his defeat potentially disquieting. His willingness to yield without necessarily accepting that accommodation as a permanent solution was characteristic of his affectionate but often vacillating nature.

But the poem "Reflections on Having Left a Place of Retirement" (I, 106–8) gives no hint that expectations had been shattered during the first months of marriage. Indeed his depiction of their idyllic home became the recollection of a terrestrial paradise, where flowers associated with blossoming love flourished in a permanent summer. The rose, which he subsequently identified with passionate consummation (the only plant our first parents transported out of Eden) unashamedly "peep'd at the chamber-window" in acknowledgment of their sexual gratification. The skylark, emblem of domestic peace, sang to them "The inobtrusive song of Happiness." Especially breathtaking was the view from a nearby mount, which assured them of God's presence. Indeed a religious aura suffused the entire atmosphere, symbolizing hallowed love in harmony with nature.

Coleridge and Sara Fricker had originally considered themselves partners-to-be in the pantisocratic society; moreover, there is strong indication that during the engagement and early marriage they genuinely thought they were in love. Only three days after the wedding Coleridge wrote Thomas Poole about his contentment with the woman he loved "best of all created Beings" (I, 160). Nor had the honeymoon ended when, six weeks later, he assured Southey: "I love and I am beloved, and I am happy" (I, 164). That physical gratification converting lover into parent was a prominent aspect of this happiness is revealed in several poems written after children were born. Absence from his wife while he was in

Germany during the winter of 1798–99 intensified the pleasant memories of affection solidified by parenthood. In "The Day-Dream" (I, 386–87) he imagines that her spirit hovers over his lips, as a sleeping mother might dream that she were about to kiss her infant, loved not only for itself but as the permanent union of her own life with that of its father. The protective instinct felt by parent for offspring, which Coleridge repeatedly symbolizes by the mother dove's wing, is in keeping with the theological tradition that God's spirit brooding on chaos created life through a supernal act of love. Hence Coleridge, remembering Milton's account of divine creation (*Paradise Lost*, I, 19–22), used the figure of the guardian spirit calling new life into existence not only in his sonnet to Bowles (I, 84–85) but also in his implied correlation between sexual passion and parental fondness.

But this early rapture did not last, and its transformation into wretchedness he sadly recorded in "The Keepsake" (I, 345–46), which associates love with the language of flowers. The rose of passion has become "In vain the darling of successful love" for its blossoms have vanished, leaving only tormenting thorns. Similarly the forget-me-not, symbol of hope, has perished. By this time, the understanding which Coleridge thought he had found in his wife had gradually hardened into distrust and antipathy. Many years later, when enumerating the four notable sorrows of his life in a letter to Allsop, he pronounced the first to have been destruction of his "Vision of a Happy Home." [11] Thereafter it was impossible "to hope for domestic happiness under the name of Husband when [he] was doomed to know 'That names but seldom meet with Love,/ And Love wants courage without a name.'" The emotional rupture was aggravated by Mrs. Coleridge's resentment at being excluded from the Wordsworths' literary domain; and the estrangement was further accentuated by Coleridge's immediate attraction to Sara Hutchinson, whom he met on 26 October 1799 and thereafter addressed poetically by the anagram "Asra." She was genial, vivacious, and sufficiently interested in poetry to share his intellectual life. After the accidental drowning in 1805 of Captain John Wordsworth, to whom Coleridge had apparently hoped she would be "blessedly married" and therefore incorporated permanently within his innermost circle of friends, he wrote: "If Sense, Sensibility, sweetness of Temper, perfect Simplicity and an unpretending nature, joined to shrewdness & entertainingness, make a valuable Woman, Sara H. is so" (III, 76).

Association with Asra brought anguish as well as ineffable delight, since he yearned unwisely during a period of ten years for a lasting relationship despite certainty that only marriage would enable it to flourish. The ambivalence of his attitude is conspicuous even in the poem "Love" (I, 330–35), composed soon after their first meeting and identified with that brief happiness in proscribed affection which both knew could lead nowhere. That he was unfortunately the thrall of love is expressed in the opening stanza:

> All thoughts, all passions, all delights,
> Whatever stirs this mortal frame,
> All are but ministers of Love,
>   And feed his sacred flame. (ll. 1–4)

The dual narrative which follows, offering diverse solutions to the problem of winning a seemingly unattainable lady, juxtaposes the realistic fears and impossible hopes contending within Coleridge. Though the love-crazed knight of the inner tale finally impresses his disdainful beloved through a valiant rescue, her pitying response comes too late to achieve more than consolation for his dying moments. On the other hand, the poet-lover of the framework story, by recounting the agonies of unrequited love, so moves his Genevieve that she consents immediately to be his bride. (Pity in Coleridgean, as in medieval, romance is often recognized as the first step toward love, and much of his desire for the unattainable suggests *amour courtois moralisé*.) This poem was originally published as an introductory companion piece to the earlier "Ballad of the Dark Ladié" (I, 293–95), which reveals another insight into its author's personal dilemma. Dealing with extramarital passion, a topic extremely rare in Coleridge's work, it sympathetically depicts the anxieties of a woman who, having granted her betrothed knight more than can be recalled, insists upon honorable marriage as her just recompense. Once this unfortunate lady became associated in the poet's mind with Asra, the fragmentary ballad could never be completed, locked as it was in ethical impasse reflecting potential dangers from the feminine viewpoint.

The shadow that Asra cast upon his home life was extremely unfortunate, as "A Letter to ——" demonstrates, for it forced him to recognize that he was as blameworthy as his mismatched wife. This verse epistle,

---

11. Allsop, *Letters*, II, 140.

which Coleridge prudently depersonalized to aesthetic and rhetorical advantage as "Dejection: An Ode," bemoans the oppressive grief in which disillusionment with his marriage had left him and for which he finds no alleviatory outlet. His "coarse" domesticity has actually deadened his responsive sensibility through ". . . those habitual Ills/ That wear out Life, when two unequal Minds/ Meet in one House, & two discordant Wills" (ll. 243–45) create a situation numbing beyond cure.[12] Even his young children, by affording temporary glimpses of familial bliss, become a source of woe; when they inadvertently impede the soaring potentialities of his mind so that he wishes "they never had been born," his gloom increases. In rhetoric so eloquent as to undermine his contention, he denies the ability to re-establish emotional contact with the external world of either man or nature. Obviously a lament for irrevocable powers in a poem of the highest imaginative caliber suggests a tendency to overdramatize the negative, proving beyond question that Coleridge reveled in self-pity as a substitute for success. This destructive habit only compounded his mental depression.

While the poem denies any expectation that Coleridge himself will ever be restored to connubial blessedness, it reaffirms his requirements for that goal and the exalted hopes attached to fulfillment. The poet still believes that others can achieve marital blessedness — particularly Asra, who satisfies all the preliminary conditions for domestic success. She is innocent, affectionate, and (unlike the fretful man who adores her) bolstered by a sense of rectitude that frees her from anxious care. Though he would no doubt be excluded from her family circle, he unselfishly wishes her a "happy Home" with those she cherishes. Obviously Coleridge still retains the belief in a sympathetic, closely knit group fixed in a definite location. Nor will he begrudge in the slightest her domestic tranquility marked by

> Peace in thy Heart, & Quiet in thy Dwelling,
> Health in thy Limbs, & in thine Eyes the Light
> Of Love, & Hope, & honorable Feeling. (ll. 145–47)

Even though these circumstances be realized where he can never see her, he will be content in the knowledge that she is safely ensconced in such an environment. As one who prefers "the Permanent" or the security assured by minimal change, he would in fact rather have that situation obtain than be tantalized by its obverse. For him only sporadic association with one he deeply loves produces such misery afterwards that its pleasure is reduced to "a dim Dream of Pain to follow" (l. 162).

Unfortunately his emotional response to such conditions is equivalent to the Eolian lute's "dull sobbing." Presumably he too would have been better off either mute or purged of all feeling by a liberating storm of passion. Yet avoidance of all further contact with Asra seemed as unlikely as eradicating her from his thoughts, and though Coleridge's inherent weakness may be deplorable, one must admit that he probably could not force himself to take such a drastic measure. If he was no better at flushing a beloved's image from his consciousness than was the speaker in "Lewti" (I, 253–56), then he was wise not to attempt that feat in the verse "Letter." In his impotent state even the union of his mental perceptions with external nature, which he appropriately describes in connubial metaphors (ll. 298, 316), has suffered the same fate as his foundering marriage. As he admits, "we receive but what we give," and the parallels between love, imagination, and epistemology are highly significant. Since the necessary interchange cannot continue once the power of projecting one's own luminous vitality upon nature has been extinguished, viable stimulation from the outside world, like connubial satisfaction, is dead to him. Though aware that both still exist and are beautiful, he can no longer respond to them. Similarly, Coleridge employs, as evidence of inner harmony and strength, the power of joy, which Schiller had celebrated in the hymn *"An die Freude"* as the divine force instilling life throughout the universe. Upon it depends the effluence of all vital feelings, including love; and of course the poet feels totally deprived. Without joy the "new Earth" and "new Heaven" promised by the union of mind and matter (or man and woman) cannot exist. Without it he lacks the ability to restore contentment in daily emotional attachments, on which his spiritual and emotional creativity depends.

How then can the poet reconcile himself to deterioration — to the widening separation between his psyche and outer stimuli, which leaves him increasingly dejected? Memories of happier, more inspiring feelings offer him no restorative power (whatever they might have proffered Wordsworth), and often by contrast to present suffering they become instruments of torment. Even the emotional tumult which he expects to

12. All citations of this verse epistle are from George Whalley's edition in *Coleridge and Sara Hutchinson* (London, 1955), pp. 155–64.

liberate his soul from dull torpor does not alleviate his sorrows, though it grants him limited resignation. Asra alone, addressed as "Sister & Friend of my devoutest Choice" and "dear, as Light & Impulse from above," offers a modicum of salvation in a spiritual love re-establishing unity not so much with earth as with heaven. So long as she is unblemished, affectionate, and joyful, she can participate in the mutual interplay of life that produces happiness, which he represents in the celebrated image of eddying motion creating an unbroken circle.

The apparent failure of earth-bound aspirations prompted him, in typically Romantic fashion, to seek gratification in the world beyond the senses. His devotion to Asra was not the fixation of preconceived ideal to mortal woman — the deceptive but all too common habit to which he in a letter ascribed the failure of many love matches (IV, 906–7) — but rather the abstraction of the ideal from the actual. Though far more intense, this distillation followed much the same pattern as his earlier attachment to Mary Evans, whom he had admired without any expectation of reciprocal feeling until it was too late. The tendency to etherealize his fondness for Asra produced increasing self-analysis in an attempt to prove their relationship an infinitely superior marriage of true minds. Confidently reassured that his feelings were the product of most admirable sentiments, he strove to demonstrate that they represented spiritual longing for absolute goodness. Like Dante, who claimed that "the Good . . . kindles love, and all the greater in proportion to its degree of goodness" (Huse translation of *Paradise*, XXVI, 28–30), he tried to identify his devotion to a particular woman with his soul's affinity for supreme benevolence. "The best, the truly lovely," he maintained, "in each & all is God. Therefore the truly Beloved is the symbol of God to whomever it is truly beloved by!"[13] For Coleridge Asra was the God-bearing vessel, proof that divine life existed in him, and assurance that he would ultimately achieve union with divinity. As he observed in an eloquent paean entered in his notebook,

> I hold it . . . neither impiety on the one hand nor superstition on the other that you are the God within me, even as the best and most religious men have called their conscience the God within them. . . . you alone have been my conscience — in what form . . . can I imagine God to work upon me, in which *you* have not worked? . . . the sum of all your influence and benignant grace has been horror of whatever is base, shame and compunction for

whatever is weak and unworthy, fervent aspirations after good and great honourable and beautiful things, and the unconquerable necessity of making myself worthy of being happy as the one indispensable condition of possessing the one only happiness — your love, your esteem, and *you*.[14]

Such extravagant claims could not long withstand the abrasion of everyday experience; and soon after writing the preceding entry he made another recording his terrible disillusionment. The harshest pain stemmed from realization that his self-effacing love had been reciprocated only by friendship — an idea later deplored poetically as "Kindness counterfeiting absent Love" (I, 459). The rupture in the autumn of 1810 of his longstanding acquaintance with Asra and the Wordsworths completely demolished his insubstantial amatory castle, and once again he indulged in tearful self-pity for never having been loved, even though several people had relished his devotion. "One human being, *entirely* loving me (this, of course, must have been a woman)," he wrote, "would not only have satisfied all my hopes, but would have rendered me happy and grateful even tho' I had had no friend on earth, herself excepted."[15] This intimate union need not have been a marriage in the conventional sense, which he regarded as only a social contract ratified for the manifestation of esteem and friendship.[16] What he had vainly sought was "a *Wife*, in the purest, holiest sense of the word" though circumstance might prevent the sacrament of mundane union.[17] The same entry asserted that for a decade he had striven to achieve this apotheosis of love — one totally without shame, yet one that only an angel would understand. Consequently he could only rationalize his failure on the grounds that "voluntary self-humiliation," "habitual abasement," and self-identification with pain rather than pleasure might indeed have won an angel. But Asra, he had discovered, was largely woman.

These disappointments, however, in no way diminished his theoretical interest in marriage or modified his assumption that he could offer sound advice on the subject. Most of his counsel reveals a pragmatic effort, at

13. For this entry in notebook "24," see Whalley, p. 99.
14. Notebook entry soon after 24 October 1810. See Thomas M. Raysor, "Coleridge and 'Asra,'" *SP*, 26 (1929), 319.
15. Notebook entry of 3 November 1810. See Raysor, p. 321.
16. Allsop, II, 17.
17. Notebook entry of 3 November 1810. See Raysor, pp. 321–22.

least in his public voice, to accommodate in some way to reality. He even declared that, though the possibility of discovering the ideal mate was remote, anyone willing to settle for less than perfection might find contentment.[18] Believing that young people, especially girls, optimistically rush into marriage unaware of its inherent obligations and pitfalls, he contemplated writing a book on the duties of wives, designed to expose both men and women to the unglossed facts of conjugal relations prior to the wedding.[19] Though this intended volume never materialized, he did express similar thoughts in a letter to a young lady on the brink of matrimony.[20] Unless she took this irretrievable step with careful forethought, he warned, it might be tantamount to suicide. Those desiring the conditions of Eden to continue beyond courtship — those determined to cultivate more than just a "Kitchen-garden, a thing of Profit and convenience, in an even temperature between *indifference* and *liking*" — should take special care so that true love will perennially blossom. Therefore anyone seeking beyond "animal comforts" and respectability must have a soul mate rather than a yokemate. Since much of one's future usefulness depends upon wise selection of a partner, he advised his correspondent to choose a husband who was morally righteous, affectionate, and adaptable. He especially admonished her against one who by constitutional disposition was inclined to "mournful complaints" even though, as it often happened, afflictions of this sort were accompanied by "the highest worth and the most winning attractions." Mindful of his own predisposition to anxiety and self-pity, he urged rejection of any suitor who might through such infection reduce a whole family to misery. In retrospect Coleridge perceived the futility of endless worrying and convincingly transmitted the incisive wisdom learned through his own domestic nightmare.

But while his lofty views on marriage were tempered in later years by acceptance of its limitations, his interpretation of *das ewige Weibliche* grew ever more exalted. Whether or not his conceptual models had any permanent contact with flesh and blood, he enjoyed contemplating the *idea* of feminine love.[21] After the halo suffusing Mrs. Clarkson in celestial light had dimmed, he transferred it with rekindled brilliance to a Mrs. Crompton, whom he described as an "angel without wings." Concerning her he wrote John Morgan on 18 February 1812: "She explains to my feelings that most venial, because most beautiful, of all forms of Idolatry, the adoration of maiden Motherhood visualized & realized in the Virgin & Child" (III, 370). Coleridge obviously felt that woman as virgin, wife, and mother had potentialities in love that man could not possibly achieve. In a religion extolling *caritas* as its ultimate virtue the symbol of the Blessed Virgin was the most appealing representation of the divinity in mankind.

In his lonely declining years, sheltered though he was by his foster family, the Gillmans of Highgate, Coleridge's laments for lost domestic happiness grew increasingly pathetic.[22] His nostalgic reminiscences, severed from experience like blossoms cut from a nourishing plant, assumed the characteristics of pressed flowers; while unquestionably authentic, they were so rigid and lifeless as to be only sad reminders of faded beauty. Even his "Constancy to an Ideal Object" (I, 455–56) shows disillusionment in the Christian Platonism through which he strove to transcend his marital fiasco. This late poem questions that the concept of love, which admittedly exists only in the brain, should be immutable when all the rest of nature decays. Since in no earthly time can the idea be transmuted into fact, it achieves actuality only in death, when Hope and Despair (the Coleridgean equivalents of Eros and Thanatos) finally meet. The poet therefore understands that no mortal can be the constant he had worshipped. Even so, he cannot dispel the mental image, with whose embodiment he still yearns to have "an English home." Though unwilling to pronounce the ideal chimerical, he must concede that it has borne only the faintest resemblance to his experience. As a projection of his mind, it offered therapeutic relief, but it did not solve the problems of earthly love.

Whatever may have been the shortcomings of George III, marital infidelity was not one of them. In fact, it was even said that his domestic virtues enabled him to perpetrate upon his subjects detestable measures that a libertine monarch could never have inflicted.[23] Though his political acumen was often impugned, unwavering devotion to wife and children elevated him above moral reproach. Such rectitude, however, was never

18. See "The Improvisatore," *Poetical Works*, I, 462–68.

19. See Allsop, I, 190–91.

20. Allsop, II, 86–101. For similar ideas recommended to a prospective bridegroom, see Coleridge's letter of 8 January 1819 (IV, 903–9).

21. See Allsop, II, 88.

22. See "To Two Sisters" (I, 410–12), "Recollections of Love" (I, 409–10), and "Love's Apparition and Evanishment" (I, 488–89).

23. For enunciation of this view see Coleridge's letter of 31 May 1796 to John Fellows (I, 219).

ascribed to his sons, who comprised the most dissolute group of royal princes England has experienced. George IV, first as Prince of Wales, then regent, and ultimately king, denigrated the institution of marriage almost as much as he diminished the crown's popularity. His repeated vacillation between admission and denial of a morganatic union with Mrs. Fitzherbert proved only one thing — that marriage for him was of no consequence except as the means to a desired end. His agreement to marry Princess Caroline of Brunswick was openly acknowledged as financial expedience, since Parliament would not subsidize further dissipation unless he provided a legitimate grandchild to the throne of George III. After stud service had been rendered, the Prince relapsed into cohabitation with Mrs. Fitzherbert — until he tired of her and her successors in turn. In view of his own flagrant defiance of the marital code, his insistence (upon succession to the throne in 1820) that the House of Lords pass a divorce bill against his allegedly unfaithful wife made a farce of the entire proceeding. Its failure was partly hastened by the unhappy queen's assertion that her only adultery had been committed with Mrs. Fitzherbert's husband, but it is significant primarily as a reflection of aristocratic amorality.

Yet against this upper-class spectacle of profligacy ran the ever-present current of British respect for the home. It was almost as though, while the aristocracy tended toward greater debauchery, the middle classes felt increasingly obliged to uphold bourgeois morality. The popularity of Thomas Campbell's *Pleasures of Hope*, which went through nine editions between 1799 and 1807, may in part be ascribed to esteem for "Hymenean joy." Its descriptions of marital hardships and domestic love today seem either cloyingly lachrymose or insipid, but they no doubt provided what contemporary readers expected on such topics. Indeed when Francis Jeffrey noticed Campbell's *Gertrude of Wyoming* for the *Edinburgh Review* in April 1809, he commented that those who admired *The Pleasures of Hope* for "its pictures of infancy and of maternal and connubial love" would find "still higher gratification" in the author's subsequent work (XIV, 4). As though a stronger effort were needed to bolster the domestic scene, zealous reviewers and editors strove to endorse morality. That the traditional *Gentleman's Magazine* should contain many sentimental poems exalting virtue and conjugal bliss is not surprising because that periodical tended toward family enlightenment. But that *Blackwood's*, known for its vitriolic wit, should in its first year of publication include original verse of the same nature indicates that public demand was too strong for even the editors of the "Maga" to ignore. The August issue of 1817, for example, printed a mournful poem entitled "The Widow'd Mother" and a sonnet "On the Spirit of Domestic Happiness," the latter calling marital contentment Albion's "tutelary Power" very much as Burns had thought it Scotia's (I, 501). An equally sentimental story entitled "The Progress of Inconstancy; or, the Scots Tutor; a Moral Tale" in the September 1817 issue (I, 601-7) further demonstrates that while *Blackwood's* could be flippant about anything else, serious affection, particularly of the kind worthy to be sanctified by marriage, was not a subject for jest.

Adherence to ideals such as these contributed no small amount to Walter Scott's unprecedented vogue in the nineteenth century. Despite his admiration of aristocratic ways, he remained throughout life the champion of middle-class virtues, and as in other tastes his preference was an accurate weather vane of majority opinion. Even though he was the favorite poet of the Prince of Wales, Scott had serious misgivings about a future sovereign whose scandalous private life had set a dismal example for his subjects. Consequently when King George suffered a serious illness in August 1811, Scott voiced grave apprehension about the heir apparent. As he wrote his friend Joanna Baillie, ". . . alas! a public defiance of morality is but a bad bottoming for a new reign — it is incalculable the weight which George III derived from his domestic conduct." [24] Nor was this opinion merely designed to ingratiate him with Miss Baillie, for he embodied it not only in his life but in the works that made him extremely popular, first as poet, then as novelist. Though his own sexual voltage may not have been strong, there were other reasons for this moral stance. His sense of justice was so highly developed that sensual gratification resulting in anguish could not be countenanced; indeed sexual vice was totally alien to his nature. Hence he bore no puritanical hatred toward sin because of fears that in weaker moments he might succumb to it; he simply had little genuine interest in transgressions of the flesh. Byron, though differing radically in temperament from Scott, considered him "the most *open*, the most *honourable*, the most *amiable*" of men, "as nearly a thorough good man as man can be." [25]

To assert, as Grierson does, that Scott "had no great understanding of

24. Letter of 4 August 1811, *The Letters of Sir Walter Scott*, ed. H. J. C. Grierson (London, 1932-37), II, 529. Subsequent references to Scott's letters appear in the text.
25. *LJ*, VI, 220-21.

love as a passion" is exaggeration.[26] Yet modern critics generally deplore his lack of salacious thrills and disparage him for submitting to contemporary taste. Certainly he extolled sincere, enduring affection and condemned destructive ardor that blighted whatever it touched. There is evidence, however, that in youth his amatory fervor had been less constrained by common sense than it subsequently became in maturity. The extant letters addressed to his first sweetheart, a tradesman's daughter in Kelso, show him as completely enraptured with this otherwise unknown Jessie as any other adolescent of seventeen or eighteen. His earliest surviving message to her demonstrates that young Walter was no Dryasdust suitor. "I cannot sufficiently express," he wrote, "the impression your lovely features have made on my heart . . . . Your gentleness, your goodness, your kindness have filled me with the sweetest feelings I have ever known" (I, 1). Though their friendship burgeoned for a while, Walter for reasons that cannot now be determined, apparently lost interest in her as a prospective wife. Since for him no other amatory culmination was possible, he abruptly ended the relationship in a manner so painfully honest as to make her forever resentful.[27]

His treatment of Jessie should theoretically have prepared him for the terrible disappointment in his next love, Williamina, who, as the daughter of Sir John and Lady Jane Belsches, was as much above him socially as he had been above Jessie. For five years, though without much real encouragement, he was ecstatically hopeful of someday making her his bride. By the autumn of 1795, however, he grew despondent upon learning that William Forbes, son of a wealthy banker and heir to his father's baronetcy, was also seriously interested in her. When she did in fact select Forbes, the desolate Walter assumed that she had acquiesced to the materialistic advice of her mother, who later declared William to have been her daughter's first and only love.[28] Whatever the reasons for Williamina's choice, Scott felt that for the sake of worldly security and social rank she had betrayed her heart; and to commemorate his disillusionment in her faithless behavior he wrote "The Violet." Though Williamina cannot have been oblivious to the Forbes assets, she may well have discerned (in addition to the imminent coronet) a kind heart to which her rejected suitor was then understandably blind. Some seventeen years after her death, it was Sir William Forbes who in 1827 generously aided Scott in his desperate financial plight, when hostile creditors held him at bay, by anonymously paying off the beleaguered author's most pressing debts.

Because Williamina remained in Scott's memory the perfection of what might have been, her image was never tarnished by the unflattering light of common day or worn by the attrition of domesticity. After her death, he let recollections of her occupy his mind enough to inspire depiction of various heroines, and he himself acknowledged that she served as the model for Matilda in *Rokeby* (1813). Obviously with love, as well as history, the past became additionally romantic, and it grew increasingly idealistic as he projected himself into a purified version of the affair distilled of all unpleasantness. He was further consoled by interpreting this disheartening experience as a paradigm for all callow love. "Scarce one person out of twenty marries his first love," he wrote George Huntly Gordon on 12 June 1820, "and scarce one out of twenty of the remainder has cause to rejoice at having done so. What we love in those early days is generally rather a fanciful creation of our own than a reality. We build statues of snow, and weep when they melt" (VI, 208).

That he was not one to be destroyed by amatory languor is demonstrated not only by his own resolution to bypass failure but by later commentary in his novels. When one of his most winsome heroes, Quentin Durward, suffers "mental dejection" upon first being separated from his beloved, Scott emphasizes the salutariness of occupying one's mind with sanguine thoughts. "Melancholy, even love-melancholy, is not so deeply seated," he observes, "at least in minds of a manly and elastic character, as the soft enthusiasts who suffer under it are fond of believing."[29] And indeed Quentin soon becomes so immersed in the active life around him that sadness is dispelled. Similarly, in *St. Ronan's Well* the Rev. Josiah Cargill recovers from a grave disappointment in love. Scott, poking gentle fun at feminine sentimentalists, remarks that Josiah does not remain "for years the victim of an unfortunate and misplaced passion," for a "well-constituted mind, which is itself desirous to *will* its freedom," does not permanently succumb to hopeless dedication.[30] Instead he wisely turns his attention to pursuit of an even nobler mistress — Knowledge. Another of Scott's characters, the charming Rebecca of *Ivanhoe*, reconciles herself

26. *Sir Walter Scott, Bart.* (New York, 1938), p. 160.
27. See Grierson's introduction to *Letters*, I, lviii.
28. Grierson, *Scott*, p. 31.
29. *Quentin Durward*, ch. XIX, in the "Caledonian Edition" of *The Works of Sir Walter Scott* (Boston and New York, 1912–13), XXX, 23.
30. *St. Ronan's Well*, ch. XVI, *Works*, XXXI, 249.

to unattainable love through adherence to filial obligation. But Scott warns in the 1830 introduction to the novel that one should not expect self-denial or "the sacrifice of passion to principle" to be compensated by worldly justice.[31] Rather, "the internal consciousness of . . . high-minded discharge of duty produces . . . a more adequate recompense, in the form of that peace which the world cannot give or take away."

Scott's avoidance of rapturous love in literary works was quite deliberate, not only because he feared its detrimental effects upon the young but because he lacked sympathy with characters overwhelmed by passion. As he wrote Matthew Weld Hartstonge on 29 October 1812, "your true Lover . . . is in my opinion the dullest of human mortals, unless to his mistress — I know nothing I dread more in poetry than a Love scene unless it be a *battle which is equally unmanegeable*" (III, 185–86). Such an attitude justifiably prompted a feminine acquaintance of Lady Abercorn to ask whether the poet had himself ever been in love since his heroes seemed so inept at it. Responding to Lady Abercorn's provocative letter on 21 January 1810, he candidly rejected the kind of love women expected in poetical narratives because he had through sad experience found it disadvantageous (II, 284n, 286–87). If his own marriage admittedly lacked the intense fervor that occurred only once in a lifetime — a man who has almost drowned, he asserted, does not thereafter venture beyond his depth — it nevertheless had emanated from "the most sincere affection," which through twelve years continued to increase.

His courtship of Charlotte Carpenter might indeed have provided the model for that of his most admirable characters. Soon after meeting her in September 1797 he declared in a letter that their "hearts were formd for each other" and stated with typical resoluteness his intentions and worldly prospects (I, 65–68). Despite their brief acquaintance, Walter also felt obliged to write his mother explaining the seriousness of his interest in Charlotte, whom he commended not for beauty but for a cheerful temper, admirable understanding, proper religious principles, and anticipated fortune (I, 68–70). He had apparently learned, after two disappointing love affairs, that a lasting relationship must be based on something other than physical attraction. Charlotte's conduct was equally circumspect. Though already twenty-seven years of age, she would not accept the proposal until her erstwhile guardian had approved, and throughout their engagement her behavior (though by no means lacking in ardor) was restrained and level-headed.

Marriage for them was a further means of cultivating noble qualities — the underlying condition for developing the *bona indoles* through which fulfillment of duty, self-sacrifice, and mutual understanding became not a burden but a routine pleasure. During the early years of marriage, Charlotte was sociable, gay, and warm-hearted. Whenever possible, she aided her husband in his work and in the active social life both of them seemed to require. Moreover, their two sons and two daughters became a focus of great familial love. If Charlotte did not bear the financial catastrophe of 1827 with equanimity, her bad health may have been largely responsible. After her death, when Scott and his daughter Anne passed through Carlisle, they visited the cathedral where he and Charlotte had been married. Commenting on this nostalgic visit in his journal, he noted: "It is something to have lived and loved; and our poor children are so hopeful and affectionate, that it chastens the sadness attending the thoughts of our separation."[32]

Scott's highly conventional treatment of love in his artistic creations is well illustrated by *The Lady of the Lake*, which has as its central problem one similar to that of his two preceding metrical romances, *The Lay of the Last Minstrel* and *Marmion*. The poet must arrange, despite numerous obstacles posed by faction and warfare, to marry his heroine to the man of her choice. Were she less resolute, she might easily settle for another suitor. But a determination to take the course of extraordinary resistance contributes not only to her character but also to the adventurous excitement serving as the plot's backbone. While the narrative is propelled chiefly by forces of destruction, true love and the magnanimity it inspires ultimately triumph over conflicting loyalties that threaten to bestow Ellen's heart where it would be unhappy.

Ellen's attachment to the youthful Malcolm is never rhetorically argued. Though he seems handsome, valiant, and honorable, we are forced to rely chiefly on her estimate of his inherent worth. Obviously her "heart has its reasons" that lie beyond dispute. Her initial predicament arises from the fact that the clan-chieftain, Roderick Dhu, also loves her. But, despite acknowledged debts to him for sheltering her outlawed father in his island lair and to his mother for having reared her, Ellen never confuses obliga-

31. *Works*, XV, xxii.
32. *The Journal of Sir Walter Scott* (New York, 1890–91), II, 150–51. See also John Gibson Lockhart, *Memoirs of the Life of Sir Walter Scott, Bart.* (Edinburgh, 1839), IX, 256.

tion with love. Though willing to fulfill her duties even to the extent of death, she insists upon the absolute freedom of her affections. Indeed she would prefer to be a nun or a hapless exile rather "Than wed the man she cannot love." With her ingenuous charm, she has also won the admiration of the disguised monarch, whose gift of a ring entitles her to any boon she may request from the crown. In a *beau geste*, such as Scott particularly enjoyed, the king subsequently awards Malcolm to her. Thus with fairytale justice, virtue bolstered by forgiveness, constancy, and sympathetic understanding is poetically rewarded.

In *The Heart of Midlothian* Scott has more to say about love than anywhere else, owing largely to a juxtaposition of rational affection with destructive passion. Though his antithetical depictions are conspicuously overstated for the sake of emphasis, they are nevertheless saved from absurdity by a tongue-in-cheek whimsicality and by insight into the shortcomings of both polarities. Furthermore, his empathic humor prevents a solemnly didactic tone while permitting an unequivocal moral stance. Perhaps more than any other of his works, this novel demonstrates that man's behavior in love is congruous with his general demeanor; and the much maligned fourth book, long though it may be, is justifiable as the necessary elaboration of this doctrine. According to Scott's implied view, someone like the Spectator Club's Will Honeycomb, who was honest and worthy in all matters except those concerning women, was a neoclassical fantasy. Nor could he accept the popular Romantic concept of a despicable cad whose virtues in love would redeem his misdeeds in other affairs. As a man loves so too does he live.

No better embodiment of this idea is afforded than David Deans, the lovable but eccentric cow-feeder, who is devoted to a rigid code of Calvinistic ethics governed by the Lord's injunctions, by man's legalistic efforts to enforce them, and by obedience to a well-developed conscience. Never does he entertain the possibility that extramarital intimacies might be mistaken for love, and his peremptory disowning of his younger daughter for her transgression is especially significant in view of the strong familial bonds of his Cameronian faith. True to type, he retains an "Auld Licht" Presbyterian attitude toward marriage, which he pronounces "a necessary evil" since in his view it is a compromise with the world and the flesh against possible inroads of the devil. It is a regrettable tie in that it prevents man from soaring toward spirituality by binding him to creature comforts such as wife, bairns, and property; yet its legality minimizes both the stigma and sinfulness of carnal desire, and for those incapable of adhering to the Pauline counsel toward virginal continence, the married state is definitely preferable to internal combustion. Though he is always generous with advice against a precipitous union — his admonitions to his elder daughter and her betrothed on this score are ironically comical after their Joblike patience — he concedes that wedlock is an honorable condition, however disappointing it may sometimes prove to be.

While Jeanie and Reuben do not share her father's cynicism, they do approach marriage with prudence. Their love, though not of an exciting variety, has ripened slowly since childhood, based as it is upon shared interests, common backgrounds, and respect for obligation. Outwardly Reuben is reserved, and not until his worldly ambitions are within sight of attainment does he allow himself to grow emotionally committed to Jeanie. Even then, they agree that marriage must be postponed until his education is completed and he has some steady means of support. The novelist describes this seemingly Platonic love with conscious detachment. "Fortunately for the lovers," he asserts, "their passion was of no ardent or enthusiastic cast; and a sense of duty on both sides induced them to bear with patient fortitude the protracted interval which divided them from each other." [33] Physically Jeanie is no more alluring than Reuben. With plain face and rustic manners, "her only peculiar charm" is "an air of inexpressible serenity, with a good conscience, kind feelings, contented temper, and the regular discharge of all her duties, spread over her features." [34] In short, her personality is one that only another with similar traits would fully appreciate.

An excellent foil to Jeanie is her younger half-sister, Effie, who by being exquisitely beautiful is irresistibly attractive to men. But having been reared more indulgently than her elder sister, she acts according to impulse rather than by any rational code of ethics — like an "untaught child of nature" — and Scott obviously trusted the "natural man" no more than

---

33. *The Heart of Midlothian*, ch. IX, *Works*, XI, 126. The section entitled "Marriages" (Part II) of George Crabbe's *Parish Register* (1807) has several interesting vignettes illustrating different kinds of wedded (and unwedded) couples that may well have furnished ideas for Scott's novel. As epigraph for Chapter IX of *The Heart of Midlothian* he uses a passage about the prudent lovers Reuben and Rachel from that section of Crabbe's work. To begin Chapter X Scott quotes from the tragic story of Phoebe Dawson, who seems to have been the prototype for Effie (*Parish Register*, II, 131–228).

34. *The Heart of Midlothian*, ch. IX, *Works*, XI, 119–20.

he did the unpredictable vagaries of the elements. Her secret infatuation with a charming but equally wayward young man and an ensuing pregnancy further estrange Effie from her morally stringent family, so that she admits her condition to no one. This fact, combined with the child's disappearance, causes the indictment for infanticide. The deplorable situation provides a definite index to Scott's view of what can happen even when both lovers do all within their power to avert the catastrophes which their unlawful relationship sets in motion, for all Staunton's efforts to free Effie from prison or to marry her prove unsuccessful. Despite the author's obvious sympathy with the misfortunes of his errant characters, his grave mistrust of any love unbridled by reason is clearly shown by the consequences of uncontrolled passion.

Though it is not in accord with Jeanie's conscience to bear the necessary false witness that would save her sister's life, she heroically seeks a pardon, and her firm conviction that Effie is innocent of child murder prevails with a queen who admires her virtues. What especially ingratiates the simple Scots girl with Queen Caroline is an accidental mention of the cutty stool as a means of publicly disgracing adulterers, for the queen is so delighted with the obvious chagrin felt by her attendant Lady Suffolk (who is also the king's mistress) that she directs her sympathy wholeheartedly toward Jeanie's cause. By evoking an empathic response between two chaste hearts, Scott, ever the righteous crusader for sexual morality, enables virtue to succeed.

While the pardon would seem to eliminate major obstacles to a favorable denouement, the pattern of the characters' lives has already been set by their varying responses to love. Though Effie achieves both respectability and material advantages through marriage to Staunton, she and her husband, guilt-ridden and ever fearful of exposure, lack the spiritual peace necessary to happiness. Not until Staunton has been killed, in a rather heavy-handed stroke of retribution, by the son he could not care for at birth, does she find solace (as Scott predicted Bryon might) in the rituals and penances of Roman Catholicism. By contrast, Jeanie's reward is one of genuine happiness in marriage, for she and Reuben are united after he is well established in his parish. Respected by all who know them and blessed by children, they live quietly content, requiring little more than their own well-being.

The Bride of Lammermoor, on the other hand, suggests that sentimental love, when detached from practical considerations, may provide the *ha-*

martia of tragedy. Far from idealizing passion that can lead only to disaster, Scott in this novel demonstrates the inadvisability of an unwise attachment, either an engagement that cannot culminate in marriage or a union unhallowed by love. Nevertheless, he does not condemn the young lovers' folly. Just as he understands Caleb Balderstone's preference for illusion (in his case, the verities of past grandeur) to the harsh realities of present degradation, so too he sympathizes with the failure of Edgar and Lucy to overcome insurmountable obstacles. They are caught in an insoluble deadlock between two families cyclically out of phase — the once lofty Ravenswoods approaching their nadir, the aspiring Ashtons nearing their zenith. Whereas Edgar is constrained by an aristocratic code demanding openly respectable behavior, Lucy's opportunistic family is bound by no ethics. In a rapacious manner, the Ashtons resort to unconscionable trickery in attaining their goals, and from this conflict of irreconcilable standards death alone can provide escape for the lovers.

Their own natures also contribute to final annihilation. The serenely beautiful Lucy is at seventeen strangely indifferent to "the tinsel of worldly pleasure." Unlike other members of her grasping family, she admires chivalric ideals and seems oblivious to intrigue. So docile does she appear that her domineering mother condescendingly calls her the "Lammermoor Shepherdess," but as Scott reminds us, lest she appear spiritually anemic, well-bred young girls of the seventeenth century were expected to abide by parental governance. Beneath her ostensible compliance, however, there exists a latent germ of passion requiring only the proper stimulus for development. It is quite logical, then, that she responds emotionally to the handsome young man who saves her and her father from a wild bull and later entertains them in his ruined castle. Edgar is, in fact, all that one might expect in a fascinating Byronic hero: he is proud, melancholy, and filled with a desire for vengeance demanding supralegal justice. His fatal attraction to Lucy is all the more devastating because she is one of the inimical Ashtons, who by virtue of Machiavellian scheming have usurped his ancestral domains. Hence destiny has trapped him between love and obligation, so that he must become either a fool or a villain. His honorable compliance with Lucy's desire first to secure her parents' consent to the engagement is what subjects him to those whose only interest is in his destruction.

Only in the minds of self-deceiving readers like Emma Bovary could Scott's treatment of love be regarded as an invitation to romance that compensates for humdrum existence. If *The Bride of Lammermoor* teaches any object lesson, it is that love must be carefully guided and supported by rational judgment. Fools alone assume that it can flourish in hostile or sterile environments; and, as Edgar and Lucy might have perceived, willful tenacity to its impossible hopes causes not merely disappointment but complete havoc. Unless lovers are strong enough to resolve impediments to marriage, they are better off not to embark upon a sea of passion. The world of successful love has no place for illusion, fairy tale enchantments, or exotic escapism. Emma Bovary's self-identification with the operatic Lucia is perhaps more justifiable than with the novelistic prototype, for Donizetti's *Lucia di Lammermoor* accentuates both the lurid sentimentality and Gothic melodrama of its original. Though Emma's convent reading of Scott may well have given her a glamorized view of history and famous heroines, his novels cannot be justly indicted for misleading her about rapturous love. Careful study of his work might indeed have saved her from being engulfed in the quicksands of fantasy, for his narratives provide cogent arguments in favor of emotional stability.

PART THREE

Love Without Marriage

CHAPTER V

The New Moralists

I N AN AGE when mankind was zealously establishing freedom from political oppression, enlightened women inevitably adapted many libertarian concepts to their own purposes and envisioned their ultimate emancipation from domestic tyranny. Since in all respects other than physical prowess they were potentially the equals of men, marriage came under stringent reconsideration. Even though liberal-minded interpreters of the Bible regarded the two divinely inflicted punishments of Eve — suffering in childbirth and subjugation to man — as nothing more than a primitive attempt to rationalize the status quo, many contemporary daughters of Eve were scarcely more fortunate than their first ancestress. Their servile dependence upon man, even more deplorable than reliance upon capricious fate, is tragically epitomized in Donna Julia's farewell letter to Juan: "Man's love is of man's life a thing apart,/ 'Tis woman's whole existence" (I, 194:1–2). But if some women, deprived of men's career opportunities, resigned themselves to being repeatedly undone, others strove actively to remedy the inequity.

The most eloquently determined of these was Mary Wollstonecraft, whose *Vindication of the Rights of Woman* (1792) urged liberation of the downtrodden sex not only for its own sake but for the general improvement of society. Striking at the root of the trouble, she declared that women had been enslaved to love. By accepting the foolish notion that the chief justification for their existence was being useful to the other half of humanity, they had tacitly approved their own subservience. So long as the one socially endorsed career was respectable marriage, young maidens' only ambitions were directed toward ensnaring desirable husbands even while pretending disinterest. After this goal was achieved through duplicity, their business was then to keep spouses interested by whatever was expected of wives in particular stations. Though Mary Wollstonecraft considered genuine affection essential to any attachment and was unwilling to dispense with marriage unless society was ready to abandon all social virtues, she nevertheless urged the same rights for women that men assumed as their prerogatives. Not the least of these depended upon acknowledgment of a single moral standard for both sexes.

While granting that society was primarily responsible for making women the sportive toys of men, she also blamed those of her sex who acceded to the traditional concept of womanhood. Young girls were falsely educated to become "alluring mistresses" rather "than affectionate wives and rational mothers." [1] Wishing only to inspire love in a potential catch, they preoccupied themselves with personal beauty and elegant dress. Instead of preparing for life in a way that would "strengthen the body and form the heart," they became little more than debased lures concerned with ingenious ways of trapping their prey. [2] Not surprisingly, then, their empty minds were governed by indolent vanity and a desire for pleasure. In this puerile state (which unfortunately men were conditioned to prefer) most of these vapid creatures remained unless some inadvertent catastrophe forced them to mature.

Nor was the situation any better after marriage. An industrious woman, devoted to household obligations, often found the reward of unremitting diligence to be loss of her husband's affections. Sometimes, fondly hoping to rekindle his ardor by the stratagem of teasing restraint, she inadvertently drove him to prostitutes, who succeeded where affected propriety had failed. On the other hand, the naïvely romantic woman, who regarded love as her sole profession, became equally disillusioned when she ceased to enflame conjugal passion or to receive the trifling compliments she expected as evidence of fondness. Such a wife might even prefer a rake to an exemplary husband because the former, constantly playing the role of seducer, conformed to her preconceived idea of an interested male. Furthermore, as a result of hypocritical society, she was likely to confuse integrity with reputation and assume that feminine virtue was unsullied as long as public honor was unstained. Indeed many a woman apparently lacked the awareness that married love progressed into something quite different from that of youthful courtship. As Mary Wollstonecraft astutely perceived, though in a rather old-maidish way, "Love, considered as an animal appetite" could not "long feed on itself without expiring."[3] If a married woman's inequality produced such deplorable consequences, the widow was reduced to an even more intolerable state of dependency. Without an honorable vocation, she was unable to work and ashamed to beg; she could only throw herself upon the mercy of some male relative for protective custody.

To resolve these problems Mary Wollstonecraft advanced a number of sound recommendations. Her proposals for a national system of coeducation, wherein the youth of both sexes were to acquire liberal knowledge and physical training, seemed daring at the time, though her obvious distrust of the human body would have marked her as a Hebraist rather than a Hellenist according to Matthew Arnold's dichotomy. Specifically, she suggested that women ought to cultivate their intellectual abilities, which would ultimately be more appealing and enduring than physical charms. Matches founded on mutual esteem and understanding would be much more successful than those based on romantic ardor. Having no real objection to a strong, unwavering passion, she nevertheless disapproved of the irrational sensuality often identified as love but actually, in her opinion, the enemy of virtue and friendship. Yet even well-intentioned individuals would continue to be frustrated unless society as a whole improved. Since, according to orthodox belief, virtue stemmed from exclusive adherence to reason rather than to emotional impulses, morality had entrenched itself in an impregnable fortress against which the storms of passion were constantly raging. So long as religion provided a refuge for weakness and fanaticism rather than a positive approach to human ethics, it would never be the governing principle of conduct that, ideally, it should be. Until the antagonism between heart and mind was properly resolved, there could be no just peace between man and woman.[4]

1. Mary Wollstonecraft, *A Vindication of the Rights of Woman*, ed. Charles W. Hagelman, Jr. (New York, 1967), pp. 23–24.
2. *A Vindication*, p. 52.
3. *A Vindication*, p. 121.
4. In *The Wrongs of Woman; or, Maria* (1798), Mary Wollstonecraft implicitly sanctions divorce when husband and wife can no longer cherish one another.

Perhaps it was inevitable that two of the most sensitive defenders of human rights — Mary Wollstonecraft and William Godwin — should have been attracted to one another, crotchety though both were inclined to be. What began merely as intellectual admiration led to cozy intimacy, occasional cohabitation, marriage (though with separate domiciles since neither wished to monopolize the other), and even parenthood. Having been driven twice to attempt suicide by the disintegration of her liaison with Gilbert Imlay, Mary was well aware when she became intimate with Godwin in 1796 that a thorny path might lie ahead. Even more painful was the stigma of bastardy attached to her daughter Fanny Imlay; and it was especially because prejudiced society did not accept illegitimate children that Mary and Godwin, who at first had absolutely no intention of being married, decided to submit to the routine ceremony when Mary became pregnant.[5] That Godwin, after having published strictures against matrimony, felt obliged to defend his apparent inconsistency is obvious from a letter of 19 April 1797.[6] As he explained, he had previously asserted (in *Political Justice*) that the attachment between two persons of opposite sexes ought to be "in some degree permanent" though matrimony as then practiced in European countries was despicable. Consequently, after protesting that the iniquitous institution of wedlock ought to be abolished, he recommended that his fellow men enter into it only "with the greatest caution." Though in his particular instance he had yielded to what was "necessary for the peace and respectability" of Mary, he declared himself no more irrevocably bound by the utterance of a few words than he had been prior to that formality.

Godwin's *Enquiry Concerning Political Justice* (1793), which was generally regarded as one of the most inflammatory works of the period, had indeed touched lightly upon marriage — and then, significantly, in the subdivision entitled "Of Property."[7] The widespread attention these meager comments received was far beyond the importance their author attached to them, but they were nevertheless of great relevance under that particular heading, not only because he regarded marriage as a fraudulent title of ownership in people but also as the primary means of passing on accumulated wealth to perpetuate a class structure. It was these proprietary functions and the abuses they encouraged that Godwin determined to eradicate. Though in the subsequent editions of 1796 and 1798 he softened some of his earlier pronouncements — his short, happy marriage to Mary may have had some influence on emendations for the third edition — he never wavered in his antipathy toward matrimony as frequently practiced in an acquisitive society.[8]

Particularly condemned was the manner in which it was ordinarily arranged. Usually, "thoughtless and romantic youth" met on several occasions far removed from the realities of everyday life and vowed "eternal attachment" to one another. Not until too late did they discover the imprudence of their choices; yet the inexorable standards of society forced them to make the best of unwise selections. Rationalizing that their original decisions must have been correct, they proceeded to live a corrupting lie. Since men who deliberately deceived themselves in domestic relations were strongly inclined to carry that folly over into other endeavors, the fraud of marriage led to debased judgments in numerous concerns. To counteract these impostures, Godwin advised unhappily married people to admit their mistakes and dissolve the union. They should search for compatible association rather than let connubial ties, like a set of blinders on a horse, keep them from seeing "the most attractive and admirable objects." Regardless of legal restrictions, they should seek connections with worthy people from whose acquaintance they would "derive the greatest improvement." This freedom, far from inviting promiscuity, would in a reasonable society such as Godwin endorsed enable partners to adhere only as long as both individuals so desired.

If marriage was, in a sense, a matter of proprietary rights, there would be attendant evils. Enforced cohabitation, Godwin believed, would check "the independent progress of mind." Furthermore, he thought it inconsistent with the present imperfections of men, particularly the propensity to oppose all inflexible restraints, including the sexual. "It is absurd," he declared, "to expect that the inclinations and wishes of two human beings should coincide through any long period of time. To oblige them to act and to live together, is to subject them to some inevitable portion of thwarting, bickering and unhappiness."[9] He also felt that should a man

5. William Godwin, *Memoirs of the Author of "A Vindication of the Rights of Woman"* (London, 1798), pp. 154–58.

6. Charles Kegan Paul, *William Godwin: His Friends and Contemporaries* (Boston, 1876), I, 235.

7. London, 1793, II, 848–52.

8. For textual variants in the later editions see *Enquiry Concerning Political Justice*, ed. F. E. L. Priestley (Toronto, 1946). Priestley's text is that of the 1798 edition.

9. *Political Justice* (1793), II, 849.

arrogate one woman to himself, prohibiting his neighbors from proving their superior desert, he would be "guilty of the most odious of all monopolies" (II, 850). The guarding of connubial treasures in miserly fashion only caused ill effects, for nothing so inflamed the envy and desire of a potential transgressor as a jealous husband's vigilance. While trespassers were incited to overcome fenced-in claims, owners became preoccupied with constructing marital hedgerows. Many men indeed became so obsessed with protecting their conjugal gardens that they ceased to tend them properly and thereby abrogated their right to possession. Consequently, Godwin believed, marriage under such conditions produced the very antithesis of reason — destructive passion, adultery, and legalized rape.

Despite expressed fears that depravity would follow the abolition of matrimony, Godwin prophesied the very opposite. Conjugal infidelity, he carefully explained in subsequent editions, would be considered only a venial lapse and not such a heinous crime that it became all the more exciting by clandestine practice. As usual, he felt that laws which were created to restrain vices merely increased them. In his egalitarian society of the future sensual enjoyments could be so minimized that intellectual pleasures would be preferred and relations between the sexes would become similar to bonds of friendship. A man might "cultivate the intercourse of that woman whose accomplishments" he found most impressive. If other men felt the same attraction for her, then they too could enjoy her conversation and "be wise enough to consider the sensual intercourse as a very trivial object." Sexual relations "in each successive instance" were to be determined by the willing consent of both parties. Just as people eat not solely for pleasure but to ensure health, so too men and women were to have physical relations "because it is right the species should be propagated." If the child's paternity were uncertain, that would be of no consequence because in a classless society family name would have no relevance and unessential property could not be inherited. In fact, even in strictly personal matters Godwin recommended that people evaluate others objectively on the basis of worth and not allow familial ties to bias impartial judgment. In 1793, though to a lesser degree in 1796 and 1798, he apparently felt that marriage was too firmly entrenched to admit reform. If the public and private ills entailed by proprietary ownership were to be eliminated, the connubial relationship as then perpetrated would have to be abolished entirely.

Against Godwin's views on human perfectibility, as well as those of the French philosopher Condorcet, Thomas Robert Malthus wrote his rebuttal entitled *An Essay on the Principle of Population* (1798). Therein he pronounced the rational, egalitarian society envisaged by *Political Justice* to be nothing more than "a dream, a beautiful phantom of the imagination."[10] Far more than his predecessors on the subject, Malthus succeeded in dramatizing the fears about a growing demographic problem and, as an economist, attempted to devise an explanation for the alleged discrepancy between food and population increments. Since, according to his postulate, man's sex drive would always produce people more abundantly than the means of subsistence could possibly be increased to feed them, the ensuing misery and vice (nature's *ex post facto* way of restricting humanity) would always prevent the Godwinian utopia from being realized. His second, revised edition of the *Essay* (1803) mitigated the initial gloomy predictions, partly with the hope that "moral restraint" under the guidance of reason might save mankind from impending disaster. Specifically he suggested that if everyone were able to remain celibate by means of self-imposed chastity until such time as he and his beloved could properly care for the fruits of their passion, then the world might avoid the prophesied dilemma. Contrary to popular opinion, however, he at no time recommended any artificial restraints upon a couple after marriage. Whether or not Malthus's enemies were placated by his emphasis on rational control, they could neither ignore him nor dispel the fear that some truth might exist in his Delphic utterances, which in successive editions were bolstered by increasingly voluminous tables of statistics.

Malthus, an ordained clergyman, was also scornful of Godwin's latitudinarian views on cohabitation because he thought such practices would lead to even greater production of illegitimate children. Illicit relations "without improper arts" (as Malthus presumably called contraception, abortion, and other unmentionable practices) would just increase the burdens on society. Early attachments, if entered into by young people who thought they could easily break them, would merely invite irresponsibility toward provision for offspring. The only obvious check was the moral compunction a man ought to feel about bringing into this world children for whom he could not provide. Should this curb be removed, women

10. *Essay* (London, 1798), p. 175.

would suffer all the more from inability to support their progeny while men would proceed to indulge their passions with the impunity of tom-cats. Denying that a commerce between the sexes could, except in a few rare instances, ever be sublimated to an intellectual one such as Godwin depicted, Malthus argued that the property-oriented institution of marriage was the only sound one devised for taking care of the young and for limiting their number to a manageable figure. In the revised edition of 1803 he asserted that one of the main reasons preventing his contemporaries from acknowledging the demographic problem he had outlined was "a great unwillingness to believe, that the Deity would, by the laws of nature, bring beings into existence, which, by the laws of nature, could not be supported in that existence." [11] To this contention he replied that mankind's awareness of the dilemma, as well as the dire consequences of ignoring moral restraints instilled by common sense and revelation, should remove "all apparent imputation on the goodness of the Deity." In fact, the competitive "struggle for existence," which Charles Darwin would later reinterpret scientifically without the blessing of religion, was defended in the *Essay* as the divinely ordained impetus to human advancement.

However much the superannuated, the frigid, the impotent, and the remorsefully overindulgent might inveigh against passion, Malthus saw no evidence that it was waning. He readily conceded that "the pleasures of pure love [would] bear the contemplation of the most improved reason, and the most exalted virtue." [12] Since reason enabled men to consider the results of any enjoyment, it was for some, admittedly, the ideal guide and check against possible abuses. Nevertheless, he was unable to believe that cultivation of the intellect would cause an eclipse of sensuality. "Virtuous love, exalted by friendship," he declared, "seems to be that sort of mixture of sensual and intellectual enjoyment particularly suited to the nature of man." [13] Certainly he could not imagine that the common mass of humanity would ever achieve such an improved condition of intellectual and rational control that instinctual drives would appreciably decline.

Malthus's concisely phrased hypotheses were so famous in his day that thoughtful contemporaries were obliged to read his work. If for no other reason, idealists such as Wordsworth, Southey, Coleridge, Scott, Hazlitt, and Shelley acquainted themselves with the *Essay* in order to refute the voice of necessitarian despair. Many opponents denounced him, quite unjustly, as the spokesman of an Establishment trying to shun its responsibility toward the poor or arguing that only the rich were entitled to connubial love. More than other literary men of his time, Byron (if we may pass over Keats's "hungry generations" in "Ode to a Nightingale" as a rather questionable allusion) was receptive to Malthusian concepts, though not without serious misgivings. His epistolary comments show that he was aware of the discrepancy between an acceptance of human suffering as biologically necessary and a religious endorsement of it as providential; hence he associated Malthus's observation of reality with an amazing ability to deceive oneself about its true theological implications.[14] Moreover, no matter how much he respected the professorial parson's contributions to economic theory, he obviously regarded "moral restraint" as a potentially dangerous self-delusion, for in his view sex was the temptation man could least likely resist, even when starving.

Whereas traditional ethics had been concerned with the authorization of love by civil or religious ceremony, William Blake believed that a valid union could be legitimatized only by love. Any determination of rightness by criteria external to lovers was therefore false; deeds of love were justified by sincere inner feelings. Both in his own day and later, Blake was famous for unconventional views on marriage, though much of that reputation derives from unverifiable anecdotes. One of the most trustworthy raconteurs, Henry Crabb Robinson, noted in his diary that Blake claimed Biblical authority for proposing a communality of wives. When Robinson, whose stodginess Blake delighted in twitting, responded rather priggishly that marriage seemed to be "a divine institution," the poet countered that "from the beginning it was not so."[15] Yet despite currency of this tale, as well as far more lurid ones supposedly illustrating his antagonism toward nuptial bonds, there is no evidence in his surviving works that he condoned harems or sexual promiscuity. However, his numerous comments on love and connubial relations show that he had many trenchant insights into both subjects.

Though Blake's first volume, *Poetical Sketches* (1783), gives little hint

11. *Essay* (London, 1803), p. 494.
12. *Essay* (1798), p. 211.
13. *Essay* (1798), pp. 213–14.
14. For an elaborated treatment of this subject see my "Byron on Malthus and the Population Problem," *Keats-Shelley Journal*, 18 (1969), 17–26.
15. *Henry Crabb Robinson on Books and Their Writers*, ed. Edith J. Morley (London, 1938), I, 337.

of his later attacks on marriage conventions, it nevertheless shows deep concern with various facets of the matrimonial relationship.[16] Probably the simplest expression of this interest appears in four poems to the seasons describing earth's love affair with cyclical nature. Also in the pastoral tradition of neoclassicism, "To the Evening Star" invites the planet Venus to smile upon "our evening bed" and draw the "Blue curtains of the sky" so that a state of fulfilled marital quiescence (later to be developed as the concept of Beulah) may be achieved. A blissful, euphoric state of conjugal love is suggested by the song beginning "Love and harmony combine," in which sexual implications are undeniable: "While thy branches mix with mine,/ And our roots together join." Countering this idealism, in a way that was to become much more characteristic of Blake, is the treacherous perversity of Dalila in "Samson." Most predictive of Blake's future treatment of love, however, is the song beginning "How sweet I roam'd," because it describes the sexual trap into which a young girl has fallen. During courtship her beloved strives to please with sensuous delights, but having caught her "in his silken net," he sadistically locks her in "his golden cage" and treats her as his private toy. This theme is reiterated satirically in a song from *An Island in the Moon*.[17] Beginning with a mock-heroic apostrophe to "Matrimony made of Love," the poem hails wedded life as a universal poultice; yet the jolting reference to it as a deluding snare, into which the hopeful are most readily beguiled, wrenches the starry-eyed view.

The tendency to be easily deceived is ordinarily associated with guileless purity; and though Blake in his *Songs of Innocence* eloquently celebrates the limited virtue of the naïve state, he maintains elsewhere that innocence when associated with proscriptive religion ceases to be winningly childlike and becomes repugnantly childish. A refusal to progress into the world of generation is as contrary to the course of human life as Milton's "cloistered virtue." Though man may regard the Fall as an inevitable consequence of incarnation, to be human is to pass from innocence into experience and, hopefully, into redemption. The obstruction of such development is presented in *The Book of Thel* (1789). The poem's motto, read in context, suggests that one can learn accurately only from those in intimate contact with any desired truth; the mole, and not the eagle of the skies, knows the pit representing both the grave and the world of process. Furthermore, in answer to the motto's final questions, wisdom and love are shown to be inherent even in the male and female generative organs — the "silver rod" and "golden bowl" that deserve the esteem ordinarily granted precious metals.

The lament of Thel, an unborn soul on the threshold of embodiment, concerns the transience and seeming lack of purpose in earthly existence. Through her experiences Blake presents some of his basic tenets concerning love. The created beings who attempt to console Thel find no cause to grieve in their own evanescence but rather rejoice in being part of cyclical nature. The cloud in particular regards his life as emanating from the same source which renews Luvah, emblem of love and sexual regeneration, and justifies his rapidly changing condition with the belief that "every thing that lives,/ Lives not alone, nor for itself" (II, 25–27). Even the insignificant worm, symbolizing both the phallus through which human life comes into being and fleshly corruption by which man returns to the elements, is shown to have a usefulness. The clod of clay offers further encouragement by unquestioning acceptance of her role as the material from which the creator has lovingly fashioned his children. Though unable to comprehend her own function completely, she is content to serve her purpose, realizing that true love does not seek to please only itself. It is into her house that Thel enters on a temporary basis, with the provision that should it prove distasteful the "virgin of the skies" may still return to a pre-existent state. Thel's disillusionment in the world of generation becomes the vehicle for Blake's indictment of a deplorable situation, particularly with regard to the fallen senses that, instead of being portals of unmitigated joy, are, as a result of frustrations, sources of pointless suffering. Especially the sexual restraints dictated by absurd notions of chastity cause the horrified Thel to flee back into the realms of the unborn, believing that the usefulness she had expected to justify existence is apparently denied. Preferring to remain forever within the limitations of innocence rather than progress into experience, she rejects the challenge of fallen life, only to regress into atrophy. Her plight brilliantly demonstrates Blake's contention that body and soul divided from each other become sterile.

Further implications for Blake's love ethic appear in *The Marriage of Heaven and Hell*. Many of the contraries, which are conspicuously symbolized in the title imagery and without which he felt there could be no

16. All citations of Blake are from *The Poetry and Prose of William Blake*, ed. David V. Erdman and Harold Bloom (Garden City, N.Y., 1965).
17. Erdman, pp. 450–51.

progress, are particularly applicable to marital union — an alliance supposedly not of opposites that would annihilate or cancel out one another but rather of two contrary aspects of a single entity. Man and woman, radically different yet complementary expressions of the same species, tend when ideally united to advance humanity. So too, attraction and repulsion, reason and energy, love and hate are necessary antitheses that propel earthly life. Blake believed that these somewhat paradoxical relationships had been oversimplified by a "natural religion" that associated goodness with rationalistic passivity and evil with energetic action. Thus orthodoxy had become the purveyor of a Urizenic hindrance to human endeavor: those who did nothing would be rewarded in heaven, and those who acted would be punished. To the contrary, he argued that man's energies should not be repressed or negated but channeled into creative achievement; the only real vice was either failing to translate one's own thoughts into action or impeding someone else's intended deeds. Since he believed sex to be one of the surest methods of stimulating imagination, he considered sensual restraint a heinous crime in preventing this godlike activity. Therefore a belief that physical love was sinful became an affront to divinity.

According to the edifying devil who serves as Blake's whimsical spokesman in *The Marriage*, theists have also been misled by a belief in the dualism of flesh and spirit, associating libidinous energy with the body and rationality with the soul. Emasculated priests, who themselves have virtually no desire or pervert it into fearful lechery, place a "curse upon the fairest joys." But Blake insists that body and soul are inseparable, the body providing merely the "chief inlets" and the perceptible outward manifestation of soul during earthly existence. Nor should there be any final division between energy and reason. Rather energy, springing from the bodily portion of a unified man, should be recognized as the only vitality and reason as its outward boundary. Hence those who give vent to exuberance are not necessarily courting eternal damnation; more likely, if granted unconstrained opportunity, they will convert their powers into eternal delight. Blake cites examples of those originally endowed with remarkable fervor — the poet Milton and the rebellious Lucifer — who by following the Orc-into-Urizen progression became so subdued that they used the vestigial remnants of life merely to rationalize their subjugation. Only when such men break repressive bonds do they express that divine fire which makes them artists, poets, or lovers.

The proverbs of hell, which invite acceptance of the moderately unusual through startling hyperbole, expand Blake's concept of physical man reawakened through sensual perception. Sexual fulfillment becomes the first step toward apocalypse, and even excessive indulgence will result in a higher wisdom than abnegation. His terse maxims make unmistakably clear the deleterious effects resulting from denial of divinely implanted creativity. Restraints merely breed psychic pestilence, stimulating what they seek to hinder: "Prisons are built with stones of Law, Brothels with bricks of Religion." Blake therefore recommends that humanity reject this proscriptive attitude and return to the pristine relationship of man and woman which existed before the Fall blighted sexual consciousness with shame. As a result of the division between male and female selfhoods, Eve, according to the poet's later elaboration, ceased to be the Emanation of Adam and became instead a Spectre totally outside him. This impasse may be resolved by sexual communion, a fiery consummation which cannot be dishonorable, for "The soul of sweet delight, can never be defil'd." Man, by experiencing such heightened enjoyment, is enabled to recognize the infinite in the finite and to become more genuinely like the divinity residing within him.

Blake further identifies the true God with the prolific and active; those in whom the divine urge is weak he calls the devourers, who merely receive the excess of delight from the prolific. The devourers do have a rightful place in the universal scheme, for without them to receive the overflow of energy the prolific would cease to be productive. A disjunctive effect occurs when the devourers, assuming with myopic vision that their portion is the whole, seek to operate alone and to bring the prolific under their control. This, by Blake's diagnosis, is what religion has done in trying to reconcile necessarily opposite principles. The church has made of the rational devourer an equivalent of what the poet would later call the mocking Spectre, the ghostly selfhood, which of itself can make no contribution but which, by setting itself apart from the prolific, actually stifles existence. But Jesus, who understood the proper balance between contraries, opposed rigid categories separating good from evil and acted virtuously by impulse rather than adherence to the decalogue. To subject men of entirely different natures (Blake's lion and ox) to one invariable law enforced tyranny upon all.

Many of the *Songs of Experience*, translating these gnomic principles into concrete reality, deal specifically with problems arising from the enslavement of love in a fallen world. As prophet and reformer, the Bard of the "Introduction" beseeches Earth to return to an unspoiled state, to arise from debasement and renew her now extinguished light. But Earth replies in despair from a dark prison on the "watry shore," symbolizing her chaos until the apocalyptic dawn. Immured in this den by "Starry Jealousy," she blames her condition on the extraneous tyranny of the "Selfish father of men," the Urizenic deity whom she fears but never loves. Her incarceration has, of course, repressed what ought to be joys of earthly life; and she particularly bewails the proscriptions against sex, which have chained delight and caused the sensual pleasures to be regarded as disgusting — never to be indulged except in dark secrecy. Consequently human affection is in bondage and, like the speaker of "Earth's Answer," incapable of liberating itself. Probably to correct this despondent view, Blake much later added the poem "To Tirzah," which implies that redemption might actually take place in an individual sufficiently resolute to overcome the constraints of nature. Hence it provides a hopeful solution to the problem delineated by Earth. Tirzah, representing the protective maternal principle of Innocence as well as a rapacious natural goddess who has confined man's experiences to sensory perceptions, signifies the inevitable death of all life committed to the world of generation. But the twice-uttered line — "Then what have I to do with thee?" — which recalls Jesus' words to his mother (John ii:4), expresses a determination to break through the limitations of the physical body though not in the orthodox Christian sense of minimizing the corporeal to exalt the spiritual since in Blake that dualism does not rightfully exist. Admittedly Tirzah has bound four of the human senses in such a way that man cannot escape self-deception any more than he can avoid mortality. Yet Blake intimates that the sense of touch, enabling man's body to transcend imprisonment in the "Mortal part" governed by Tirzah, will, through awakened imagination, achieve the resurrection promised by Jesus.

Though hope for the freeing of love underlies much of Blake's thinking, most of the poems in *Songs of Experience* explore its depraved condition in the present world. "The Clod and the Pebble," for example, illustrates two widely held amatory viewpoints that instead of being contraries are actually antinomies negating one another. The clod of clay, trodden by cattle's feet until it epitomizes plastic malleability, maintains that true love, having no care for itself, is completely self-effacing. From the ingredients of hell, it builds its own illusion of heaven. Yet the flinty pebble of the brook contends that self-gratification is the only meaningful form of love, and it finds joy in proprietorship's triumph at "anothers loss of ease." In place of an extant heaven, it constructs a hell. Too often in the human world such differing attitudes are openly advocated, especially by martyr-prone women and hedonistic men. The combination, though superficially tolerable, drives each extreme to a more contemptible position, producing an impossible "heaven" and an unacceptable "hell." At the crux of both problems is Blake's archvillain, selfhood, which is glorified by either suffering or pleasure but not obliterated as it ought to be in an ideally sympathetic relationship.

Another unhealthy attitude encountered in the world of experience is the idolizing of chastity, which often leads to bitter frustration. The speaker in "The Angel" dreams of being what every young girl is taught to admire — "a maiden Queen" angelically shielded — only to discover that her ideal is self-defeating. In the passage of dream time, her continued defense of maidenhood becomes a mockery, for advanced age is sufficient to protect her. A comparable sense of wasted life as the result of abnormal restraint or calculated guile appears prominently in several manuscript poems, including "I feard the fury of my wind," "An old maid early eer I knew," and "Long John Brown & Little Mary Bell." Especially deserving of their just punishment are the foolish lovers in the last poem, who have converted themselves into cesspools of self-denial. Coquettish Mary has "a Fairy in a Nut," symbolic of the seductive beauty with which she deliberately entices John Brown. He, on the other hand, has "the Devil in his Gut," which represents his identification of love with ulcerous torment because he cannot eradicate a belief in the sinfulness of physical desire. Hence the sprite that Mary usually controls within the nut takes special delight in skipping out to tease John's devil into frustrated rage. The more John attempts to divert his psychological distress with food and drink, the more he is consumed by internal suffering until finally he dies. Yet after the appealing charms have departed from an aging Mary, the devil that beset John takes possession of her and dwells in the nut previously occupied by the fairy. At this point, whether or not love is sin for an old maid like Miss Bell is a purely academic question.

Through enlarged perspective, "Ah! Sun-flower" also diagnoses the willful curtailment of natural energy. In the first stanza the heliotropic blossom, wishing liberation from time and space, reacts with intense longing for the source of its power; yet while turning its head toward the sun it must remain sadly earth-bound. The human analogue — man's inherent yearning to respond to divine illumination and warmth through love — is treated in the other stanza primarily as the sexual exuberance of youth. The young man who pined away in frustrated desire and the pale virgin who shrouded herself in frigidity now arise from their graves vainly hoping to achieve the happiness promised as a reward for thwarting their material bodies. By refusing to express divine impulses on earth, they have actually denied the real God in order to purchase a specious salvation. As "The Garden of Love" suggests more directly, false interpreters of Christianity have prohibited sexual relations which Blake, like Milton, felt must surely have existed in Eden. According to Crabb Robinson, Milton had indeed appeared to Blake and warned him not to be misled by the fallacious doctrine expressed in *Paradise Lost* that the pleasures of physical love were of postlapsarian origin.[18] Obviously Blake assumed that the Fall, which introduced only generation and death, could not possibly have created any pleasure; it was in the ideal Garden that sex not only existed but was unmitigated delight.

These opposing views on sexual joys — one associated with the Rousseauistic concept of a sinless Arcadia, the other arising from Calvinistic condemnation of fleshly indulgence — are juxtaposed in "A Little Girl Lost." An enlightened era, Blake maintains, will hardly find its basic problem credible, that "Love! sweet Love! was thought a crime." Indeed the unalloyed pleasure of the youth and maiden who, responding to "holy light," innocently indulge their love in the openness of sunshine is condemned by her sanctimonious father as contemptible and filthy. It is precisely this authoritarian view that brings about some of the social ills described in the poem "London." Among the "mind-forg'd manacles" Blake deplores is the kind of thinking that divides sanctified conjugal relations from unregularized passion to such an extent that the former becomes moribund while the latter is infused with vitality.

The consequence of restraint, however, is not always perpetual frustration; that the opposite extreme can also result is demonstrated in "I saw a chapel all of gold." The beautiful edifice, symbol of the female principle, has been closed, denying entry to those who weep and worship outside its doors. Yet the serpent, representing the masculine principle, forces his way within solely to gratify himself in violent rape. His desecration of what had once been a place of reverence does not satisfy him, but it causes irreparable damage to the shrine. Even the bread and wine, emblematic of man's possible assimilation of divine impetus, are destroyed by the serpent's poison. The revulsion felt by the speaker is so great that he absents himself (somewhat like Gulliver) from his own kind in order to consort with swine, where presumably there are no artificial restraints that encourage ravishment. Far from blameless though the phallic snake may be, it is human society which Blake held largely responsible for inviting sexual abuses. With Godwin, he believed that whatever was interdicted became automatically more exciting in a destructive manner than it would ordinarily have been.

Often love is blighted by the fact that society's customs are stronger than an individual's ability to overcome them. "The Sick Rose" presents a woman who can neither abide by conventional ideas of chastity nor completely ignore them. The man represented as the "invisible worm" merely follows the dictates of masculine passion, for which he is to be no more condemned than the worm whose natural sustenance is the rose. The degrading aspect of their liaison is not its extramarital character but its reduction through social strictures to the sordidness of a back-street affair that neither dares acknowledge openly. The worm, though borne by the forces of nature, must be "invisible" to prevent scandal while he enjoys her "bed/ Of crimson joy." Yet the fact that his love for her is dark and furtive does not allay her conscience or her fears. On the contrary, having yielded to a proscribed attachment, she is being destroyed psychologically — though the fault is more society's than her own. Without offering a solution to an extremely knotty problem, Blake merely states the case.

But why, if these distortions are so evident, does man tolerate them? Because, as Blake explains in the manuscript version of "Infant Sorrow," [19] he is ensnared at an early stage of development into gradually accepting the ways of "natural" society. Even as an infant, this Blakean Everyman learns that struggling against swaddling bands is futile. At first naïvely sulking, he soon discovers that pleasing expressions obtain better results and henceforth employs the trickery of smiles. Growing older, he becomes conscious of appealing flowers that extend "their blossoms" tempt-

18. *On Books and Their Writers*, I, 330. For Milton's accounts of love before and after the Fall, see *Paradise Lost*, IV, 736–75; IX, 1027–45.
19. See Erdman, pp. 719–21.

ingly to him. But the hypocritical father-priest condemns him for being so attracted and binds him in symbolic marriage to a myrtle tree. That the husband bitterly resents this confinement is obvious from his exclamation in a notebook poem entitled "in a mirtle shade": "Love free love cannot be bound/ To any tree that grows on ground."[20] However sympathetic the myrtle may seem to be, she too is unable to alleviate the "heavy chain." Only liberalization of marital ties, Blake implies, might have resolved the dilemma.

Blake also attributed much of the degradation of love to woman's perverse eagerness for domination, which he called the Female Will. He apparently felt that only the apocalypse would rectify this antagonism between the sexes, for in his "Vision of the Last Judgment" he maintains: "In Eternity Woman is the Emanation of Man   she has No Will of her own   There is no such thing in Eternity as a Female Will."[21] Quite certainly virginity as a negative goal was utterly abhorrent to Blake, who could not believe that the Mother of Jesus was a virgin after impregnation by the Holy Ghost.[22] Hence much of his attack on religious orthodoxy was occasioned by what he regarded as false chastity cloaking lechery. Though the Female Will is given a more complex treatment in those poems that depict Orc's subjugation to a woman symbolizing nature, it appears also in some short manuscript poems. "The Golden Net," for example, shows how a young man becomes enthralled to the feminine wiles of three virgins who work primarily on his sympathies. The maiden clothed in flames of fire arouses his passions, the one dressed in iron evokes his distorted sense of rectitude associated with restraints, and the one covered in tears and sighs appeals to his concept of dependent womanhood. As they hang a golden net upon the branches of a tree, he is further disarmed into pitying them for all that woman must endure through sexual frustration. But when the three virgins realize his compassion, their deceitful smile hoists the net aloft and entraps him. A similar though infinitely more complex dilemma confronts the love-ensnared speaker in "The Crystal Cabinet," though he takes matters more actively in hand. Attempting to expand his consciousness outwardly by seizing "the inmost Form" rather than enlarging his mind imaginatively within, he destroys his questionable Beulah and falls back into the chaos of the Blakean hell, Ulro. The deplorable situation faced by those so deluded is one that develops mythopoeically in the prophecies as the consequence of Enitharmon's separation from Los. Divided from man, the mocking unattainable woman becomes the symbol of religious chastity and amatory deception while man himself, acquiescing to this condition, becomes her victim.

Some feminine perversity stems from woman's conditioned tendency to respond favorably to deceit but to be frightened by candor. In "Never pain to tell thy love" the artless lover, having driven away his sweetheart by a frank declaration of his true feelings, notices in nature how successful clandestine action can be, for the wind achieves its goals silently and invisibly. The implicit deduction is that in amatory matters man too can succeed by trickery rather than honesty. Similarly, in the notebook poem beginning "I asked a thief to steal me a peach" Blake's spokesman suggests that his purpose cannot be attained by honorable means. Since the woman involved is trained to approve only thieves' methods, she feels obliged to protect her image by refusing a guileless proposition; yet she passively yields to someone who employs cunning. Adding a cosmic dimension to the view is the poem "To Nobodaddy," in which Blake accuses natural religion of having fostered the desirability of subterfuge. Why is it, he asks, that man associates jealous Nobodaddy with a distant world that remains silent, inscrutable, and hidden perpetually in mysterious clouds? Why has man created an ethical scheme sanctioning duplicity such that fruits of the earthly garden are enjoyed only when offered by a wily serpent? Is it because the love about which he can be most definite, the love of woman, is gained only through deception?

One of Blake's most profound treatments of the deep-seated hostility between the sexes is contained in a fragmentary manuscript poem beginning "My Spectre around me night & day." (In *Europe* this strife is later magnified as the eighteen-hundred-year nightmare of history during which the "female dream" of Enitharmon plagues the Christian era.) The psychological alienation of man and woman, seen rather subjectively from the masculine viewpoint in the manuscript poem, has divided man against himself to such an extent that his Spectre, the portion which cannot transcend self-confined egotism and is usually associated with incorporeal spirit or despiritualized lust (in either case an incomplete entity), has gone outside him and wards off desirable contact with other human beings who might actually alleviate his problem. In other words, the

20. Erdman, p. 460.
21. Erdman, p. 552.
22. See the manuscript poem "On the Virginity of the Virgin Mary & Johanna Southcott" and *Jerusalem*, ch. 3.

Spectre, the dregs remaining behind after his Emanation has inwardly detached herself, prevents any reconciliation that might restore man to wholeness. Meanwhile his Emanation, which should be the portion that flows outward as a creative projection of his best nature, is hopelessly confined within and debilitates her own latent powers by weeping for a sin that is presumably amatory. In such unwholesome relationship the divided male and female portions of humanity wander through chaos, the Spectre tracking the feminine Emanation in response to physical needs even though there is no mental peace between them. With emotional tempests, the speaker claims, she disquiets his mornings; with jealousies and fears she turns what might have been pleasant nights into tearful experiences. Equally reprehensible is her destruction or crippling of his special interests so that he is rendered imaginatively impotent.

So that love may transform the exterior world into something admirable and adaptable to his mind, he implores the woman to cease operating as a detached unit and hopes rather self-righteously that she may pity him as he forgives her. Not surprisingly, she gives vent to a vengeful outburst of Female Will, declaring relentless animosity: "Never Never I return/ Still for Victory I burn" (ll. 33–34). Totally unrepentant, she vows to perpetuate the old game of woman fleeing and man pursuing, as Enitharmon and Los do in *The Book of Urizen*. Not only does her action preclude any forgiveness of sins, without which there could be no reunion; it erects a permanent barrier against internalizing the external and thereby restoring the state of wholeness. On the personal level this wretched separation causes endless strife between individuals, while on the social or national plane the corresponding failure to assimilate object into subject produces that monstrous antithesis of brotherly love — war, which Blake saw as a perversion of the sexual impulse.

Hoping for some resolution to this problem, the speaker of the poem decides to turn from his previous tactics, which have merely aggravated the predicament, and completely renounce the kind of love through which they have been suffering. To do so, of course, he must root up the Infernal Grove, a nocturnal forest that Blake associated with the delusions of "natural" or "deistic" religion. Furthermore, he must destroy the old image of woman as cruel mocker or capricious nature goddess and recreate her in the image of Divine Man. Most important, he realizes, is the continuing mutual forgiveness that, in Blake's view, constituted the principal message of the Redeemer. The unfinished character of the last stanzas indicates that the poet was experimenting with ideas that would make his solution to the dilemma more impressive. Obviously the divided state of Spectre and Emanation troubled him very deeply. Much of the blame he placed upon the Pauline corruption of Jesus' teaching, which he tried to set straight in "The Everlasting Gospel." The perfect resolution is again presented in *Jerusalem*, where Britannia (Albion's Emanation) is reunited with Albion in the apocalyptic state. This was obviously the ideal condition which Blake futilely attempted to explain to Crabb Robinson, who inadequately described it as a rambling argument advocating "a union of sexes in man as in God — an androgynous state." [23]

For Blake's most intrepid declaration of amatory freedom from erroneous notions of conscience, one must turn to *Visions of the Daughters of Albion*. The significance of its terse epigraph — "The Eye sees more than the Heart knows" — ultimately becomes clear through commentary on poetic events, for the limited experiential knowledge stored in the fallen man's heart proves vastly inferior to the illumination gained spontaneously through vitalized perception. Whereas the encrusted organs governed by custom falsify reality, an eye (or, for that matter, any other awakened sense) functioning as a true window of the soul enables a visionary mortal to respond instinctively to whatever is apprehended. It is this separation which the principal character of the *Visions* must overcome in order to grow wise, for so long as the tree of knowledge is distinct from the tree of life mankind cannot utilize his full potential. If, on the contrary, humanity can immediately unite sensory perception with emotional experience through what the poet boldly terms "happy copulation," then the enervating schism can be healed. Though Theotormon stumbles over obstacles to this reunification, Oothoon is victorious. Therefore whatever the latter perceives in her liberated condition cannot justifiably be prohibited as though it were some temptation to be forsworn but is translated into the instant wisdom of her consciousness.

Overthrowing the constrictive rationalism of theology, Oothoon, described as "the soft soul of America," undergoes revolutionary awakening to a new morality of love. As the prefatory "Argument" explains, her devotion to Theotormon exists without any concomitant feelings of guilt, and despite some virginal fears concerning the unknown, she is ready to give herself unquestioningly to one whose ethic regards physical love as

23. *On Books and Their Writers*, I, 330.

sin. Yet before achieving her goal, she sustains a profound psychological crisis resulting from sexual rape. The suffering that ensues leads her not only to a more enlightened concept of what is wrong with love in our society but also to concrete suggestions for remedy. The prophecy thus becomes Blake's plea for more liberal relations between the sexes — a recommendation that seemed (and may still appear) to orthodox moralists like the true voice of diabolism, though much of what he advocates has actually come into being less through tolerance than through improved contraception. In Blake sexual relations are justified, and even idealized, not on the grounds of procreation but rather for the purpose of uniting two people so that the most comprehensive expression of love obliterates selfhood and advances both lovers to a more exalted plane of existence. Man, separated from woman as well as nature by the Fall, can be temporarily redeemed when he is united with his Emanation and, from the amatory paradise of Beulah, enjoys a glimpse of Eden's restored innocence.

Obstructing this achievement are the fraudulent ethics endorsed by society, religion, and political economy. Whereas Oothoon, unlike her morally enslaved sisters, regards sexual fulfillment as the privilege of each individual to indulge according to his own consent, Bromion, the self-gratifying exploiter, interprets it as enjoyment granted the strong through subjugation of the weak. Thus passion, interpreted by his code of rapacious mercantilism, leads to nothing more than ownership in marriage or vendible pleasures for which the mighty need not pay. Consequently, once he has sated himself by ravishing Oothoon, he casts her aside as a harlot, salving his own conscience while deliberately inciting jealousy in her intended lover. Theotormon's acquiescence to such an imperialistic code inadvertently bolsters it even while debilitating him. Inhibited by conventional notions of chastity, he cannot accept the ravished Oothoon, no matter how deliberately she suffers torment in the vain hope of thereby eradicating her guilt. Realizing that Theotormon's absurd morality serves no commendable purpose, she therefore calls upon him to abandon it in favor of more enlightened views on purity, exuberance, and unfettered love.

Against the false religion and its "mistaken Demon of heaven," emancipated Oothoon brings her charge that earthly joys have been needlessly regimented by a uniform prescription of sexual behavior. Her indictment of society includes an alarming portrayal of enslaved love whereby a young girl, eager for romance, is reluctantly bound to a man she loathes and must throughout the rest of her blighted existence tolerate her husband's "weary lust." True love, on the contrary, must remain "free as the mountain wind"; nor can it be mistaken for amatory exploitation, which "drinks another as a sponge drinks water" and disturbs the "frozen marriage bed" with tribulations. To prove her point, Oothoon even demonstrates the supreme altruism: she will obtain attractive girls for Theotormon's sexual delight, never allowing so much as a "jealous cloud" to obscure "the heaven of generous love." Having herself achieved apotheosis, she calls upon all living creatures to rejoice in what life offers. Obviously she has attained that paradoxical condition described by Orc in *America*, whereby the ideals of honest virginity can be found in a harlot who, despite perpetual ravishment, remains forever chaste; for Oothoon has re-established the unity of man and nature, heart and head, body and soul, innocence and experience. Feeling no guilt whatever, she declares herself incapable of defilement through another's misdeed —

> . . . a virgin fill'd with virgin fancies
> Open to joy and to delight where ever beauty appears
> If in the morning sun I find it: there my eyes are fix'd
> In happy copulation; if in evening mild. wearied with work;
> Sit on a bank and draw the pleasures of this free born joy.[24]

But Theotormon, as lethargic as society grown accustomed to masochistic pleasures of self-torment, merely sulks. Sitting unresponsively beside the turbulent ocean, he converses with the shadows of his self-denying Urizenic religion while the English daughters of Albion sigh longingly for the liberation that their American sister has achieved. The emancipation of regenerative life, Blake recognized, would require an extraordinary union of strength and imaginative vision.

24. Erdman, p. 49.

CHAPTER VI

The Exaltation of Passion

ROMANTIC WRITERS who justified love defying either marital or blood ties did so primarily on the grounds that sincere passion minimized other considerations in proportion to its intensity. Yet in vindicating such love for reasons other than mere sensationalism they confronted, without necessarily resolving, serious moral dilemmas that are brought into sharpest focus through Leigh Hunt's redaction of the story of Francesca da Rimini. In Dante's original version pitting overwhelming emotion against both familial and connubial obligations, concern for the adulteress's plight in hell stemmed largely from awareness that a sensitive, loving heart is most readily ensnared in illicit relations. Hunt's strongly developed sympathy with life's unfortunates, however, caused him to view the catastrophe as an adversity of chance for which no individual should be held reprehensible. In his retelling, Francesca's love for Paulo originates in a noble intention to bestow her heart upon the unknown bridegroom who appears for the arranged marriage; she could not possibly know that he is only her husband's brother sent to marry the bride by proxy. Moreover, Giovanni's consistent refusal to take any interest in his wife, as compared with Paulo's sympathetic warmth, further palliates sin. But such shifting of blame from the principal characters to circumstance, when combined with Hunt's equivocal attitude toward sexual transgression and compounded by nominal incest, created an ambiguous ethical norm.[1] By altering the tradition sufficiently to absolve the lovers, the author found himself condoning an "innocent" adultery. On technical grounds alone *The Story of Rimini* (1816) merited critical denunciation; yet it was Hunt's underlying puritanism that played him the cruelest trick, for his defensiveness toward a liberal morality betrayed him into unintended prurience.

The anonymous account of *The Story of Rimini* in the *Edinburgh Review* [2] let Hunt off very gently, but John Gibson Lockhart, signing himself merely "Z," felt obliged to see that in *Blackwood's Magazine* justice would be done. The *Edinburgh* reviewer, whom Lockhart shrewdly took to be Hazlitt, was on the whole commendatory even while enumerating a variety of poetical blemishes. Since he had asserted that the author did not "belong to any of the modern schools of poetry" (XXVI, 482), Lockhart launched his infamous blast against a new school which he dubbed "the Cockney" and of which he designated Hunt "chief Doctor and Professor." [3] In his opinion, indecency was a disease with Hunt, who spoke "unclean things from perfect inanition" and whose attempt at a jaunty, almost colloquial, idiom was lascivious and vulgar — the product of "a man who has kept company with kept-mistresses" (II, 40). As though adding charm to simple seduction were not enough, Hunt had, in the hostile critic's view, gloated over it "only when accompanied with adultery and incest." Though much of the censure for technical shortcomings was deserved, the personal attack upon Hunt for limited education, bad taste, a Cockney's admiration for rural verdure, lack of patriotism, irreligion, and moral depravity surpassed the worst vituperation of nineteenth-century reviews.

Unfortunately Hunt, in the preface to *Rimini*, had himself brought about some of the disapproval by apologizing for the story as a "sublime night-mare" and by asserting that its evocation of sympathy from Dante

1. Not until 1907 was the British law repealed which prohibited a man from marrying his deceased brother's widow or his deceased wife's sister. Prior to that time the Levitical injunction against intimacies with a member of one's own family, even when that "one flesh" was established by previous marriage, still held.

2. 26 (June 1816), 476–91. Both Hazlitt and Jeffrey subsequently claimed the review. See *The Wellesley Index to Victorian Periodicals: 1824–1900*, ed. Walter Houghton (Toronto and London, 1966), I, 455.

3. See especially *Blackwood's*, 2 (October 1817), 38–41; 2 (November 1817), 194–201. "Pimpled 'azlitt," the "Cockney Aristotle," was generally held to be a charter member of the group.

proved the "melancholy absurdity of his theology." [4] Hence it was not difficult for Lockhart, in the second installment of his attack on the Cockney School (November 1817), to condemn Hunt's poem as thoroughly unethical, emphasizing particularly that violation of brotherly confidence added incest to injury. In view of well-established mythological, dramatic, and even Biblical precedent, he could hardly object to its literary propriety; in fact, he conceded that the "awful interest" aroused by totally abandoned passions had sometimes led authors to treat "such unhallowed themes." Yet he pointed to a difference between the way great writers had managed dangerous subjects and the way Hunt had cheapened them. Sophocles, for examples, had presented incest as a spectacle of "domestic horror" yet "unpolluted with guilt." His dramatic representation showed not only human weakness evoking our pity and love but also the absolute necessity for punishing evil. Other treatments of the theme — those of Euripides, Ford, Alfieri, and Schiller — elicited compassion, sometimes through a sense of overwhelming fatality, but always emphasized the need to eradicate the ghastly crime in the blood of some horrendous atonement. Not only did these dramatists studiously avoid "luxurious images" that might arouse lust, but they approached "unhallowed love with the seriousness of a judge, who narrates only that he may condemn the guilty and warn the heedless" (II, 197). It was Hunt's inability to handle a tragic theme in an elevated or edifying manner that brought Lockhart's wrath down upon him and later upon the younger poets whom he had encouraged. In the critic's view, *The Story of Rimini* completely divested forbidden love of its traditional horror, made the narrative a vehicle for light-hearted descriptions, and debased the entire subject into a "genteel comedy of incest."

As though the charge of unexpiated incest were not enough, *Blackwood's* continued to attack Hunt's unrefined treatment of love — with or without divine sanction. Years after Lockhart had tarred and feathered even Keats for indiscretions on the latter score, *Blackwood's* in December 1822 renewed its assault on the Cockneys with a seventh installment entitled "Hunt's Art of Love." The title itself was a cruel blow, suggesting that, like Ovid, the Romantic poet had treated love with mock seriousness only to encourage seduction. In addition to previous criticism of Hunt's literary morals, the review sweepingly condemned the "gross impertinence" of any Cockney presuming to write about human affection (XII, 780). Whereas in the strict sense love ought to be "a tender affair between a lady and a gentleman," Cockney authors, ignorant of respectable emotion, seemed to regard it as "merely a congress between a male and a female." In the reviewer's unalterable opinion, Hunt knew as little about making love as he did about writing English grammar. With one imperious gesture, the "Maga" swept aside such upstarts and whatever Ovidian aspirations they might have had by declaring: ". . . any Cockney who writes about love deserves to be kicked" (XII, 781).

That *Blackwood's* should have condemned Hunt's treatment of incest while praising the exemplary handling of it in *Manfred* and *Parisina* may strike the modern reader as hollow in view of the now verified relations of Byron and his half-sister, Augusta Leigh. Yet it was probably Hunt's dedication of *Rimini* to Byron, in a stilted epistle fluctuating between obsequious humility and vaunted intimacy, that impressed the reviewer as presumptuous and invited unfavorable comparison with one whom Lockhart called "the first of all living poets" (II, 195). The inherent offensiveness of the subject is alleviated in *Manfred*, according to Lockhart, by suggesting only through veiled hints that the central character's agonies result from "unlawful passion for his sister." Furthermore, the sufferer is punished so severely that he is seen as an object lesson — "a weary wasted hater of the world, and of himself." Never do we view his partner in unspeakable crime until she has already atoned for guilt and died. Also *Parisina*, which in many ways reflects Byron's profound interest in the story of Francesca da Rimini, is considered by Lockhart a model for employing incest in an artistically and morally acceptable manner. Its superior refinement is attributable to avoidance of specific "details of this unhallowed love," for the reader is scarcely permitted a glimpse of the transgression before seeing its inescapable punishment; hence pity is quickly altered into righteous indignation. Moreover, the work is imbued with a tragic sense of superhuman destiny compelling retribution, so that the principal characters seem driven to act as they do. Thus while poor Hunt, with his comparatively blameless life and noble intentions, was pilloried for indecency, Byron, the practitioner of almost every sin, was (at least before the publication of *Don Juan*) held up as the criterion of artistic propriety.

Bryon's prefatory advertisement to *Parisina* deferentially conceded that the theme might because of "the delicacy or fastidiousness" of the modern

4. London, 1816, pp. vii–viii.

135

reader be considered "unfit for the purposes of poetry." [5] All he could say in his own defense was that ancient, Renaissance, and contemporary dramatists had shown no objection to domestic tragedies of love. Byron does indeed give the supposedly unmentionable subject a classical flavor by making it (like Clytemnestra's ritualistic murder of Agamemnon as punishment for his sacrifice of Iphigenia) the consequence of Azo's own misdeeds. Illicit connection becomes retribution for a blood guilt that must gradually work its way out through suffering. By leading the reader into sympathetic identification with lovers who must steal their bliss in an evening rendezvous yet by merely hinting obliquely at what transpires between them, Byron overcomes the barrier to our acceptance of prohibited affection. The overwhelming ecstasy that Parisina and Hugo experience in the garden bower eradicates, like a dream, all compunction. Only when they must leave "The spot of guilty gladness" does the narrator suggest conscience through Parisina's fears of Heaven's condemnation. Not until she mutters her lover's name during troubled sleep and implicates herself in acts too indelicate for explicit detail does the poet explode the bombshell of incest.

Byron's treatment is further sophisticated by moral complexities admitting of no single standard, for each character has both sinned and been sinned against. The reader's compassion is directed particularly toward Hugo, not so much as a lover as an ill-treated natural son, who reveals in a final speech before execution his overwhelming sense of injustice for injuries done him and his abandoned mother, Bianca. His acknowledged wrong to Azo therefore becomes just recompense, appropriate also from Parisina's viewpoint because she had originally been destined as Hugo's bride before being pre-empted by the Prince. Hugo's reflections on these two amatory triangles in which both men are involved demonstrate that Azo's neglect of his former mistress has led inexorably to the son's hostility; the alliance of mother and son against Azo has set the pattern for a relationship in which Parisina has become the surrogate for the dead Bianca. Azo's punishment continues even after the loss of both wife and son, for the legitimate sons of his subsequent marriage are inferior to the child of love whom he beheads. As his own existence changes to living death, evil returns to its source.

The forbidden love in *Parisina* and *The Story of Rimini* involved only a superficial incest arising from matrimonial kinship, and its offense tended to be obscured by greater iniquities. Even accounts of outlawed consanguineous relations should no longer have startled early nineteenth-century readers, for in both England and Germany realistic fiction, drama, and Gothic romance of the previous century had fascinated by the sheer sensationalism of the horrendous subject.[6] Yet illicit acts as generally employed in such literature had been unconsciously committed and had, upon discovery, been considered an ultimate affront inflicted by destiny. Romantic writers, if they sought to attract attention with a slightly threadbare topic, were obliged to go one step farther; and incestuous love indulged knowingly served their purpose well since (despite what was sanctioned for the Biblical Abraham and his half-sister Sara) it could not possibly lead to connubial ties. According to inherited tradition, they believed marriage and passion to be incompatible; marital bonds, after all, required a steady constancy, and as Byron observed, "there is no such thing as a life of passion any more than a continuous earthquake, or an eternal fever." [7] In addition, sibling devotion in varying degrees seems to have been peculiarly understandable to several English Romantic writers. One need only note the affection of Wordsworth, Lamb, Byron, and Shelley for their own sisters, and of Hunt, Wordsworth, and Shelley for even their wives' sisters. These sensitive, introverted men felt closest to others like themselves, and in an era preoccupied with the need to transcend egoism by directing emotions toward others, they were inexorably drawn to members of their own families. Sometimes the first step beyond narcissism became incest.

As Byron had Childe Harold observe on his Rhine journey (III, 55), a union cemented by blood kinship ordinarily resulted in a psychological impasse that death alone could resolve. In *Manfred* he sought to explore such an ineradicable love and, by catharsis as well as public self-castigation, to extricate his conscience from its intolerable burden. The play is less a dramatic confrontation of Manichaean principles than a study of the suffering which a socially alienated individual must endure when he defies codified morality to obey the dictates of his heart. Also prominent is

5. *Poetry*, III, 503.
6. For interesting analyses of incest in this period see Otto Rank, *Das Inzest-Motiv in Dichtung und Sage*, 2nd ed. (Leipzig and Vienna, 1926); Eino Railo, "Incest and Romantic Eroticism," ch. VIII of *The Haunted Castle* (New York, 1964); and Peter L. Thorslev, Jr., "Incest as Romantic Symbol," *CLS*, 2 (1965), 41–58.
7. Letter of 5 July 1821 to Moore, *LJ*, V, 318.

the Byronic admiration for a rebel daring enough to challenge one of society's most stringent taboos.

The egocentric nature of Manfred had sought the perfect woman within his own imagination rather than in the external world, and inevitably his mental prefiguration of a beloved was the female projection of himself. The most likely embodiment of this preconceived ideal, and undoubtedly the one most similar to him, was his sister Astarte, who became, through the conceptual refining away of impurities, all that was most lovable in himself and therefore beyond the pale of mundane ethics. But his incestuous devotion, instead of overcoming the confinements of selfhood, forced him to become increasingly solipsistic. Unlike Cain in Byron's drama of that name, he could not reassure himself that loving his sister was ethically acceptable (as it might have been when the human race had to propagate or perish), since contemporary society placed the most rigid proscriptions upon such relations. He could justify his violation only on the grounds of extraordinary passion. The forbidden nature of the fruit had made it all the more tantalizing; and the indulgence of desire with full knowledge of worldly (though not necessarily eternal) punishments to follow ennobled his deed with the sanction of martyrdom. In fact, the world's censure and his ensuing disgrace, far from obliterating his love for Astarte, bound him ever more firmly to her, for by assuming all the blame for her death, he was further enslaved through mental anguish. Ultimately, Byron implies, such intense suffering has atoned for the injury he caused. As Manfred himself declares in refusing at his death to be the devil's prey, his inner torment has been so agonizing that it could not be augmented by a demon's; nor should crimes be punished "by other crimes,/ And greater criminals" (III, iv, 123–24). According to this subjective ethic, Manfred's love for his sister must be deemed forgiven.

In a much more deliberate attempt to shock the bourgeois reading public with literary incest, Shelley made the hero and heroine of *Laon and Cythna* a brother and sister whose love for one another sustains them through extraordinary trials. Moreover, the reunion of these sibling lovers after a long separation is celebrated by two days of abandonment to erotic ecstasy interpreted as true marriage. In Laon's remembrance of the event,

> There we unheeding sate, in the communion
> Of interchanged vows, which, with a rite
> Of faith most sweet and sacred, stamped our union. —

> Few were the living hearts which could unite
> Like ours, or celebrate a bridal night
> With such close sympathies. (VI, xxxix: 1–6) [8]

In two stanzas following, Shelley explains that, unless some artificial barrier is interposed, those who have been nourished by the same source of life must be forever linked; by natural law they "cannot choose but love."

By asserting in his preface to the poem that love was universally celebrated as "the sole law which should govern the moral world," Shelley indulged in shrewd rhetoric, for none dared object to that dictum.[9] But in the application of that principle to incestuous liaisons he flagrantly defied convention. With customary reformer's zeal, he assured the public that prohibited love was introduced to increase their tolerance through acquaintance with practices differing markedly from their own. He even called attention to "one circumstance" in the personal conduct of his sibling revolutionaries that was purposely "intended to startle the reader from the trance of ordinary life." His determination "to break through the crust of those outworn opinions on which established institutions depend" flaunted a belief that proscriptions against incest, which in our society rest squarely upon Levitical interdiction, were merely inherited superstition. The love of Laon and Cythna he thought innocent and benevolent because emotions deserved to be considered solely on their own merits. Imploring men not to dissipate their energies condemning forbidden passion, he appealed to the most universal of human feelings, love, in order to bolster a positive rather than a negative morality.

Though the candor of Shelley's prefatory defense was disarming, the anonymous reviewer in the *Quarterly* [10] could not conceal his revulsion from the blatant endorsement of such love. His only consolation was that the poet's application of radical theories to human experience inadvertently discredited them. Had the reviewer not known better, he would have taken the poet to be an ironic advocate of both civil order and accepted religion! Even Shelley's publishers, the Olliers, despite a reputation for broad-mindedness, felt such qualms about the incest motif that they

---

8. Citations of *Laon and Cythna* are from *The Works of Percy Bysshe Shelley in Verse and Prose*, ed. Harry Buxton Forman (London, 1880), vol. I.
9. *Works*, ed. Forman, I, 97–98.
10. 21 (April 1819), 460–71. The reviewer was John Taylor Coleridge.

insisted upon withdrawal of the poem. Though Shelley eloquently pled for courageous tolerance, they demanded drastic overhauling to delete all mention of the obnoxious relationship.[11] Hence the preface and twenty-six pages of text were canceled in order that the innocuous expurgated version might appear under a new title as *The Revolt of Islam*. In the revised form there is no blood kinship between the lovers; they have merely been inseparable friends from early youth.

Even so, Shelley continued to believe in the literary possibilities of the banned subject. On 16 November 1819, several weeks after completing *The Cenci*, he wrote Maria Gisborne his observations on Calderon's *Cabellos de Absalon*. Especially impressed by the Spanish dramatist's depiction of outlawed passion, he commented:

> Incest is like many other *incorrect* things a very poetical circumstance. It may be the excess of love or of hate. It may be that defiance of every thing for the sake of another which clothes itself in the glory of the highest heroism, or it may be that cynical rage which confounding the good & bad in existing opinions breaks through them for the purpose of rioting in selfishness & antipathy.
> (II, 154)

Count Cenci's rape of his daughter Beatrice out of perverse animosity would, as Shelley knew, outrage English critics, no matter how delicately he treated it. But that was precisely what he intended. Incest in *The Cenci* he deemed reprehensible not because of consanguinity but because the act was committed in hatred rather than love.

At a very early stage of literary development, Shelley treated the readers of *Zastrozzi* (1810) and *St. Irvyne* (1811) to love so rapturous that marital blessings promised by both Verezzi and Fitzeustace to their respective beloveds seemed not only anticlimactic but superfluous. Yet as both these virtuous, albeit overamorous, young men explained to their intended wives, marriage was one of the institutions demanded by prejudiced society. Though the brief ceremony might constrain the body, it could not fetter the soul, as love alone was capable of doing.[12] Such moral defiance, made additionally lurid against the background of melodramatic fantasies, might have been attributable to the influence of Gothic romance, to the author's inherent iconoclasm, or merely to his adolescence. Actually this antagonism toward marriage was so firmly engrained in the poet's thinking that time would not alter it.

After being jilted by his cousin Harriet Grove, he filled many of his letters to Thomas Jefferson Hogg and Elizabeth Hitchener — the "brother" and "sister" of his soul — with observations on love based upon the experience of his first heartbreak. Though he had never doubted that mere sexual gratification contained a strong element of selfishness, he was shocked to realize that his exalted passion for Harriet must have been based partially on self-interest. Since the ultimate touchstone of genuine affection, as he saw it, was eagerness to bestow happiness upon one's beloved, why then was he miserable thinking that Harriet would be happy married to the man of her choice? Chagrined that he could not extricate his thoughts from recurrent torment, he vowed in a letter to Hogg to rise above egoism (though not above self-analysis): "I *will* feel no more! it is selfish — I would feel for others" (I, 36). After another egregious failure, this time in the role of Cupid for Hogg and his sister, Shelley further admitted "what an unstable deceitfull thing Love was" (I, 104). Throughout life he would deplore the paradox that the individual inclined toward strong affection was also the one marked for most intense anguish when the illusion shattered.

Because of such amatory uncertainties, it is not surprising that marriage was thought inimical to the course of love — as foolish as an attempt to place a strait jacket on an angel. Having declared that love itself provided "the indissoluble sacred union," he confessed "sickening disgust" at the thought of confining love's energies with such a tyrannical fetter (I, 79–80). After Hogg came dangerously close to accepting theoretical matrimony, Shelley felt obliged to point out how incompatible it was with virtuous honor and how degrading the marriage service was to womanhood (I, 81). The institution itself, as he asserted in his fragmentary essay "On Marriage," still bore too many vestiges of its original purpose — a no-trespassing claim to female chattel.[13] The perpetuation of this un-

---

11. See especially his letters of 11 and 13 December 1817 to Charles Ollier and of 16 December 1817 to Thomas Moore, *The Letters of Percy Bysshe Shelley*, ed. Frederick L. Jones (Oxford, 1964), I, 578–83. Subsequent references to Shelley's letters appear in the text.

12. *The Complete Works of Percy Bysshe Shelley*, ed. Roger Ingpen and Walter E. Peck (London, 1926–30), V, 75, 197. Unless otherwise specified, all quotations from Shelley's prose refer to this edition, cited hereafter as *Works*.

13. *Works*, VII, 149–50.

natural crime he blamed primarily upon organized Christianity and its concept of irrefrangible constancy (I, 194-95). The confining of sexual joy to one partner for life he considered as objectionable as a law compelling the enjoyment of artistic and gustatory pleasures with one particular person.

Following closely in time upon such observations, his own marriage to Harriet Westbrook came as a severe shock both to his friends and to himself. His first letter to Elizabeth Hitchener after the wedding excused his own apostasy by explaining that he had married to save Harriet's reputation, since without that she could never be happy (I, 144). To Hogg, on the other hand, he admitted outright conversion to matrimony (I, 135). On the theory that in any liaison the woman inevitably sacrificed much more than the man, he had felt obliged to yield, since voluntary sacrifice, even of one's principle to insure another's happiness, was the acid test of love. Reconciled to marriage, he further palliated it by urging both Elizabeth Hitchener and Hogg to join him and his wife in a familial unit bound by love rather than legal chains. But upon learning that Hogg (who interpreted the invitation more liberally than it was intended) had subsequently tried to seduce Harriet, Shelley accused him of being led "either by false reasoning, or . . . real feeling" into a "disgusting & horrid" error (I, 167). Apparently Shelley still clung to his theories of free love, but the kind of amatory freedom he advocated required that all individuals concerned be completely willing. His objections to Hogg's advances toward his wife were based not on the fact that such affection was tinged with carnality but that a devoted friend had selfishly urged his suit contrary to Harriet's wishes. In his view, Hogg had violated the Shelleyan code by his willingness to sacrifice another's welfare to his own pleasure (I, 171). Shelley's highly emotional reaction to a friend's behavior, which after all was only accepted theory put into a rather crude attempt at practice, suggests that the husband, probably more than the wife, had been taken by surprise. (When in 1815 the poet was living with Mary Godwin, he was ostensibly willing to share his amatory wealth with Hogg, but presumably the difference in situations was spelled by Mary's consent.)[14] When Hogg, duly chastised and repentant, tried to rejoin the familial Eden from which he, snakelike, had been banished, Shelley, after considerable vacillation, decided that the plan was inadmissible (I, 175-76). Since all three of them were apparently more infected by custom than he had assumed, their wounded feelings toward one another, as well as his fear that Hogg would be unable to restrain himself, obviated any further design for triangular happiness.

In *Queen Mab* Shelley publicly reaffirmed many of these beliefs on marriage. His long footnote to the section deploring the venality of love blamed rigidity of marital laws for encouraging prostitution and all its concomitant ills.[15] Women who dared obey "the impulse of unerring nature" outside wedlock were relentlessly ostracized from society and forced to take up the loathed profession. But in time they would wreak unintentional vengeance, for into their polluted embrace were driven young men excluded by overprudent virtue from association with "modest and accomplished women." This commerce would in turn not only spread venereal disease but would debase the sensibilities of these men toward any serious attachments.

To the irrevocability of marriage Shelley also attributed many personal evils. An unhappy union, whose hated bonds could be severed only by death, often ruined two otherwise productive lives with unresolved hostility and blighted those of the miserable children. Therefore he felt that the physical relationship should last no longer than the love of which it was the ultimate expression of unity. He especially assailed the pretension of law "to govern the indisciplinable wanderings of passion," that instinctual response to loveliness over which man has no absolute control. Since by his concept love was in essence liberty, it would inevitably wither when subjected to legal enforcement. The three necessary prerequisites for its survival he listed as confidence, equality, and unreserve; but constancy he thought a positive good only when it granted the contentment toward which all ethical science strove. When any arrangement no longer contributed to the happiness of a couple — that is, "when its evils [were] greater than its benefits" — it could no longer be sacred and ought to be dissolved.

Shelley realized, however, that fulfillment of his ideal would necessitate a radical change in social and religious attitudes. In the perfected age described by the last canto of *Queen Mab*, love would be "Unchecked by

14. See Shelley's letter of ?26 April 1815 to Hogg, *Letters*, I, 426, and Jones's note 1, I, 423. See also Jones's essay in *Shelley and His Circle*, ed. Kenneth N. Cameron, III (Cambridge, Mass., 1970), 423–34.

15. See *The Complete Poetical Works of Percy Bysshe Shelley*, ed. Thomas Hutchinson (London, 1960), pp. 806–8. Unless otherwise specified, all quotations from Shelley's poetry refer to this edition, hereafter cited as *Poetical Works*.

dull and selfish chastity,/ That virtue of the cheaply virtuous" (IX, 84–85). But for the time being he did not recommend complete latitudinarianism, since as he wrote Godwin on 7 July 1812, "promiscuous sexual intercourse under the present system of thinking would inevitably lead to consequences the most injurious to the happiness of mankind" (I, 314). In fact, to forestall attacks on himself as the advocate of libertinism, he specifically stated in his note to *Queen Mab* that he was not vindicating license as an alternative to marital padlock. He did assert that abrogation of marriage would encourage a "fit and natural arrangement of sexual connection." [16] Moreover, he was confident that the love of parents for children and the latter's dependence upon domestic care would insure unions of long duration wherever they were truly functional. In any case, since choice and change could never be successfully controlled by law, he declared abolition of legal marriage preferable to the continued undermining of society.

To justify these condemnatory views, as well as his desertion of Harriet for Mary, Shelley composed "Rosalind and Helen," a "modern eclogue" that provides a striking contrast between loveless matrimony and unmarried love. Aware of the poem's artistic shortcomings, he had abandoned the project until, according to Mary Shelley's note to the 1839 edition, she had urged him to complete it.[17] As she pointed out, Shelley considered love to be the only valid "law of life." It was "the essence of our being, and all woe and pain arose from the war made against it by selfishness, or insensibility, or mistake." Though critics indeed pounced on the mawkish sentimentality and impossible melodrama inherent in the poem, Shelley's incisive observations on human affection were in Mary's eyes adequate to redeem an inferior composition. Furthermore, she naturally found gratifying the depiction of how superior a passionate attachment without matrimony could be to a regularized union without love, as portrayed in the life histories of two women, which are juxtaposed like amatory complaints of Arcadian shepherds.

But if Shelley chose to wage a frontal attack on matrimony, his assault had negligible impact on that well-fortified bastion. Byron's flanking maneuvers were a much more insidious threat, and even his early fables implied that marriage, though admittedly a sop to the frail, had never posed unassailable impediments to the strong. Though the serious import of his oriental tales may now be obscured by their melodrama and extravagance, these narratives in their own day asserted a boldly fascinating love ethic. The Turkish environment, then synonymous with contempt for womanhood, permitted the author daring opinions about extramarital passion to which the reading public was highly receptive, even when compelled to grant that such deductions might be partly valid in contemporary Christian lands. Above all, the tales reflected a mind highly sensitive to earthly inequities and a heart (like that of one of his heroes) with an unusual propensity toward emotion. Similarly they revealed an awareness that conventional absolutes of right and wrong were inapplicable where claims of love conflicted with demands of society. Under these conditions what seemed criminal according to social mores might be deemed acceptable. Byron's extraordinary sense of justice led him to depict sympathetically those who, imbued with righteous indignation, wrought vengeance manfully instead of leaving it to the dilatory grindings of some heavenly mill. Though a determination to see rewards and punishments meted out in this life could bring only limited satisfaction and might lead ultimately to catastrophe, it was nevertheless the only course of behavior open to those willing to fight for what they passionately desired. In fact, to such men the cowardly failure to take action when boldness was necessary would have constituted an alternative much more intolerable. Quite obviously, therefore, providence in Byronic terms involved not only a God of Love but also a Supreme Arbiter whose incomprehensible ways worked themselves out through the staunchly resolute — Carlylean heroes of love. These courageous, individualistic characters could perform, under divine impulse, deeds either out of intense devotion or, when the loving heart had been rendered desolate, out of comparable hatred. What distinguished them as particularly Byronic was their firm intention to act, regardless of consequences. All goals seemed possible, at least temporarily, for those intrepid enough to seize them.

The initially passive victim in the dynamic conflict of *The Giaour* is Leila, who, like many another oriental girl of exceptional beauty, has been fated to be the mere ornament of a harem. Her unusual charm seems to disprove the Prophet's assertion "that woman is but dust,/ A soulless toy for tyrant's lust" (ll. 489–90). But feminine loveliness, as Byron laments, often suffers much the same fate as an exquisite Kashmeer butterfly that invites pursuit. After the excitement of a chase to gain something beyond

16. *Poetical Works*, p. 808.
17. *Poetical Works*, pp. 188–89.

one's grasp and a fleeting sense of triumph at its seizure, there is no pleasure in subsequent possession even for the pursuer, so that the hapless prey loses not only its freedom but also "its charm by being caught." Unfortunately fragile beauty so crushed finds no joy inside a cage, nor can a demeaned captive understand the significance of love since in Byron's view that emotion belongs only to the free.[18] Though Leila is not the only miserable prisoner in the emir's collection, she receives little sympathy from her fellow sufferers, who take a self-righteous attitude toward her amatory indiscretions with a foreign Christian — the Giaour. When caught attempting to flee the palace with her beloved, she is condemned to the usual Turkish punishment for unfaithful wives: she is thrown into the sea to drown.

Though the Giaour is unable to save Leila from a watery grave, he does avenge her death in mortal combat with the emir. Byron describes their conflict as a burlesque of sexual consummation. Extreme hatred, even more than its antithesis, locks the contenders in irrevocable passion:

> . . . Love itself could never pant
> For all that Beauty sighs to grant
> With half the fervour Hate bestows
> Upon the last embrace of foes. (ll. 647–50)

Even as the Giaour kills his enemy in a necessary "act of justice," the poet emphasizes another curious interrelation of love and hate. By extraordinary irony, Leila's heart, though incapable of inspiring true affection in Hassan, had produced such devotion in another that now her beloved's sword compels the "felon heart to feel." However, this same connection between love and hate causes the avenger, in turn, to be drawn into a web of fatality from which he finds no escape. Though his last confession expresses remorse principally over failure to prevent Leila's death rather than for the slaying of her murderer, it is apparent in the delirium preceding his own death that he has never succeeded in extricating himself from feelings of guilt for the destruction of one he loathed as well as of one he adored.[19] His protests that conscience had sanctioned his behavior toward Hassan are not, in retrospect, altogether convincing.

Far more impressive is the Giaour's defense of his relationship with Leila, which is justified primarily by its intensity, for overwhelming love makes its own laws that supersede all others. Since adultery, by his implied definition, is a violation of true love rather than a breach of imposed marital vows, Leila's only sin was one forced upon her by a man to whom she was merely a slave. Treachery to an unacceptable husband therefore became truth to a lover. The Giaour insists, moreover, that her devotion to him was absolutely guiltless: she was his "life's unerring light," a vision of perfection that beckons to him even from the world beyond. In a passage recalling Burns's rationalization of errant ways in "The Vision," he claims:

> . . . Love indeed is light from heaven;
>   A spark of that immortal fire
> With angels shared, by Alla given,
>   To lift from earth our low desire. (ll. 1131–34)

The Giaour obviously feels that he and his beloved had been inspired by divinity; and since achievement of the heart's aspiration serves as evidence of divine grace, he declares himself to have been supremely blessed. Having attained the pinnacle of romantic experience, he cannot conceive of loving again and scorns those promiscuous fools whose shifting attachments indicate they have never yet found the ideal.

The Bride of Abydos also deserves attention for its typically Byronic ingredients of enmity counterbalanced against love and of sympathy with suppressed womanhood. Since the poet wished to present an accurate picture of Turkish life to those who knew nothing of Near Eastern customs, he originally intended making Selim and Zuleika brother and sister because, under the rigid formalities separating oriental men from women, no other relationship would provide the necessary "degree of intercourse leading to genuine affection." [20] But careful reflection convinced him that such a degree of kinship was too close for comfort, even though the lovers die before physical consummation is ever achieved; he prudently removed their connection one step farther so that they are merely first cousins. This shift also provided thematic advantages, permitting the author to contrast the animosity that dissolves a blood relationship (that

18. Cf. *Don Juan*, V, 126–27, and *The Corsair*, l. 1108.
19. The Giaour's state of mind in his final confession (ll. 971–1328) I take to be a concrete elaboration of the passage likening the remorse-riven mind to a scorpion encircled by fire (ll. 422–38) and a partial fulfillment of the curse pronounced upon the avenging infidel (ll. 747–86).
20. Letter of 15 December 1813 to Prof. Clarke, *LJ*, II, 309.

between Selim's father and uncle) with the fraternal devotion uniting Selim and Zuleika. What Byron's tale suggests is that familial closeness does not automatically produce affinity but may stimulate hate as well as love; consanguinity therefore has no legitimate bearing upon affection.

Of all Byron's serious lovers, Mazeppa alone seems to have suffered a tragedy of the heart without losing either his life or his equanimity. Somewhat like the Giaour, he still loves his former sweetheart and abhors her husband, who precipitously thwarted their affair; but, quite unlike the anguished avenger of Leila's death, he has allowed neither his emotions nor the burden of remorse to consume him. Though in true Byronic fashion he succeeded in vanquishing his enemy when "time at last [set] all things even," he has occupied his mind with other interests besides revenge. As an accomplished military commander, he has kept a level-headed course through the fifty years following his unforgettable amatory exploit and its nearly fatal consequences. Furthermore, he has developed — partly as a result of inherent temperament, partly from a sensible response to past circumstances — a philosophical ethic of love and human destiny that is sufficiently pragmatic to sustain the present and permit a viable future. Having accepted the impulses of life in all their natural fullness, without unnecessary torment, he is even able to recall his most crucial experiences with satisfaction.

Forming another contrast to the old Cossack is his sovereign, Charles XII of Sweden, who has perverted the need for love into a lust for power and who, as the poem begins, has suffered a crushing military defeat comparable in some respects to an amatory disaster. To encourage his leader in such straits, Mazeppa recounts a story of his own youth that provides a tactful but somewhat ironic lesson potentially useful to the wounded monarch. The episode, which occurred when Mazeppa was a page at the Polish court, resulted from his illicit amour with a beautiful young countess unhappily married to an elderly husband. Since the lovers were seriously devoted to one another, Mazeppa would have preferred to call her his own in "full view of Earth and Heaven," contrary to the general opinion that clandestine love is doubly sweet by being forbidden. But even their secret bliss was destined to end when the count discovered their relationship and punished his rival by tying him naked to a wild stallion turned loose on the countryside. Explaining how he survived the bizarre journey on horseback and thereby "learned to ride," Mazeppa turns his horsemanship into a metaphor for the conduct of life and draws

148

the moral that a kind of divine arbitration aids those strong enough to change defeat into victory. Unfortunately the weary king derives from the tale only what is of immediate benefit — sleep.

However, the central monologue does provide the reader with several revealing points on Byron's attitude toward love. Significantly, Mazeppa, in describing his intimacy with the countess, feels obliged to explain their surrender to emotional rapture as a weakness, since his royal listener presumably had never known an overwhelming attachment. In what is ostensibly a compliment to the king, the grizzled warrior declares that the greatest rulers are those who exert unwavering dominion over both their subjects and their passions. Yet this flattery is at variance with deductions that he later draws from the narrative itself. While recalling those moments when the end of his life seemed imminent, he concludes that only the man who has gratified the urge to love and who has learned that control over passions does not mean renunciation of them is, as Byron was later to show in *Sardanapalus*, capable of facing adversity — even death — in "hopeless certainty of mind." Such an individual, obviously, is Mazeppa, whose simple acceptance of life seems to account for his survival.

In two of his most mature productions (the Haidée episode of *Don Juan* and *The Island*) Byron succeeded, when temporarily relieved of the need to create dazzling adventures, in drawing together many of the views on love suggested rather sketchily in earlier works. Though his elaboration of such ideas presumably did little to impress Goethe with an ability to philosophize, one must also consider that Byron scornfully avoided organized systems of thought which, according to his assertions in *Don Juan* (XIV, 1–2), prove their invalidity by being superseded. Metaphysics, unlike science and religion, merely raised questions that it could not answer. Nebulous speculation (particularly that of Plato) he regarded as a dangerously deceptive veil over reality. Indeed the narrator's first mention of "philosophy" links it uncomfortably (like husbands and lapdogs) to the other stimulus for Juan's awakening — puberty. In view of repeated avowals throughout the poem that he is "fond of true philosophy," his deliberate curbs upon a tendency to reason abstractly seem difficult to reconcile. However, the inconsistency dissolves once we realize the poet's distinction between useless theory and practical psychology. To experience, the greatest of all teachers, he attributed his own superiority of insight (XV, 17:5–6). By attacking established schemata, he attempted to cover up his shortcomings as a systematic thinker while presenting sound views on human behavior.

But whereas most of Byron's narrative writing was devoted to a realistic depiction of man and his corrupt society, in these notable exceptions he laid down his scalpel to dream of what man's nature might be like under highly specialized conditions. Just as Voltaire used the Eldorado interlude for a refreshingly positive viewpoint, Byron described the possibilities of love under favorable circumstances and sharpened the vision with contrasting situations in modern society. The elaborate care devoted to these portrayals indicates that he was, in his own fashion, a constructive philosopher concerned with those rare instances when the ideal and the real coincide.

Not only did Byron write out of the depths of his own feelings, but he also reflected the works of certain authors who struck in him a sympathetic chord by their portrayals of love. Although Wieland's *Agathon* proved useful for some amatory details, Rousseau's *Julie, ou la Nouvelle Héloïse* especially impressed him and acquired additional lustre after he had visited many of the Swiss scenes hallowed by association with its characters. Some of the most eloquent stanzas in the third canto of *Childe Harold's Pilgrimage* are addressed to "the self-torturing sophist, wild Rousseau,/ The apostle of Affliction, he who threw/ Enchantment over Passion" (77:1–3). Of special interest is Byron's subjective interpretation of Rousseau the lover: "as a tree/ On fire by lightning; with ethereal flame/ Kindled he was, and blasted" (78:1–3). Inspired by dedication not to mortal woman but to ideal beauty, he breathed life into the imaginary Julie, investing her "with all that's wild and sweet" (79:2).

In both the Haidée episode and *The Island* Byron asserts, like his French mentor, that the political and economic corruption of civilization is inimical to true love. In the former, however, the social background, while always an impending threat, is held in abeyance long enough for Juan and Haidée to enjoy their brief paradise. The island retreat, which ever since Homer's day has served as a possible escape from the community of man, permits the lovers a moratorium on laws that operate elsewhere in the world. Even so, there is never any doubt that Lambro, as an amalgamation of Milton's God and Satan, will destroy their Cycladean Garden of Eden. Despite his charming manner, the unscrupulous pirate symbolizes predatory materialism, which, like the mercantile empires whose doom Byron was fond of sounding, flourishes by exploiting others' wealth. Though Haidée is the "greatest heiress of the Eastern Isles" and enjoys a superior status based on her father's ill-gotten riches, she has remained relatively uncontaminated. At least all the services she renders Juan are for love and not for money. And, whereas the free-born children of nature are happy when alone, they are "Unfit to mix in these thick solitudes/ Call'd social, haunts of Hate, and Vice, and Care" (IV, 28:3-4). Their Edenic joy is destroyed by the tyranny of unjust society, to which they cannot adapt.

Byron's depiction of Toobonai in *The Island* is, on the other hand, a much more positive view of political equality and material plenty. This imaginary utopia of the South Seas — one that deliberately rejects all the harsh anthropological and factual details of Mariner's *Account of the Natives of the Tonga Islands* (1817) and Bligh's *Narrative of the Mutiny and Seizure of the Bounty* (1790) — becomes "the equal land without a lord" (I, 36). Individual liberty is such that laws are unnecessary, and the only plaintiff is "the small voice within," which Byron terms "the Oracle of God." Moreover, the usual greed for material goods is unknown "Where none contest the fields, the woods, the streams" (I, 215). Nature's bounty in a land of endless summer affords such "promiscuous Plenty" that there is no need to struggle for the essentials of life. The islanders live in a "goldless Age, where Gold disturbs no dreams" (I, 216) and where there is neither avarice nor incentive to marry for money.

Closely allied to political freedom is the right of the individual to bestow his affections where he pleases. In *The Island* that privilege is taken for granted, and there is no obstacle to the fulfillment of Neuha's love for Torquil except the threat from the outside world. But in the Haidée episode paternal interference spells the lovers' doom. Though this situation was also a well-worn cliché of plot, it must have been prevalent enough in contemporary Europe to justify condemnation by Mary Wollstonecraft in her *Vindication of the Rights of Woman*.[21] Similarly, Rousseau's Lord Bomston maintains that everyone should be entitled to marry whomever he desires and that parents who try to break or form the sacred ties of nature are not only domestic tyrants but enemies of society.[22] Julie optimistically writes her lover: ". . . the heart gives law to itself . . . and

21. See especially ch. XI: "Duty to Parents."
22. *Eloisa: or, a Series of Original Letters*, tr. from the French, 2nd ed. (London, 1761), I, 255-56. Subsequent references to this work appear in the text.

bestows itself at its own pleasure" (I, 286). Unfortunate Haidée, whose predicament parallels Julie's, is able to love only when her father is away, and upon his departure from the island (the narrator observes sardonically) she becomes as free as a married woman in Christian lands (II, 175). Later her prophetic dream, in which she is chained to a rock as the tide rises and drowns her, symbolizes the catastrophe caused by her lack of freedom in love.

As a rule, Byron suggests that man can liberate and rehabilitate himself if he is able to exclude from his existence the artificialities of civilization. Juan, to be sure, is so much the natural man when he meets Haidée that he does not know how to dissemble and clearly follows impulse in doing what comes naturally. Haidée, lacking the world's sophisticated learning, possesses the intuitive perspicacity of childhood. Though illiterate, she can read in Juan's face what is far more important — the emotions of his heart. Consequently they understand each other perfectly even before she teaches him Romaic for verbal communication. While they are both very much aware of nature's divinity and their union with it, their love is consummated on the seashore, and all is fulfilled "after nature's fashion" — with stars serving as nuptial torches, ocean as their witness, and solitude their priest. Neuha and Torquil are also children of unspoiled environments — she "The infant of an infant world" (II, 127) and he a product of the wild Hebrides; hence they are able to respond completely to the spectacular beauty of the South Seas. Indeed it was "Nature, and Nature's goddess — Woman" that initially lured the mutineers to this lotus land not yet debased by contact with Europe. Here the natives lived in such perfect harmony with their surroundings that even "Their art seemed nature" (III, 181).

A corollary of this return to prelapsarian virtue is the resurrection of those vital forces which effete civilization has crucified. Hence in all Byron's literary amours — whether triangular, parallel, or merely horizontal — the fundamental ingredient of love is passion, as it is in the *Nouvelle Héloïse*. Part of Julie's difficulty stems from the inability of custom and obligation to eradicate her frustrated love for Saint-Preux. In her dying farewell to him she writes: "Long have I indulged myself in the salutary delusion, that my passion was extinguished. . . . In vain, alas! . . . it was interwoven with my heart-strings" (IV, 244–45). Byron, in both his accounts of ideal love, used the word *passion* to indicate its dynamic quality; and the imagery — involving torrents, tempests, earthquake, fire, and lightning — is highly appropriate to his concept of elemental love, since it derives largely from the kinetic energies of nature. When Juan and Haidée indulge in their kiss of immeasurable length and strength, it seems as though youth, love, and beauty are "all concentrating like rays/ Into one focus, kindled from above." The blood under such conditions becomes "lava, and the pulse a blaze,/ Each kiss a heart-quake" (II, 186:1–8). Indeed the most frequent symbol of love is the sun, customarily associated not only with divine illumination but also the fire of passion. Debasing this tradition, the narrator in *Don Juan* identifies heaven's brightest light with lust and, anthropomorphizing the burning star, asserts that "Sol's heat is/ Quenched in the lap of the salt Sea, or Thetis" (IX, 69:7–8). Obversely he associates chastity with the chill, virtuous North.[23] Yet Byron in all earnestness condemns the moral hypocrisy of northern Europe and admires instead the emotional fervor of sun-drenched lands. Whereas in frigid countries nothing ripens "rapidly save crime," Neuha and Haidée have matured early in southerly latitudes and both exude the inner warmth that the poet correlates with the sun's intensity.

The inevitable result of such passion is, of course, inebriation of the senses, as Rousseau also testifies. The sentimental Saint-Preux recalls those days when he gave himself "to the transports of a mutual passion; in which [he] drank its intoxicating draughts," and lost his rational faculties "in the rapture, the extasy, the delirium of love" (IV, 47). In *Don Juan* this exalted goal of inebriation is thoroughly undercut, however, by the hedonistic narrator, who advocates having "wine and woman": "Man, being reasonable, must get drunk;/ The best of life is but intoxication" (II, 179:1–2). His later reference to the drunkenness of sensuality in the affair with Catherine the Great (IX, 67) underscores this corporeal aspect of love. Indeed the narrator, whose pleasures tend toward the carnal, seems to care little how the effect is achieved so long as reason and its stepchild dullness are overcome.

Obviously the total amatory involvement that Byron dreamed of can thrive only in youth and innocence. Though Haidée at the age of seventeen had already rejected several suitors, her acquaintance with the art

---

23. Comparing *l'amour italien* with that of England, Byron told Thomas Medwin: "Love is not the same dull, cold, calculating feeling here as in the North. It is the business, the serious occupation of their lives . . . ." See *Medwin's Conversations of Lord Byron*, ed. Ernest J. Lovell, Jr. (Princeton, 1966), p. 23.

of love is limited, for Byron refers unequivocally to her virginal condition. She seems as "pure as Psyche ere she grew a wife —/ Too pure even for the purest human ties" (III, 74:5–6). Also Neuha, a child in years though mature in appearance, knows nothing of passion until Torquil initiates her, and the simplicity of her unfallen world is repeatedly emphasized. Both women realize first love, "that all/ Which Eve has left her daughters since her fall" and supposedly the only true love women ever have.[24] In both cases the poet stresses the innocence of youth before the progressive disillusionment known as experience can terminate love's magic. Nothing is revealed about Torquil's previous encounters, but Juan has learned something from Donna Julia. Yet much of his charm derives from an unspoiled naïveté reflected in his perennially "virgin face" (XVII, 13:8). As Byron conceives the Cycladean lovers, they are "so young, and one so innocent" that Juan's nude bathing every day passes "for nothing" (II, 172:1–2). He arrives on the seashore virtually unclothed and remains so (except for "a tatter'd/ Pair of scarce decent trowsers") until attired in Turkish garments. Following their natural marriage on the seashore the narrator counterbalances sentimentality by describing the two as "a group that's quite antique,/ Half naked, loving, natural, and Greek" (II, 194:7–8). Nakedness becomes the trademark of innocence, and as with Adam and Eve before the Fall, there is no awareness of shame.

Despite the fact that innocence in these two island romances is paradoxically linked with guilt, as in the real world, many critics have mistakenly tried to interpret the Haidée episode as a Miltonic return to a totally uncorrupted Eden. But what appears to the lovers as another Saturnian age is only fleeting. Byron's concept of sin diametrically opposes the defense of connubial relations in Book IV of *Paradise Lost*, for he maintains in a crucial passage about the union of Juan and Haidée: "till then never,/ Excepting our first parents, such a pair/ Had run the risk of being damn'd for ever" (II, 193:2–4). Despite nature's sanctification, sexual intercourse is the forbidden fruit in Byron's garden; once it has been enjoyed, the dissolution of Eden begins. As the poet explains this marriage of heaven and hell, the heart "Prompts deeds eternity can not annul,/ But pays off moments in an endless shower/ Of hell-fire" (II, 192:5–7). Later in the episode Haidée still seems unaware that Juan has "soil'd the current of her sinless years" (III, 1:7); temporarily they are "happy in the illicit/ Indulgence of their innocent desires" (III, 13:1–2). This paradox is further expressed in the lament for Haidée's unborn child as "a fair and sinless child of sin" (IV, 70:3). That Byron interpreted Rousseau's concept of love as both elevated and sinful is shown by a canceled line from *Childe Harold's Pilgrimage*. What finally became "O'er erring deeds and thoughts, a heavenly hue" was originally "O'er sinful deeds and thoughts the heavenly hue" (III, 77:7).[25] These ambivalent feelings toward sex are borne out in Byron's own experiences and pose an unresolved contradiction that can best be explained by his Presbyterian upbringing. Often tormented by thoughts of mortal sin, he simultaneously reveled in sexual delights.

Yet the most tantalizing question concerning love — that of its duration — is one which Byron seems reluctant to face. Even Rousseau would have conceded that the incandescent ardor maintained for years by Julie and Saint-Preux is at least partially kindled by obstructions hindering gratification; and certainly he argues that, since everything else fluctuates, expectation of "a constant passion" is nonsense (III, 179). Byron emphasizes a similar incongruity by making Juan and Haidée profess undying love at the same time that his narrator generalizes on infidelity as the law not only of humanity but of all nature. "The heart is like the sky, a part of heaven,/ But changes night and day too, like the sky" (II, 214:1-2). Nevertheless Haidée, like other Byronic heroines ready to sacrifice all for their beloveds, gives herself unquestioningly. She neither asks for vows nor speaks of scruples since she has "never heard/ Of plight and promises to be a spouse,/ Or perils by a loving maid incurr'd" (II, 190:1-4). One reason for their mutual fidelity, Byron explains, is that they are not married, for marriage and love, as in medieval courtly conventions, "rarely can combine." Matrimony as the sequent of passion, "like vinegar from wine —/ A sad, sour, sober beverage — by time/ Is sharpen'd from its high celestial flavour/ Down to a very homely household savour" (III, 5:5-8). Part of the difficulty, as Godwin argued in *Political Justice*, is that legal union constitutes another form of tyranny which, because of man's inherent desire for freedom, merely encourages infidelity. Untainted by civilization's hypocrisy, Haidée and Juan become "The faithful and the fairy pair" (IV, 18:2). Even time, the traditional foe of love, hates to deprive them of their joys, but there is no need to do so because they are destined not to experience the withering of this ecstasy (IV, 8-9).

24. *Don Juan*, II, 189:7-8; III, 3-4.
25. *Poetry*, II, 265n.

In *The Island*, however, Byron is far less concerned with the psychological aspects of constancy than with an artistic solution. As he well knew, happy love is a literary *cul de sac*; and unless obstacles are deliberately placed in its way, it becomes the most tedious of subjects. In our society only an adulterous liaison will automatically recharge the battery of passion by virtue of inherent (but not insurmountable) barriers. Though uttered facetiously, his comments on this principle reveal an awareness of artistic limitations:

> All tragedies are finish'd by a death,
>   All comedies are ended by a marriage;
> The future states of both are left to faith. (*Don Juan*, III, 9:1-3)

After all impediments to the happiness of Neuha and Torquil have been removed, there is nothing to do but leave them in a state of suspended bliss. What happens to their attachment should it be converted into "lawful, awful wedlock" is beyond the realm of the ideal. By cutting the tale short, Byron has created the only one of his love stories that ends happily.

There is, however, but one ultimately satisfactory conclusion, from both literary and psychological standpoints, to the transcendent emotion that Byron delineates. Paradoxically, the only fortunate resolution, if satiety or indifference be avoided, must be death. Byronic passion, retaining the basic Latin sense of suffering, is an agony so exquisite that it transcends mortal existence and becomes "a little death." Hence at its zenith it must be tantamount to complete annihilation. So Byron describes the ecstasy of Neuha and Torquil, which requires temporary obliteration of the senses, as the souls of the lovers leave their bodies to seek mystical union with the Divine Spirit (II, 370-81). The metaphor comparing their rapture to an "all-absorbing flame" and a "pure, yet funeral pile" indicates consumption of bodily features. Rousseau's Saint-Preux further characterizes passion as a sensual extinction rendering subsequent life anticlimactic (I, 183). This sentiment Byron echoes concerning Juan and Haidée when his narrator remarks: "Mix'd in each other's arms, and heart in heart,/ Why did they not then die?" (IV, 27:1-2). Premonition of physical death is apparent throughout the episode. On their last evening together the lovers experience an inexplicable sadness vaguely suggesting the end of their happiness, and Haidée, commenting on this "mutual feeling," prophesies: "I at least shall not survive to see" (IV, 23:6-8). Death is also presaged by terrifying images in her dream, from which she wakes to the very real threat of Lambro's presence. Pleading with her stern father, she declares: "On me . . . let death/ Descend. . . ./ I love him — I will die with him" (IV, 42:4–7). Juan is of course destined for another fate; yet Haidée's madness and subsequent demise become not only a sacrificial atonement for sin but also a martyr's defiance of life under intolerable conditions. Her tragic passion is in every sense consummated in a *Liebestod*.

Yet if love proves fatal, the consolation is that existence even without it must end in death; and according to Byron's view, a quickening of the heart gives life more meaning than anything else. His concept of ideal love, for which he strove but in reality never achieved, explains much about the pattern of his promiscuous and often tempestuous liaisons. The venality of society, he felt, was basically at fault. Yet the physical and spiritual union requiring innocence, youth, self-sacrifice, intense passion, and independence from social cares was one that by its very nature could not long endure even if achieved. Hence each affair that initially promised chimerical bliss was doomed, and as Byron grew older, attainment became even less likely. Nevertheless, its pursuit he held as praiseworthy as the desire for gold, glory, or the grape. To him, love, though but a shadow of the ideal, was the pulse of life.

PART FOUR

The Fantasy of Love

CHAPTER VII

Visionary Love: Shelley and Keats

W_{HEN} Don Quixote was charged with devotion to an imaginary
lady bearing little resemblance to her earthly counterpart, he replied that
his ideal image of her, whether real or fanciful, was the only Dulcinea he
could love. Though Romantic writers who became preoccupied with waking and sleeping dreams were not, like the errant knight, necessarily de-
ranged through assimilation of chivalric romances, they also revealed
their intense aspirations in visions transcending the imperfections of
earthly life. While this inclination may have been a type of insanity mani-
festing itself most prominently in *idées fixes*, it was a madness permitting
fresh viewpoints that could not have stemmed from sobriety. To the
idealistic mind, fantasy assumed such importance that it often pre-empted
the status of reality, producing stronger mental conviction than external
fact. A tendency to regard the metaphysical more worthy of consideration
than the physical grew destructive only if it so far detached those philosophically inclined from the concerns of time-and-space existence that
they were unable to cope with earth-bound problems. Admittedly, when
delightful illusion clashed with painful actuality, the choice encouraged
a retreat into the more favorable world. Even so, this propensity to flee the
here and now was prompted less by a desire to escape for pleasure's sake
than by the hope of experimentally constructing improved designs for
living unattainable amidst the frustrations of contemporary society. Con-

sequently the dream-vision, as an artistic form of wish fulfillment, proved a useful means of depicting not what is but what might or ought to be; and the poet, using his creative imagination, inevitably served as intermediary between the sphere of being and that of becoming.

It was quite natural under such conditions that visionaries should have been receptive to the doctrines of Plato, who had postulated a better world in order to elucidate this demonstrable but flawed replica. And many of the Romantics utilized his philosophy, which they knew either at first hand or at farther remove, to inform their own concepts. Socrates himself had analyzed the dream as a psychic gratification of desire (often repressed) and as a memorial reflection, however distorted, of what occupied conscious thought.[1] His attitude, however, was essentially one of distrust, for he warned that, when rational powers ceased to perform their censorial functions, the beast within man would be turned loose. Hence he recommended that during waking hours the temperate individual deliberately allay his passionate element and insure that reason assume control over the baser animalistic nature, thereby attaining sound perspective rather than irresponsible fantasy. The Romantic idealists, investing themselves in *vates'* robes and replacing Socratic reason with creative imagination, hoped that, by following a paradigm similar to the one Plato recorded, they might discern the suprarational truth transcending reality. The dream or even idle reverie became for them a means of liberating not energies that deserved to be caged but powers that should be freed.

Nor was it difficult under Platonic auspices to establish an affinity between love, poetry, and prophecy since Socrates had declared all three to be products of inspired madness.[2] Much that was applicable to prophetic dreams was equally valid for what he paradoxically termed both amatory insanity and "the greatest of heaven's blessings." In his view the lover, being possessed of and impelled by a god, was truly divine.[3] However, Eros, according to the priestess Diotima, whom Socrates paraphrased, was neither divine nor mortal but rather a daemon mediating between the two realms.[4] One of the most famous passages in the *Symposium*, which Shelley with meticulous care translated into English, describes the method by which love impels man to seek possession of the good in its various manifestations of beauty until by mounting a developmental ladder he ultimately rises to a vision of the celestial ideal. Underlying this progression is the postulate that man, desiring immortality, seeks spiritual and physical rebirth in the beautiful. Anyone eager to proceed correctly in the mysteries of intellectual love should therefore begin by admiring beauty embodied in one highly attractive individual, from whose image he then creates fair thoughts and respect for all physical loveliness. Having also learned to esteem the spiritual beauty of this particular mortal, he must then enlarge his conscious appreciation to include the spiritual beauty in all humanity. Moving from the concrete to the abstract, he will realize that the charms of the mind are infinitely preferable to those of the body. Therefore he will be drawn to virtue and hence to laws, traditions, philosophy, and ultimately science — all part of what, in Shelley's translation, is termed "the wide ocean of intellectual beauty." Thus, under proper stimulus of love, the perceiver of absolute beauty will make his pilgrimage from earth to heaven, where he will achieve his final vision — not a knowing about love but a direct apprehension of it.

This pursuit of love, beauty, and truth was later adapted by medieval writers to their own devices. The love-vision became an extraordinarily popular frame for allegorical poems; and romances of knight errantry, in which some worthy quest usually served as narrative backbone, often depicted heroes seeking the embodiments of their amatory fancies. Yet in very un-Platonic fashion the mentally conceived beauty impelling such adventurers was only the initial impetus, the goal being a damsel of voluptuous appeal. This search for some lady who materialized in a dream indeed became such a cliché by Chaucer's time that he unashamedly ridiculed it in "Sir Thopas," debasing the chaste knight who rejected mortal women and would have nothing less for his paramour than an elfin queen. As a result of more serious treatments, however, the essence of *amour courtois* was repedestaled during the Renaissance by being converted to a secular cult of love and beauty. Without apology Spenser in *The Faerie Queene* had the magnanimous Arthur recount his moving vision of Gloriana as she appeared to him in sleep (I, ix, 13–14). Thereafter the Prince forsook all other attachments and vowed that, no matter how arduous the endeavor, he would not rest until he found her somewhere in fairyland. Interest in "fine fabling" such as this was stimulated by Richard Hurd's *Letters on Chivalry and Romance* (1762); and throughout the

1. Plato, *The Republic*, 571–72.
2. *Phaedrus*, 244–45. The suprarational inspiration of the rhapsode is especially emphasized in the *Ion*.
3. *Symposium*, 180.
4. *Symposium*, 202–3.

nineteenth century Spenser, as well as his Italian predecessors, Boiardo and Ariosto, continued to be essential reading. To the Romantics, therefore, the motif of the amatory quest seemed a natural part of living tradition in a way that it no longer is.

Shelley, speculating on the change in poetic orientation between pagan and medieval times, argued that Christ's teachings on equality, combined with chivalry, produced a spiritual feeling toward elevated woman that would have been impossible in classical days. To this feminine liberation he ascribed the poetry of sexual love, which, by his analysis in *A Defence of Poetry*, had "become a religion, the idols of whose worship were ever present" such that "earth became peopled by the inhabitants of a diviner world" (VII, 127–28). Rousseau's account of that phenomenon in his life testifies to the survival of medieval traditions, whereby visionary concepts were made flesh, though he himself linked it with a Greek myth of the creative artist. In his *Confessions*, he describes how he mentally conceived the perfections of Julie for *La Nouvelle Héloïse* and then realized, upon meeting the Comtesse d'Houdetot, that this charming friend was the incarnation of his imaginary heroine. Hence he transferred to the Comtesse the qualities of his literary creation and, conversely, while finishing the novel, attributed to Julie the characteristics of his earthly beloved. This amalgamation he likened to the story of Pygmalion, who fell in love with the product of his own prefigurative mind only to discover that his ideal Galatea had assumed human existence. The experience obviously fascinated him, for on its theme he based a lyrical monodrama. The fact that his *Pygmalion* impressed Goethe (as evidenced in *Dichtung und Wahrheit*) suggests that it coincided with a *Zeitgeist* highly receptive to *Liebesträume*. Though Romanticists who employed the device often associated it loosely with Plato or his adapters because it involved a "beau ideal" and minimized the physical, the phenomenon was actually closer to Rousseau and medieval romances. For instead of progressing from concrete to abstract and from corporeal to spiritual, as Socrates recommended, it proceeded rather from heaven to earth and from soul to body — without, however, completely losing traces of its divine origin.

Even before he acquired a first-hand acquaintance with Plato's writings, Shelley cherished what many another love-sick boy with philosophical pretensions has termed the search for his soul's companion. Among the melancholy Gothic poems addressed to his cousin Harriet Grove,

"To St Irvyne" demonstrates that in early youth he pictured her as the none too stable incarnation of an amorous fantasy:

> My Harriet is fled like a fast-fading dream,
>   Which fades ere the vision is fixed on the mind,
> But has left a firm love and a lasting esteem,
>   That my soul to her soul must eternally bind. (ll. 17–20) [5]

Obviously there was, as James A. Notopoulos maintained, a "natural Platonism" in Shelley from the very beginning of his literary career. His pursuit of the ideal in physical reality and his dissatisfaction with mundane imperfection were outgrowths of this temperament.

Though the most comprehensive treatment of the love-quest appears in "Alastor," some of Shelley's prose statements detail it even more explicitly. As early as 1811 he explained in a letter that all true lovers seek the embodiment of a mental aspiration. Attempting to console Hogg after the shattering of an amatory illusion, he wrote: "You loved . . . an idea in your own mind which had no real existence. You concreted this abstract of perfection . . ." (I, 95). That Shelley saw this situation as the one underlying all spiritualized attachments is further evidenced by his analysis of sentimental passion in "A Discourse on the Manners of the Ancient Greeks Relative to the Subject of Love," a work not published in entirety until the twentieth century because it dared to account for sublimated homosexuality. As he interpreted the dilemma peculiar to classical Greece, men had, by cultivating only the masculine population and debasing the feminine to virtual savagery, deprived themselves of love's "legitimate object," for ideal unions do not exist with degraded inferiors. Man naturally selects another most like that "object or its archetype" existing forever in his mind.[6] In the advanced stages of civilization, as Shelley analyzed the progress, the importance of sensual gratification is proportionally diminished as man realizes that the "profound and complicated sentiment" also necessitates intellect and imagination. The sexual connection, though never completely eliminated, is reduced to an auxiliary function as the more refined modes of amatory converse increase.

After Shelley himself had experienced disenchantment in love, he read

5. Though Harriet Shelley dated the poem 28 February 1805, Kenneth Neill Cameron, in his edition of *The Esdaile Notebook* (New York, 1964), pp. 305–9, suggests a later date — 1809–10.
6. *Shelley's Prose*, ed. David Lee Clark (Albuquerque, 1954), p. 220.

St. Augustine's *Confessions*, which showed how a sensitive individual might quench bodily fires with spiritual inundation. The use of a Latin quotation from that work as an epigraph for "Alastor" proclaims the kinship that the young author felt with another Platonist, Christian though the latter ultimately became. Since Shelley seemed perpetually enamored of love and ever seeking some object for his ardor, St. Augustine's description of himself upon arrival in Carthage was appropriate. It is significant, moreover, that the great Church Father believed in the reality of visions, having himself been disturbed by erotic dreams. Yet the marked difference between the prelate and the central figure of "Alastor" is that the former found his progress toward divine love impeded by devotion to carnality, while the latter seemed unable to cope with mundane problems because of attachment to an ideal. Whereas St. Augustine converted his physical desires into spiritual yearning for God, whom in his Platonic moments he called "that supreme Loveliness," the Shelleyan hero met untimely death because he could not reconcile fleshly illusion to visionary reality. Yet the validity of the quest, despite inevitable disappointment, was beyond doubt. That life, not only for the lover but for all aspiring men, consisted of striving for illusory goals is clear from a letter Shelley wrote Hogg shortly before composing "Alastor": ". . . who is there that will not pursue phantoms, spend his choicest hours in hunting after dreams, and wake only to perceive his error and regret that death is so near?" (I, 429–30). Therefore it seemed no idle fabrication to claim in the preface to "Alastor" that the poem was "allegorical of one of the most interesting situations of the human mind." [7]

For the principal character in his first visionary quest Shelley chose a young poet who lived, sang, and died in solitude. Whereas in youth nature's loving harmony and philosophy's stimulus had adequately satisfied emotional and intellectual needs, these nourishments proved inadequate to the mature man. Unable to respond to mortal woman, however, he sought after a Being encountered in an erotic dream, but one who led him to death rather than fulfillment. It is almost as though, in the manner of medieval romances, Eros wrought this form of vengeance upon one "who spurned/ His choicest gifts." What made his amatory vision seem worth the search was that in their brief rhapsodic union she gratified all the unsatiated longings of philosopher, poet, and lover within him by fulfilling in a single image the three Shelleyan requisites — intellect, imagination, and sense. Once he had successfully apprehended this superior reality, his estrangement from the worlds of man and nature became even more pronounced. Dedication to a visionary goal inevitably produced self-inflicted loneliness, for, though other mortals offered him love and sympathy during his frantic wanderings, he yearned for what they could not grant. Unlike the more practical idealist in Shelley's essay "On Love," who would wisely seek for the antitype of his epipsyche (VI, 202), the poet in "Alastor" desired only the prototype, the ideal itself, which could never be embodied. That the dream of love took precedence over all else is vividly pictured in his last desperate effort to find his elusive beloved. Despite the exquisite beauty of the sylvan spot at which he arrived, even the Spirit of Nature, to which his soul had been attuned in youth, could not long divert his attention. Two starry eyes (presumably of the visionary maiden) beckoned him to follow, and as the dim lights of his unattainable goal extinguished themselves in darkness, he could only resign himself to death.

Nevertheless, the lonely poet's failure to attain the "prototype of his conception" by no means invalidates the search. Nor did Shelley intend it to. The apparent discrepancy which many critics have detected between poem and retrospective preface stems largely from shifted emphasis, possibly because Shelley thought his poetic message not absolutely clear. Though the introductory note obviously stresses punitive effects of withdrawal as the poem does not, there is no evidence that the author had radically altered his intent. Certainly he would not have called the work "Alastor; or the Spirit of Solitude" — despite Peacock's suggestion of the title — unless he had felt that designation appropriate. Several times he had acknowledged his own phobia of loneliness. In a letter of 8 May 1811 to Hogg, he had declared solitude to be "most horrible," because of "the evil which comes to *self*" in that state (I, 77). The inherent destructiveness of companionless life is further emphasized by an assertion in *The Revolt of Islam* that "solitude is like despair" (l. 67) and by a reference in *Prometheus Unbound* to "self-torturing solitude" (I, 295).

Yet Shelley recognized it as an autogenous pitfall to the oversensitive soul, which experienced more exquisite pleasure and excruciating pain than did "meaner spirits." Presumably he was aware of what was becoming a popular literary problem — the necessarily maladjusted relationship of the creative artist to his own society. The dilemma arose from the fact

7. *Poetical Works*, p. 14.

that in youth man nurtured his spirit on nature's sensory delights yet could not remain forever content within its limitations. As he developed intellectually, pursuit of lonely endeavors detached him from his fellow man, nature, and even his physical senses, leaving him an alienated, divided individual. The genius, like the criminal (though Shelley did not correlate the two as Dostoevski, Nietzsche, and Mann would), must by his very temperament be a nonconformist at odds with his own breed, though miserable in such estrangement. Cultivation of inner depths was inevitably purchased at the expense of human contact; for in an effort to expand his latent talents, he unavoidably would become spellbound by his own dream. Without self-absorbed withdrawal he could not succeed; yet this very seclusion would hasten his demise.

Before proceeding to other seminarrative accounts of the search for an ideal, Shelley epitomized his basic concept in the "Hymn to Intellectual Beauty." Addressed to the only divinity he found worthy of prayer — the one constant he knew through its variable manifestations — this paean also celebrates a love-quest, yet one for a strangely disembodied vision. In Shelley's view, though the unseen power visiting the evanescent beauties of earth consecrates by its immanence all that it enhances, the decay of both the beautiful and the good has never been satisfactorily explained from a "sublimer world." Consequently "Demon, Ghost, and Heaven" continue to represent the futile attempts of poets and sages to wrest an answer from that transcendent power of which man has only fleeting awareness. If indeed the Spirit serving as messenger of sympathies, inspirer of human love, and light-bearer in life's darkness might be soundly fixed in the human heart, man would be immortal and omnipotent — even as a god. Therefore Shelley prays that the Spirit may be more enduring than its shadows, lest the grave be as disappointing as life itself. By addressing his divinity as "awful Loveliness," Shelley demonstrates that the philosophical identification of emotion and aesthetics is inherent in our language since the term "loveliness" implies an attractive quality that inspires love. With Intellectual Beauty, ordinarily a spiritual stimulus, he integrates the beauty of earth, which evokes a sensuous response. Accordingly, thought and sense, like mind and matter, are not totally separable from one another. And while this concept of love bears certain resemblances to other Shelleyan treatments of the theme, the poet is concerned in his "Hymn" not so much with capture of an elusive image as with the guarantee of its permanence, which adds "grace and truth to life's unquiet dream."

Reshaping the material of "Alastor," he translated some of its implications into a garden parable entitled "The Sensitive Plant." The poem's botanical hero, flourishing in an "undefiled Paradise," awakens to life in spring just as a poetic soul responds to love. But it is distinct from the other vegetation in two vital respects. Though all the plants react not only to the sun's increasing warmth but also to one another very much like reciprocating lovers, the Sensitive Plant yearns for affection more than do its neighbors. Yet, though it has unlimited capacity for admitting love, it lacks an attractive, scented flower with which to radiate inner feelings conspicuously. In truly Platonic fashion it desires what it does not possess — the Beautiful. This need is temporarily satisfied by the garden's "ruling Grace," a lady personifying Intellectual Beauty, who tends the plants in spring and summer but in fall dies or at least ceases to exist as the inhabitants of the garden have known her. Her departure proves fatal to the Sensitive Plant, which is but a "leafless wreck" when the hardier growths revive the following spring.

In the conclusion Shelley makes the lesson of his fable unmistakably clear. Assuming the role of an objective reporter, he pretends to be uncertain whether the Sensitive Plant or its spirit felt radical transformation before decaying. Nor does he know if the lady's gentle mind, parted from the form that scattered love, found sadness where it previously gave delight. Yet he is convinced that on earth, "Where nothing is, but all things seem,/ And we the shadows of the dream," death itself must be a mockery. The garden, its attendant, and all its sweetness have not perished. "For love, and beauty, and delight," he claims, "There is no death nor change." Since he does not wish to blame the plant or the beautiful gardener for disintegration of the amatory dream, the seasonal variation representing mundane necessity serves as a useful device revealing man's inability to sustain his vision. The spiritual estrangement signaled by the lady's departure therefore occurs as inevitably as cyclic alteration, but the most sensitive are unfortunately least capable of reviving after love has been shattered. Nevertheless, though the Eve of this horticultural Eden may have ceased to be the manifestation of the unchanging ideal, what she even temporally embodied can never perish.

Shelley's most exuberant treatment of a visionary Aphrodite appears in "The Witch of Atlas," a whimsical frolic transcending stereotyped myths.

In his unique personification of a sportive divinity, he has incorporated most of his previous assertions about the power of love. But this daemonic intermediary between the natural and the supernatural lures no solitary dreamers to destruction; rather, she inspires all who know her. Unlike the cold, elusive prototype in "Alastor," she is a warm, life-engendering spirit, whose most obvious aspect is brightness. "Garmented in light/ From her own beauty," she is so radiant that by comparison the rest of the world seems "like the fleeting image of a shade." Realizing that her appearance is too exquisite for mortal eyes, she weaves herself a veil, the usual Shelleyan division between the absolute and the mutable, to serve as "A shadow for the splendour of her love." In the description of the Witch's habitat, the paramount significance of light imagery is again emphasized by the luminous fountain and the well of flame, both of which reflect Shelley's preoccupation with the incredible mingling of fire and water accomplished only through love's efficacy.

The actions of this playful divinity show her unusual powers, especially in the creation of Hermaphroditus to be her companion. Though not reclusive by nature, she at first lives alone because her immortality obviates any permanent relationship with the transient spirits of earth who admire her. Hence, like Pygmalion, she makes a living creature, molding it of fire and snow and tempering the unlikely mixture with liquid affection. The result is a pure hermaphrodite symbolizing lovers so perfectly whole that in their androgynous union they become not only double-sexed but spiritually unsexed. This gentle winged creature, a Shelleyan Cupid who reconciles antithetical elements without obliterating them, accompanies the Witch as she sails about the universe scattering visions upon sleeping humanity. Her amazing perspicacity enables her to see into the very profundities of men, so that she may detect worthy souls beneath the rudest exteriors and eternize them, purge evil from the flawed, and (whenever necessary) break down inhibitions hindering lovers' gratification. By such infusion of her miraculous power, she brings about the fulfillment of mortals, who realize her spirit through the flesh.

By the time Shelley composed his most affirmative enunciation of the visionary theme in "Epipsychidion," he had reflected upon it so intensely that even borrowed ideas assumed an original character. His fragmentary essay "On Love" had previously defined its subject as a "powerful attraction" to something beyond self which occurs when man, aware of inner emptiness, desires an understanding response to his own experiences.

Of special import to this concept was the need to sympathize, even empathize, with another — like the strings of two lyres harmonized "to the accompaniment of one delightful voice." Quite naturally every man tends to be drawn to his own likeness or at least to one who will complement him. In principle, this affinity is akin to Aristotle's definition in the *Nicomachean Ethics* (IX, ix) of a friend as "a second self." Or in Shelley's analysis, "We dimly see within our intellectual nature a miniature as it were of our entire self, yet deprived of all that we condemn or despise, the ideal prototype of every thing excellent or lovely . . ." (VI, 201-2). The antitype of this "soul within our soul," an inner life extending beyond one's own existence, is what man seeks in love, attempting to "resemble or correspond with it" through intellect, imagination, and sense — those phases necessary to complete fulfillment. The threefold progression is not one in which the steps may be interchanged, nor can the first and second stages be abandoned after the third is reached if the totality of amatory experience is to be maintained.

Shortly before incorporating these principles into "Epipsychidion," however, Shelley wrote his *Defence of Poetry*, which draws many parallels between love and poetry. Accordingly, the goal of the poet appears as essentially that of the Platonic lover, for ". . . to be a poet is to apprehend the true and the beautiful, in a word, the good" (VII, 111). Just as the Witch of Atlas perceives spiritual loveliness behind rude exteriors, so too "Poetry lifts the veil from the hidden beauty of the world" (VII, 117). Such perspicacity can also effect ethical improvement, for he who employs imagination, which Shelley calls "The great instrument of moral good," must, like the lover, "put himself in the place of another." Shelley similarly explains love as "a going out of our own nature, and an identification of ourselves with the beautiful which exists in thought, action, or person, not our own" (VII, 118). Negatively, when social corruption infects the poetry of any age, it does so by attacking the three ingredients of Shelleyan love — first the imagination, then the intellect, and ultimately the senses. The final stage in this deterioration is represented by erotic poets, who are inferior to such giants as Homer and Sophocles because they lack the harmonious union of the two mental faculties with the physical. The correspondence between love and poetry is again obvious when Shelley describes moments of poetical inspiration as "evanescent visitations of thought and feeling . . . always arising unforeseen and departing unbidden, but elevating and delightful beyond all expression" (VII, 136);

for emphemeral visions of love have the same characteristics. And Shelley's further claim that poetry "transmutes all that it touches . . . by wondrous sympathy to an incarnation of the spirit which it breathes" (VII, 137) can with equal justification be applied to human affection.

Since Shelley began "Epipsychidion" shortly after completing his *Defence*, it was natural that he should have pursued many of the similarities already postulated. Though ostensibly addressed to Emilia Viviani, the poem utilizes "flesh and blood" symbolism primarily to illustrate the abstract. At the time of its composition, Emilia's substance was thought to be love and beauty, her accident mere womanhood. Nevertheless, many critics have bogged down in biographical identifications to such an extent that they fail to realize the poet's overriding concern with a theoretical, visionary ideal. By 18 June 1822 Shelley wrote his friend John Gisborne that he could no longer look at the poem because "the person whom it celebrates" by then had turned out to be "a cloud instead of a Juno" (II, 434). His disillusionment, as he explained it, proved once more the human error of "seeking in a mortal image the likeness of what is perhaps eternal." Yet there had obviously been a time when Emilia was in some respects the equivalent of Dante's Beatrice — vessel of divine grace, mortal emblem of perfection, and inspiration for a hymn to the Source of Love. Moreover, she was the vision of his youth made perfect in the flesh since she fulfilled the conditions of the antitype for which the poet had sought.

Like a visitant from a superior world, Emilia becomes in the poem

> . . . too gentle to be human,
> Veiling beneath that radiant form of Woman
> All that is insupportable . . .
> Of light, and love, and immortality! (ll. 21–24)

From her inner being there radiates "one intense/ Diffusion, one serene Omnipresence" — in the same way that emanations of Intellectual Beauty interpenetrate the world. And in a sequence of enraptured analogies, which attempt to suggest concepts beyond the ordinary reach of language, Shelley praises her ability to affect all his senses and simultaneously to transcend them. Though his wish that she might have been his twin or his wife's sister signifies a yearning for irrevocable closeness, his relationship with her is actually stronger, he insists, than that of belonging. He *is* a portion of her, the counterpart of her soul. He even seems to imply

172

that since she represents a reality more permanent than the physical, his response to her guarantees eternal life.

The "idealized history" of Shelley's visionary quest follows the definite progression required by his concept of love — one generally slighted by those treating that portion of "Epipsychidion" as merely veiled autobiography. His initial encounter is with the prototype, a Being too glorious to be seen yet revealing herself through nature, art, and even silence. But his search for the pure vision becomes vain as she gradually fades into the shadows of routine existence; and his attempt to find her in "many mortal forms," whose appeal is chiefly sensuous, results only in successive disillusionments. Ultimately "the glorious shape" of his dreams does reappear, though not as one entity but in diverse aspects. As the moon, she is indeed the reflection of ideal light, but with obvious limitations. Since the rays cast from her lunar sphere cannot warm him, he is neither dead nor alive under the intellectual spell of her "chaste cold bed." As the sun, she is most like his youthful vision, radiating such imaginative illumination that his frozen spirit responds to her. These "Twin Spheres of light" he implores to remain and invites a third, the sensually appealing comet, to return to his "azure heaven." By invoking love's three manifestations to make their home in his heart, he tacitly admits that no one woman in his life has satisfied simultaneously the three planes required for complete gratification.

Nor should it be necessary, according to his scheme of love, to restrict oneself to a single beloved. Hence Shelley, in contrast to the multitude, does not recommend loving one mistress or friend to the complete exclusion of others; for that devotion which spiritually creates only one object is narrowly, even unnaturally, confined. Too frequently love of the sort that progresses toward marriage, as he explained earlier in letters to Elizabeth Hitchener, becomes selfishly possessive and devoid of the altruistic sympathy identified with friendship.[8] True love, on the contrary, differs from physical matter in that it may be subdivided numerous times without diminishing any portion of it. Like human understanding, which grows through contemplation of increasingly numerous perceptions, it develops according to sustenance received. In explaining this phenomenon, Shelley originally used the more accurate term "free love" but because of unfavorable connotations canceled it. Characteristically, he also compares

8. *Letters*, I, 173, 182, 194–95.

valid affections to the light of imagination, which "fills/ The Universe with glorious beams, and kills/ Error." Since pleasure, love, and thought actually increase by having no limits set upon them, the poet hopes that through them the regeneration of a corrupt world can be effected.

In the last section of the poem, Shelley envisions a situation that both lover and poet would consider ideal though it could likely be achieved only in a never-never land. The consummate union on an Aegean island is in some ways comparable to the coalescence Dante imagined with his "God-bearing image" in heaven. Since true love cannot experience artificial restraint, Shelley invites Emilia, though admittedly enjoined to remain a "vestal sister," to become the bride of his imperishable spirit. Thus he has made an apologue of the condition postulated in his essay "On Love," in which he refers to "a soul within our soul that describes a circle around its proper paradise, which pain, and sorrow, and evil dare not overleap" (VII, 202). This idyllic state, where perfect correspondence with the antitype exists on all three planes of love, is termed in the essay "the invisible and unattainable point to which Love tends"; and the desired condition will be theoretically possible for the poet and his spiritual complement, Emilia, when the surroundings are sufficiently in harmony to express nature's inherent love. Apart from humanity's discord, they will achieve mutual absorption by progressing from an intellectual exchange to the equivalent of sexual consummation, whereby the fountains of their deepest life become "Confused in Passion's golden purity." And responding to the radiant emanation of nature's spirit, their united souls will merge with the "living soul of this Elysian isle" to achieve immortality through assimilation into the Platonic One. After such exalted flights of verbal ecstasy, Shelley returns to earth just enough to admit that attainment of his vision might have to wait for the world beyond.

The association of visionary love with its apotheosis in death was indeed one toward which Shelley moved in later years. His belief is given its most concrete elaboration in the allegorical prose tale "Una Favola," written about 1820, which distinguishes between two kinds of love — the one temporary and fraudulent, the other eternal and perfect. The deceitful enchantress named Life, as the questing youth discovers, provides nothing more than disillusionment. Yet Death, in spite of her inability to respond to someone deliberately seeking her, faithfully promises a fulfillment in eternity to lovers whose earthly devotion has been constant. Though the tale breaks off before any resolution in its narrative, Shelley's addition to the usual pattern of the quest is remarkably clear. The Pandemian attraction even at its best is untrustworthy, and only beyond the veil of mundane illusion can love avoid annihilation of its hopes. Explaining unmistakably why in Shelley's sombre view life is the fickle enslaver and death the liberator, "Una Favola" serves as enlightening prelude to his final poem.

The unfinished "Triumph of Life," though it may not utterly repudiate Shelley's earlier pronouncements, certainly treats many of the early themes in a skeptical, even ironic, manner, acknowledging limitations on creative faculties. For this purpose, Rousseau represents a poetic sensibility stultified not by death but rather by life, that "contagion of the world's slow stain" which the idealized Adonais had avoided. Rousseau's undoing is blamed on the failure of life to match his lofty expectations; by his assessment,

> . . . if the spark with which Heaven lit my spirit
> Earth had with purer nutriment supplied
> Corruption would not now thus much inherit
> Of what was once Rousseau. . . . (ll. 201-4) [9]

Translated to the moral plane this disillusionment becomes the irreconcilable discrepancy between goodness and the means toward that goal (ll. 230-31); and unfortunately the most avid seeker is the one most bitterly disappointed. The grim, withered wraith admits that in life he was "overcome/ By [his] own heart alone" (ll. 240-41). This view agrees with what Shelley, presumably from reading the *Confessions*, had asserted in his *Proposals for an Association* (1812): "Rousseau gave license by his writings, to passions that only incapacitate and contract the human heart: — so far hath he prepared the necks of his fellow-beings for that yoke of galling and dishonourable servitude, which at this moment, it bears" (V, 265).

As the wizened form explains, his downfall proceeded from an unwise reaction to his vision of a "shape all light." So captivated did he become with this epipsychal ideal, who also served as catalyst to his imagination, that he made conflicting demands of her — that she might explain the mysteries of this world and yet not be subject to its mutability. But the

9. All citations of "The Triumph of Life" are from the edition of Donald H. Reiman (Urbana, 1965).

nepenthe she provided to quench his desire for knowledge obliterated the heavenly ideal, and his "brain became as sand." [10] A new and inferior vision superseded the Uranian dream, stimulating within him mundane appetites. Once he capitulated to the blandishments of earth, he was swept with the multitude of humanity into "that cold light, whose airs too soon deform" (l. 468) and was borne along in the sadistically triumphant procession of life that includes all whose sensitivities have been crushed by the world. In short, he became much like Byron's description of himself: his heart grew prematurely old and frigid as a result of disenchanting jolts.

Obviously then, abrogation of the earthly quest through death is not the worst fate that can befall an aspiring soul. The only reprehensible failure results from being overcome by Life, which Shelley represents allegorically as a grim conqueror, from whose chariot emanates a harsh, glaring light. Only those "sacred few" of Athens and Jerusalem "who could not tame/ Their spirits," even while they "touched the world with living flame," escaped its captivity (ll. 128–31). Significantly, a large number of Life's prisoners are those who yielded to earthly passion; indeed the vanguard of the procession, composed of a frantic group impelled by lust ("agonizing pleasure"), is ultimately ground beneath the car. Even more poignant, however, is the subjugation of philosophers who could not live the love they expounded. Failing to transcend the illusory beauty of earth, they did not achieve union with the One, as Adonais did. Plato is chained to Life's "triumphal chair" because in advanced years he is said to have fallen passionately in love with a youth. Rousseau, by Shelley's interpretation, was apparently so desperate to translate his vision into concrete reality that he lost sight of Julie in settling for Thérèse. And Shelley feared that he himself had been undermined by seeking the eternal in human form. Though vision by its very nature, like Rousseau's rainbow, refracts the light from heaven to infuse earth with additional splendor, it proves to be both insubstantial and transient in physical manifestations. Hence love in the material world, dependent as it is upon life itself, must be subject to the same disintegration that besets the world of process. For the constancy of Uranian love, which rarely visits earth, the questing soul must await assimilation into eternity.

When Keats wrote "I Stood Tip-toe" in 1816, he was still under the spell of *The Excursion*; consequently his attempt to account for the origin

of myth on psychological grounds is very Wordsworthian. According to
his view, the mythmaker by means of imagination transcends the simple,
pleasurable response to natural beauty in order to humanize and even
spiritualize the powers of nature. This endeavor, far from being abstruse
or vaguely symbolic, actually makes the forces more significant to man by
animating the inanimate. Keats offers his own surmise that a Greek poet,
who was "sure a lover too," first invented the myth of Endymion to give
the amorously deprived Cynthia what any compassionate human being
would think she deserved. Such an arbiter of poetic justice, he concludes,
must by means of visions or dreams have "burst our mortal bars": through
his quest for suprahuman knowledge he found the spiritual and physical
reality that Keats calls "truth." Presumably the Greek poet's intuition,
"bringing/ Shapes from the invisible world, unearthly singing/ From out
the middle air" (ll. 185–87),[11] functioned very much as the charioteer in
Keats's "Sleep and Poetry." Both mediate between the natural and the
supernatural or between the mind's inner realm and the external world.
What particularly intrigued Keats with the story of Endymion, as the
conclusion of "I Stood Tip-toe" demonstrates, is that the union of shepherd and lunar goddess was traditionally intended to serve all mankind —
to uplift humanity not only through a quickening of love and philanthropic sympathy but by a poetical loosening of human tongues. Thus the
consummation effected by mortal and divine love was also the therapeutic
goal of poetry — "To sooth the cares, and lift the thoughts of man"
("Sleep and Poetry," ll. 246–47).

Seminal themes such as these, potentially too complex for short poems,
demanded more elaborate treatment; and Keats determined to expand
them in a work that, whether or not it was consciously a reply to "Alastor," furnished a positive solution to the difficulties of that poem. Characteristically Keats rejected a poet whose quest compelled the repudiation
of humanity and made his Endymion an active participant in the experiential world, a man who would strive to overcome his problems by facing
up to them, though admittedly with the aid of a *dea ex machina*. Furthermore, the narrative invited a number of philosophical speculations that
Keats wanted to explore. He was aware that sleep, without the curtailment

10. In *Prometheus Unbound* nepenthe is identified with unfading Elysian
flowers (II, iv, 60–61) and with love itself (III, iv, 163).
11. All citations of Keats's poetry are from *The Poetical Works of John
Keats*, ed. H. W. Garrod, 2nd ed. (Oxford, 1958).

of reason, produced dreams quite similar to those which the Romantic poet utilized in the composition of poetry. But what was the difference between dream, especially when it was a *Liebestraum*, and poetic vision? The psychological process of artistic creation through imagination seemed in some mysterious way comparable to love, whereby the human being experienced an enlargement of compassionate understanding and an extinction of selfhood through empathic projection into others. That Keats identified the poet's attainment of truth with the lover's objective is unequivocally stated in his oft-labored account of 22 November 1817, written to Benjamin Bailey:

> I am certain of nothing but of the holiness of the Heart's affections and the truth of Imagination — What the imagination seizes as Beauty must be truth — whether it existed before or not — for I have the same Idea of all our Passions as of Love they are all in their sublime, creative of essential Beauty (I, 184).

For this goal, *Endymion* presents two elaborately extended and sometimes interwoven metaphors — one chiefly applicable to the poet, the other especially appropriate to the lover. Instead of protracted allegory, in which abstractions are consistently presented in terms of the material world, the poem often fuses these conceptual metaphors, thereby creating what is sometimes rather loosely interpreted as allegorical.[12] Evidently Keats believed there was no essential difference between them since the development of human faculties that apotheosized the lover also developed the poetical character.

The problem of transforming an ordinary mortal into a lover-poet through distended narrative was what Keats had to solve in *Endymion*. Therefore his selection of the pastoral deity Pan as emblem and agent of the sensuous imagination was a felicitous one, especially since that sportive divinity had been regarded as an amateur poet. Furthermore, despite the satyr-god's notable lack of amatory success (the objects of his fancy having been made inanimate to escape ravishment), his propensities were well known; and the Arcadian chorus's appeal to him as one who would naturally be sympathetic with other lovers is apt. Yet what made Pan especially useful was his traditional association with universal nature — his upper human portion representing the nobler aspirations toward the spiritual, his lower goatlike parts acknowledging attachment to earth. This union was exactly what Keats thought the imagination and love ought to strive for, and in the last stanza of the hymn Pan is fittingly implored to remain the link between divine heaven and mundane life —

> the unimaginable lodge
> For solitary thinkings; such as dodge
> Conception to the very bourne of heaven,
> Then leave the naked brain. (I, 293–96)

The first narrative attempt to correlate beauty, imagination, and love is Endymion's intricately wrought dream-vision, in which his soul achieves an almost mystical union with the moon as his response to her beauty temporarily liberates him from selfhood. Though resigned to death in this consuming experience of love, he discovers that the result of self-annihilation is "to live,/ To take in draughts of life from the gold fount/ Of kind and passionate looks" (I, 655–57). In this way he establishes the reciprocity of taking into himself the objective world and giving out the subjective inner being that Keats associated with both love and imagination.

His awaking to earth's imperfections after such an exalted encounter must necessarily be unpleasant, and he justifies his disinterest in the noble actions expected of him on the grounds that the goal of love is higher than that of worldly ambition. The speech to his sister, which Keats carefully revised upon realizing that the extenuated narrative needed a more explicit statement of direction, clearly enunciates the purpose of the love-quest. In a letter to his publisher John Taylor, Keats described the additional passage as "a regular stepping of the Imagination towards a Truth" and emphasized the practical function it performed in his own mind by setting forth "the gradations of Happiness even like a kind of Pleasure Thermometer" (I, 218). Use of the phrase "Pleasure Thermometer," though often labeled hedonistic, was natural not only to a man well versed in science but to one who conceived of psychic happiness as an aim reached (as outlined in "The Fall of Hyperion") through a gradual upward progression. Even a moralist like Spenser in his Garden of Adonis had given the name Pleasure to the offspring of Cupid and Psyche, acknowledging allegorically that the human soul when united with love

---

12. For evaluation of allegorical interpretations, see Stuart M. Sperry, Jr., "The Allegory of *Endymion*," *SIR*, 2 (1962–63), 38–53. For analysis of *Endymion* in terms of associationist dream psychology, see James R. Caldwell, *John Keats' Fancy* (New York, 1965), pp. 91–131.

unabashedly generates delight. The desired end of Keats's poetic lover, however, lies in the union with essence, a divine fellowship with all existence, wherein the natural and supernatural elements are one. In this ultimate state man becomes "alchemiz'd, and free of space" (I, 780).

The initial stages, as elucidated by Endymion, involve advancement from a rather Wordsworthian absorption in nature to an understanding of its personified forces as mythopoeic art. Reaching this second rung, man achieves such harmony with his inanimate surroundings that he may properly be designated as a "floating spirit." But this development, should it proceed no farther, would be conducive primarily to undesirable self-aggrandizement — an arrogation rather than an offering of good. Since Keats was becoming increasingly concerned with the obliteration of solipsism, he insisted that his poet-lover advance to

> Richer entanglements, enthralments far
> More self-destroying, leading, by degrees,
> To the chief intensity. (I, 798–800).

This zenith of energic realization was highly significant for the creative artist because it defined "the excellence of every Art" and could make "all disagreeables evaporate, from their being in close relationship with Beauty & Truth." [13] It was equally important to the consummate fulfillment of love. The desired crown, as Endymion metaphorically calls the pinnacle of happiness, consists of "love and friendship, and sits high/ Upon the forehead of humanity" (I, 801–2). From its basic structure, representing friendship, a "steady splendour" emanates; and from its apex hangs "an orbed drop/ Of light," symbolizing love. The latter, when first perceived, evokes only "a novel sense" of perplexing delight; but ultimately our souls mingle indistinguishably with its radiance so that, like the young pelican feeding on its own parent, we are nourished by that ardor which originally generated us.

So fervently does Endymion believe in this miraculous sustenance that he regards all other aspirations well sacrificed in its behalf. He hopes that, just as the nightingale's song inspires even those for whom it is not intended, this passionate intensity of man and woman may bring concomitant benefits to all mankind. Though unable to prove his hypothesis, he assumes that human love is an expression of the life-force animating the entire universe and that it must of necessity manifest itself on earth in a way suitable to mortals. If a mere earthly love can immortalize man

and eradicate ambition, how much more does an immortal attachment de-
grade a "poor endeavour after fame"! So confident is Endymion of the
practical advantages accruing from his visionary experience that he cannot
accept it as only a dream.

The second book, which explores mythic art, presents a further symbolizing of love's triumph over mortality in the story of Venus and
Adonis. Of special significance to the poetical process is the Keatsian addition to the myth: while the beautiful youth is in his somnolent hiberna-
tion, the goddess of love and beauty acts very much like the creative
imagination by filling his sleep with visions (II, 486). Venus also serves
to encourage Endymion in his quest by promising success if he perseveres.
Certainly a temporary fulfillment occurs when the shepherd-king dreams
of making love to his visionary lady. At this point Keats, by trying to
convey the effect of rapture without describing the sex act, unfortunately
produced some of his most cloying poetry. Yet he also succeeded in con-
veying the repugnance that overindulgence in passion evokes against its
own surfeit. It is interesting that Lockhart, in his infamous attack on
Endymion in *Blackwood's* for August 1818, quoted lines from Keats's
1817 volume that he thought "prurient and vulgar" (III, 521) but regis-
tered no objection to the descriptions of love in the poem he was actually
reviewing. What critics have condemned as slipshod artistry in this section
and what probably led Byron to term Keats's erotic poetry the "mental
masturbation" of frustrated virility [14] is, however, not the ideal love for
which Endymion strives but only his initiation into its physical satisfaction. If this consummation were the goal itself, the quest would be ended.
As yet he is unprepared for the apotheosis of love, but his goddess (who
at this point is a fusion of the dream-lady and Cynthia, though he does
not know it) realizes this and promises him only what he can now understand as an "immortality of passion." [15] His later sympathy with the amatory frustrations of the river-god Alpheus and the nymph Arethusa
indicates, however, that he has been a worthy recipient of sexual com-

13. Letter of 21, 27 (?) December 1817 to George and Tom Keats (I, 192).
14. See Marchand, *Byron*, II, 873, 886 for the unexpurgated texts of Byron's
epistolary comments on Keats's early poetry. According to Byron, Keats was
"always f——gg——g his *Imagination*."
15. Benjamin Bailey's assertion that *Endymion* was indefensibly blotched
by Keats's acceptance of "*Sensual Love*" as "the principle of *things*" (Rollins,
Keats Circle, I, 35) may reveal as much about the poet's desire to supply a
needed corrective for Platonic love as it shows about his moralistic friend.

munion and can progress to his next step — self-effacing dedication to humanity.

The undersea adventures of the third book provide Endymion an opportunity to expand his consciousness through altruistic service, so that he may be redeemed from the pitfall of self-gratification in love and may taste "a pure wine/ Of happiness" (III, 801–2). Furthermore, the piteous story of Glaucus, whom he liberates from a thousand years of bondage, provides an oblique commentary on the main narrative. Whereas in the inherited Ovidian myth Glaucus had resisted Circe's temptations, Keats shrewdly altered the tale in order to show how degrading sexuality could ultimately become when indulged for its own sake. In what is evidently meant to be an object lesson for Endymion, who had recently surrendered to physical pleasure, Glaucus warns of the catastrophe that occurs when the objects of love and of sexual desire do not coincide. For he eventually discovered that Circe's sensuality had converted her previous lovers into beasts, changing a "specious heaven" into a "real hell" by enslaving her victims to their own physical desires.

Enlarged by humanitarian sympathy, Endymion is ready for the Indian maid, whom Keats artfully introduced to draw together the various developmental stages of the quester's experiences. Through the intense suffering from which she has learned the importance of love, the poet justifies sorrow as a means of stimulating imagination. Just as eighteenth-century theorists on the sublime deemed pain conducive to aesthetic pleasure, Keats apparently thought sorrow capable of heightening sensibility to produce a kind of elation among lovers and poets. Endymion's devotion to the mortal woman does not, however, obliterate or even diminish his heavenly attachments. Rather, he has "a triple soul" (IV, 95), for his affections are divided among the dream-goddess, the Indian maid, and Cynthia. Paradoxically, love of the real and love of the ideal by no means contradict one another since even the visionary goal must be firmly anchored in sensuous reality. But Endymion is not yet able to apprehend the real and the ideal simultaneously; nor does he understand the unity of his three loves. Hence the disturbing series of events in which one beloved vanishes as another reappears until he is left completely desolate. At this point he suffers the dilemma of the poetic wanderer in "Alastor," who allows visionary aspiration to sever him from humanity only to discover that in so doing he has lost reality as well.

Not until Endymion has experienced a fallow condition in the den of quietude is he sufficiently revitalized to solve the predicament. Conceding that no mortal ought to aspire beyond his natural sphere, he is then able to make a painful adjustment to mundane existence. Accepting even the loss of his mortal beloved, he vows to dedicate himself to the contemplative life, whereby he may still enhance the welfare of humanity. It is this self-renunciation — the loss of "self-passion or identity" (IV, 477) — that qualifies him for the ultimate union and makes possible the miraculous transformation of his dark lady into the epitome of heavenly light and earthly love. She can at last bring together her partial manifestations into one complete whole representing sensual love, compassion, and beauty since the "spiritualiz'd" Endymion has become a unified entity through coalescence of his mortal and spiritual desires. Having thus proved himself, the lover-poet transcends mortality and can be united permanently with the object of his quest.

Keats more artistically bridged the gap between illusion and reality in "The Eve of St. Agnes," owing largely to a simple narrative and a fairy tale atmosphere. Its setting in the Middle Ages, when acceptance of otherworldliness united religion with superstition and when the terminology of worship permeated the language of love, was especially useful in providing a matrix for interweaving the natural and the supernatural. Implicit faith — especially that which regarded the sensory and the supersensory as necessary complements — became in this work the counterpart of creative imagination. Just as in *Märchen* generally a childlike credence made all things possible for believers, so in "The Eve of St. Agnes" it was unquestioning trust in human affection that made congruous the planes of spirituality and earthly existence. Porphyro's acknowledgment after sexual consummation that his quest is ended and the pilgrim shrine reached weakens any interpretation of the poem as a purely spiritual ascendance. Rather, his comments reiterate the poet's conviction that body and soul must be amalgamated. To Keats, a dream without subsequent awaking was idle self-delusion; hence abstract spirituality, as represented by the Beadsman, seemed coldly meaningless until translated into practical action. Indeed the poem suggests that the physical realm makes the metaphysical worthy of contemplation just as reality lends substance to dreams.

Within reasonable limits the two lovers represent these complementary worlds, which successfully meet and reinforce one another as Madeline and Porphyro achieve the highest intensity of their passion. Madeline, though obviously of flesh and blood, is a maiden "free from mortal taint." Typifying the spiritual, she anticipates "visions of delight,/ And soft adorings" from her future husband after compliance with prescribed rituals on St. Agnes' Eve. So preoccupied is she with her awaited pleasure that, like the old Beadsman, she loses contact with physical environment; in that sense she is indeed "Hoodwink'd with faery fancy." Porphyro, on the other hand, has no discernible concept of vision as fulfillment, though Keats has granted him sufficient ethereal touches (most of them admittedly verbal echoes of the medieval cult of love) to show him capable of spiritual regeneration. His fervent hopes, which he himself has not fully analyzed, are based largely upon sensory expectations, and the numerous appeals to the five senses emphasize the voluptuous possibilities of the situation.

Angela, the earth-bound antithesis of the Beadsman, facetiously suggests that Porphyro must have employed witchcraft to enter the castle of his enemies and that Madeline herself is tonight playing the conjuror — "good angels her deceive!" Angela's use of "deceive" in this instance shows what little faith she has in spiritual gratification, though she does respect practical morality where her lady's chastity is concerned. She inevitably regards as wicked the young lover's "stratagem," whereby he may become the substance of Madeline's empty dream. Yet when he promises not to harm Madeline and threatens otherwise to challenge all his foes in the hall, the old woman agrees to conceal him in a closet so that he may not only see his sweetheart but

> . . . win perhaps that night a peerless bride,
> While legion'd faeries pac'd the coverlet,
> And pale enchantment held her sleepy-eyed. (xix:5–7)

Madeline is so enraptured with her dream-vision that its spell is not completely broken even when Porphyro bids her partake of a sumptuous feast. In the indefinite limbo where she still dreams yet half-perceives the outer world, she both recognizes him as "the vision of her sleep" and apprehends him in real life. But the contrast is so painful, "the blisses of her dream" having been "so pure and deep," that she can only weep and speak confusedly. Recovering more of her conscious wits, she explains that in her fantasy his voice pledged "every sweetest vow" while his eyes appeared "spiritual and clear." The superiority of the vision (in her present judgment at least) is heightened by his deathlike appearance as she beholds him kneeling at her bedside. However, his amorous responses in the subsequent consummation of their love prove that he is not only alive but very much awake. As he is absorbed into her dream, illusion and reality, as well as the metaphysical and physical, become absolutely indistinguishable for Madeline.

When she indeed awakes to reality, he allays her fears of abandonment, and together they flee from a hostile environment into the "elfin-storm from faery land," which he implies has been sent providentially to effect their escape. Whether or not they safely reach the home he promises, the lovers have achieved through the medium of the heart their Keatsian identity in this "vale of Soul-making,"[16] and they have done so not by denying life but rather by responding boldly to its pleasures and sorrows. By contrast, neither the Beadsman nor Angela, each of whom dies that night without satisfactory fulfillment, has apparently ever succeeded in uniting the spiritual and physical planes of mortal existence. The poem therefore remains a triumphant hymn honoring gratified desire, a canonization of human love. The question of how long the visionary experience might last remained for future exploration.

The failure to perpetuate vision beyond a fleeting period of ecstasy became the subject of "La Belle Dame sans Merci." From medieval ballads and romances Keats inherited not only the artistic dilemma of a knight's attachment to some bewitching fairy but also the technique of presenting its psychological impact before its cause. Consequently the poem is strikingly introduced by a questioner who seeks to know why the knight-at-arms has lost his former powers and even his determination to survive the approaching onslaught of winter. The reason for utter debilitation, he explains, was an unforgettable love affair into which he entered thoughtlessly for its momentary rapture rather than through any rational consideration of consequences. Though the exquisitely beautiful lady he met in the meads exchanged with him the customary tokens of human devotion, she was obviously "a faery's child" singing a "faery's song"; and his recollections of her demeanor are now tinged with justifiable doubts concerning her sincerity. To be sure, she looked at him "as she did love,/ And made sweet moan." Certainly she fed him woodland delicacies (appropriate to her though apparently not to him) and led him "to her elfin grot," where they shared further bliss. Not until he dreamed

16. *Letters*, II, 102.

of other mortals whom she had enthralled did he realize her true nature and, by implication, his own fate. With the conclusion of that futile warning his amatory vision was also shattered, and he awoke to find himself desolate "On the cold hill's side."

Unfortunately this abrupt failure after an equally sudden elevation to the zenith of passion does not lead through suffering to superior wisdom but rather to destruction. Whatever the supernatural enchantress symbolizes, her influence blights men who might otherwise fulfill their worldly promise. Only in retrospect, however, do her self-deceived victims understand that devotion to this beguiler yields only transient delight at the cost of permanent enslavement. Never asking that she abide in their world, they foolishly try to adapt themselves to her diet, language, and habitat without realizing that she is unconciliatory. But their "starved lips" clearly indicate that her nourishment will not sustain human beings; and those who briefly reach their illusory aspiration discover that the union is too unnatural to endure. When inevitable disintegration follows, the alteration of personality is so radical that mortals are thereafter rendered unfit for earth.

Not only do the characters of Keats's imagination experience visions of love; the poet himself must have done so, for one such event he even transmuted into art. Having been mightily impressed with Dante's account of Paolo and Francesca in the second circle of hell, he actually dreamed of being in that infernal region where adulterers are punished. As he recorded on 16 April 1819 in one of his long journal letters to the George Keatses, "I floated about the whirling atmosphere as it is described with a beautiful figure to whose lips mine were joined" (II, 91). So pleasurable did he find the extraordinary "punishment" that he wished to repeat it every night, and he subsequently composed the sonnet "On a Dream" (therein transcribed) immortalizing the adventure that permitted him to escape the "dragon world" and indulge his amatory fancy amidst passion's "melancholy storm." The inhospitable environment accompanying that restless kiss (in "the whirlwind and the flaw/ Of Rain and hailstones") may well have led him to conceive the more idyllic circumstances under which lovers caress in another poem transcribed for the first time in the same journal letter — the "Ode to Psyche." Concerning the latter instance Keats was uncertain whether he actually dreamed the vision or saw it "with awaken'd eyes." Yet he felt quite sure that in some form of consciousness he spied a couple reposing on the grass of an exquisite sylvan bower. Though Cupid was immediately recognizable, the god's companion seemed unknown to the poet until recollection of the myth compelled her identity — "latest born and loveliest vision far/ Of all Olympus' faded hierarchy" — Psyche, the human soul embraced by love.

Since she entered Graeco-Roman mythology too late for those "happy pieties" associated with the worship of personified natural forces, Keats wishes to make amends for the neglect of Psyche in classical times. Hence he will sing to her devotional praise and imaginatively create a temple within the recesses of his own mind. In addition to the ritualistic tribute that his thoughts can bestow, there will be "A bright torch, and a casement ope at night,/ To let the warm Love in" (ll. 64–67). The open window of the shrine is appropriate not only as a reminiscence of Cupid's secret, nocturnal visits but also as indication that the human soul must be constantly receptive to further stimulus from love if it is to attain complete realization. Quite significantly, in the letter which first contained this "Ode" Keats speculates on the need for the heart's experiential development before man's immaterial part can achieve an individual identity of its own (II, 102–4). Indeed Psyche (as the soul), by remaining utterly devoted to Eros despite long suffering, has been successfully tested and therefore awarded immortality. Keats, psychologizing the myth into an epitome of viable theology, apparently regarded the favorable result of this trial as the prototype for salvation — indeed a better "system of Spirit-creation" than that of orthodox Christianity. The poet's tribute to this delightful goddess also implies a comparison between love and imagination — both creative, conducive to an expansion of human insight, and resulting in an existence that transcends the flux of ordinary process. Furthermore, there is an interaction between these analogous powers, for it was Keats's love-vision that impelled his imagination to create an appropriate fane to Psyche. By both assimilating and projecting his experience, he has performed as a poet an act similar to the fulfillment of lovers.

But the most impressive treatment of the amatory dream and its subsequent dissolution is found in "Lamia," where passion culminates not in life but in death. The conflict that it dramatizes — arising from a juxtaposition of intuitive emotion and analytical thought — had long fascinated, even worried, Keats, who fluctuated between desire for philosophic profundity and the more comfortable inspiration of natural phenomena. His famous letter to Bailey which expresses preference "for a Life of Sensations rather than of Thoughts" attributes the digressive tendency of his own writing to lack of "a complex Mind — one that is imaginative and at the same time careful of its fruits — who would exist partly on sensation partly on thought — to whom it is necessary that years should bring the philosophic Mind" (I, 185–86). Aware that simple enjoyment of nature was automatically congenial to his temperament, he nevertheless considered "staid Philosophy," of which he wrote in "God of the Meridian" on 31 January 1818, essential for the sort of poetry to which he aspired. And though the feathered speaker of his poem "What the Thrush Said" might advise against fretting after knowledge as an avian corollary to productive indolence, Keats thought a poet's song should convey more substance than a spontaneous response to vernal warmth. Yet by 25 March 1818 he was still expressing diffidence toward his philosophic capacities when he addressed a verse epistle to J. H. Reynolds:

> . . . to philosophize
> I dare not yet! — Oh never will the prize,
> High reason, and the lore of good and ill
> Be my award. Things cannot to the will
> Be settled, but they tease us out of thought.
> . . . .
> It is a flaw
> In happiness to see beyond our bourn —
> It forces us in Summer skies to mourn:
> It spoils the singing of the Nightingale. (ll. 73–77, 82–85)

Apparently, however, he found the sensuous to be rather inadequate by itself, for on 24 April 1818 he wrote Taylor: "I have been hovering for some time between an exquisite sense of the luxurious and a love for Philosophy — were I calculated for the former I should be glad — but as I am not I shall turn my soul to the latter" (I, 271). Though awareness of human suffering darkened his "Chamber of Maiden-Thought," it also prompted him to explore those gloomy passageways leading beyond that apartment, to contribute his illuminating thought to their amelioration.[17] And his letter to Sarah Jeffrey on 9 June 1819, composed shortly before he started "Lamia," acknowledges satisfaction at having become through diligent effort "more of a Philosopher" and "less of a versifying Pet-lamb" (II, 116).

Combined with this tenuous achievement of purpose was the terrible

188

apprehension lest acquired wisdom drive out innate talent, lest he destroy his native bent without ever attaining the grandeur of poets like Milton and Wordsworth, those wise physicians to the human race. Quite naturally the insecurities of his own life caused him to associate obsessive fears with a poet's existence, and much of what he wrote — from the early description of the charioteer in "Sleep and Poetry" who "Looks out upon the winds with glorious fear" to his familiar sonnet beginning "When I have fears that I may cease to be" — might be analyzed as an attempt to overcome anxiety. In the sonnet addressed to Fanny Brawne late in January 1818, some of his misgivings arise from the assumption that emotion and reflective thought are essentially incompatible. His reference to "the faery power/ Of unreflecting love" implies that only under suprarational or supernatural conditions can love be protected against deliberate thought. Since Keatsian love, far from being a theoretical or purely spiritual phenomenon, is inextricably bound up with sensuous pleasure, Fanny Brawne even in her absence exerted what the poet termed a "luxurious power over [his] senses."[18] It should not be surprising then that analytical thought, toward which poetry and love inevitably progress in the course of their development, was mistrusted for its ultimate consequences.

To demonstrate by contrast the dire shortcomings of visionary experience for mortal lovers and poets, Keats invented as an introduction to "Lamia" the anecdote involving "ever-smitten Hermes" and a nymph. That materialization of the sylvan beauty, who has hitherto been nothing more than a mental image in Hermes' mind, is not just a passing illusion such as man often experiences in vision becomes absolutely clear from the passage "Real are the dreams of Gods, and smoothly pass/ Their pleasures in a long immortal dream" (I, 127–28). Though the Olympian deity and his beloved act like typical Keatsian lovers full of "adoring tears," "blandishment," and "fearful sobs," presumably there is no anguish because the dream, in which everything desirable is also possible, cannot dissolve. While they seem almost human in their characteristic mixture of ecstatic joy and exquisite pain, their amatory experience is essentially the unbroken delight of a fairy tale without the subsequent disillusionment that Keats ordinarily indicated by human pallor. As they proceed to the privacy of the woods, they retain their blush of ardor instead of growing wan as mortal lovers do.

17. See letter of 3 May 1818 to Reynolds (I, 281).
18. Letter of 8 July 1819 (II, 126).

Once Lamia is transformed from serpent into woman, a virgin yet "deep learned" in the ways of love, she too can successfully achieve what mortals merely vex themselves by attempting — to "unperplex bliss from its neighbour pain." [19] This she accomplishes with the Corinthian Lycius, who is completely entranced with her charms. So intoxicated is he by amorous rapture that his rational powers are allayed; and during his life amid the sensuous delights of Lamia's illusory palace, he leads a dream-like existence without ever wondering how it has been achieved. Isolated from the stimuli of humanity and external reality, he dwells in the rarefied atmosphere of pure imagination. So long as he cannot think, this condition of "unperplex'd delight and pleasure" will not deteriorate. Thus far the introductory tale of Hermes and the nymph seems merely to be repeated in a coarser tone, but the conditions of mortality obviate the permanence attainable through mythic art. For man, even in optimum luxury, passion divorced from reality proves to be insufficient. Neither love nor imagination, though capable of attaining the highest intensity, can be maintained indefinitely at such a pitch. Though Lycius' enthrallment causes him initially to avoid his former mentor, Apollonius, through fear that "cold philosophy" and "consequitive reasoning" will shatter his vision, he refers to the old man not only as "The ghost of folly haunting [his] sweet dreams" but also as his "trusty guide and good instructor" — revealing ambivalence toward both Apollonius and his present existence.

Actually he feels a twinge of conscience for being so content within his *Venusberg*, and the sound of trumpets from the outer, active world causes him to remember the environment he had "almost forsworn." His determination to translate the amatory dream into permanence by openly acknowledging his union with the beautiful enchantress is of course the fatal mistake. Even the reasoning from which it arises is specious, for his pride in her is so great that he wants to proclaim ownership — a desire comparable to the poet's lust for public acclaim, which Milton called "That last infirmity of noble mind." (Ambition, with Love and Poesy, is one of three allegorical figures who threaten Keats's idleness in the "Ode on Indolence" and his letter describing that condition.) [20] Lamia's accession to the public wedding is qualified by one stipulation, that Apollonius be excluded from the celebration. She feels compelled to shun him, for without analyzing she intuitively perceives thought to be inimical to her enchantment. Indeed the old philosopher, who intrudes unbidden at the feast, would make "Lamia melt into a shade":

> Philosophy will clip an Angel's wings,
> Conquer all mysteries by rule and line,
> Empty the haunted air, and gnomed mine —
> Unweave a rainbow. (II, 234–37)

The appeals to sensuous imagination that amaze the unquestioning guests do not impress one of his coldly rational nature, and amid the voluptuous splendors wrought by Lamia's magic he laughs as a mathematician might upon suddenly discovering the solution to a baffling problem.

The latent fears of the ambitious lover-poet are horrifyingly realized in the final scene, as Apollonius transfixes the bride with his eye, causing her loveliness to disintegrate. Despite Lycius' rebuke, the sophist self-righteously defends his action on the grounds that he cannot allow his pupil to become "a serpent's prey." But Lamia's disappearance precipitates Lycius' death. By dissecting the dream of love, the philosopher has also murdered the lover, much as Keats feared that his own powers would be destroyed. The creation of "Lamia" was for its author then not a dream of wish fulfillment but an anxiety reaction. His genuine ambivalence toward the symbolic characters achieves an objectivity or poetic "disinterestedness" eliminating any fixed point of view, and this shifting attitude is reflected throughout the story by the mixture of admiration and derision. Lamia, Lycius, and Apollonius each contain antithetic qualities that unite benefit and detriment paradoxically; but Apollonius, with his "irritable reaching after fact and reason," destroys the uneasy equipoise in which they are temporarily suspended. While Lycius has been able to adapt himself in turn to both the sensuous imagination and philosophy, he has not successfully reconciled the two. By yielding to ambition and conscience, he enables Apollonius, who is imbued with a fanatic's zeal for doing "the right thing," to annihilate all.

19. According to Moneta in "The Fall of Hyperion," the useless dreamer needlessly "venoms all his days" by mixing pain with joy (I, 172–76).
20. See *Letters*, II, 78–79.

CHAPTER VIII

Amatory Nymphs and Spectres

T HOUGH NYMPHOLEPSY has generally been diagnosed as a Romantic malady, the tendency had excellent precedent in one of the earliest classical writers, the practical-minded Hesiod, whose attachment to a supernatural ideal is said to have estranged him from his Boeotian countrymen. By his own account in the *Theogony*, he was shepherding lambs beneath Mount Helicon when in an ecstatic vision the Muses appeared and, breathing a divine voice into his rhapsodic utterance, taught him to sing. Unquestionably in his mind these charming daughters of Mnemosyne were as appealing as nymphs, but his encounter with them, far from unsettling him (as the sight of tantalizing nymphs was supposed to derange a mortal), caused Hesiod to feel extraordinarily blessed. In this crucial respect his desire for the unattainable, perhaps also reflected in the *Eoeae* by tales of women mating with gods, differed sharply from that of nineteenth-century Romantics. For the latter, an evanescent dream of love tended to debilitate its recipient, made him additionally miserable once he discovered its hopelessness, and rendered him unfit to cope with life. Contributing to the problem was an implied assumption that the less likely goals were of being achieved the more desirable they became; in that way the real would not be compared unfavorably with the ideal, and celestial forms could never be tarnished by contact with earth. This concept is given its most succinct expression in lines by Shelley:

> The desire of the moth for the star,
>> Of the night for the morrow,
> The devotion to something afar
>> From the sphere of our sorrow. (ll. 13–16) [1]

However, there were also contemporaries of Shelley and Keats who treated the visionary experience in a somewhat less ethereal manner, notably Byron. The historical cycles of achievement and destruction, which in Canto IV of *Childe Harold's Pilgrimage* he associated not only with civilization but also with individual men, are saved from total dissolution by the "Beings of the Mind," who

>> create
> And multiply in us a brighter ray
> And more beloved existence: that which Fate
> Prohibits to dull life in this our state
> Of mortal bondage, by these Spirits supplied,
> First exiles, then replaces what we hate;
> Watering the heart whose early flowers have died,
And with a fresher growth replenishing the void. (*CHP*, IV, 5:2–9)

Yet Byron assumes an essentially distrustful attitude toward unbridled imagination, for what comes to the mind "like Truth" often disappears "like dreams" (IV, 7:2). In his view, "waking Reason" proves such forms unreliable because their reality is insubstantial.

Characteristically he approaches the question of visionary love with acerbic skepticism when compelled to reflect upon the phenomenon by Harold's visit to a sacred spring along the Appian Way. According to Roman history it was at this hallowed spot that the legendary King Numa often met his beloved Egeria, goddess of fountains and childbirth. Since his just and peaceful reign was supposedly indebted to her wise counsels, the attachment, at least for the people of Rome, proved highly useful. Byron, however, employs the story for a different purpose; bringing into sharp focus many recurrent themes developed throughout the canto, he reinterprets the legend of Romulus' successor as a myth concerning the artist and his mental creation. Perhaps, the poet intimates, Egeria may have been the product of frenzied nympholepsy in the heart of one who

---

1. "To ——— (One word is too often profaned)," *Poetical Works*, p. 645.

"found no mortal resting-place so fair" as her "ideal breast" (IV, 115:1–5). Or possibly she was only a mortal woman (one prosaic Roman historian had indeed called her Numa's wife) so intensely adored by her lover that he metaphorically worshipped her as a goddess. Whatever her actual status, Byron concludes that she was "a beautiful Thought, and softly bodied forth"; since, as he repeatedly maintains, life exists in the act of creation rather than in the object created, Egeria becomes an excellent symbol of perfect love, mental rebirth, and immortality. As such, she has not been subject to the same destructiveness that besets mutable existence through the onslaughts of time, and her grotto prompts speculations on the relationship between nature and art. Especially significant is her association with fountains, for the spring, which shows no ravagement by temporal process, continues to represent her perpetual youth and constant regeneration. Her ruined statue, on the contrary, has decayed like its sculptor; yet, in what seems to be an incessant conflict between art and nature, the former has not been totally vanquished because the idea of the goddess is constantly reborn in the human mind just as life is reproduced in the physical world.

Even so, "holy Love — the earliest Oracle," by partaking of both mental and physical realities, must submit to the laws governing both; and Harold questions rather dubiously whether Egeria, by blending "a celestial with a human heart," could indeed lend "immortal transports" to human love, "which dies as it [is] born" (IV, 119). Could she eliminate "The dull satiety which all destroys —/ And root from out the soul the deadly weed which cloys?" Since the poet's own disheartening experience has convinced him that human affections are ordinarily wasted or misdirected, he conceives of man's longing for "some celestial fruit forbidden to our wants" as a rank growth of sensuality — "weeds of dark luxuriance," tempting but venomous. Perfect love, he asserts, is then "no habitant of earth" but, like an unseen divinity, merely the figment of human imagination; it is the mental product of the same inadequacies and frustrations that gave rise to anthropomorphic gods. Addressing the ideal, he declares: "The mind hath made thee, as it peopled Heaven,/ Even with its own desiring phantasy" (IV, 121:6–7). But since the creation does not exist outside the mind that worships such abstractions, the devotee has only further disillusionment awaiting him.

This false imagination Byron diagnoses as the mark of a diseased mind, though admittedly its art is more attractive than nature ever produced. It begins in childhood, a time of pleasant illusion, when such fevers instill the "charms and virtues" that we chase futilely throughout life. The cure for this nympholeptic disorder involves shattering the fatal spell, awakening from the dream, and acknowledging that the idols exist nowhere on earth. But so bitter is the remedy that men generally prefer to remain deluded, to be drawn onward by the phantom goal, though very few ever "find what they love or could have loved." The poet concludes his estimate of man's dismal fate with two alarming images. Personified Circumstance is presented as the real controller of love, for in Byron's reversal of the true creator, it converts man's final hopes into dust. The enormous upas tree is an expansion of the poison plant motif representing the human condition; rooted in earth, it extends into the skies, whence it rains plagues that disturb the soul.

In spite of this gloomy prospect Byron is unwilling to consign man to utter defeat. Whatever the miseries engendered by imagination, the poet finds relief from complete cynicism in the divine faculty of thought, which, though frequently ignored, has the power to liberate man from his willful blindness. Lovers and artists especially — those most sensitive to the ravages of earthly change — must pursue the creative ideal because it alone represents the immutable truth which they seek. Though the quest prove futile and the experience painful, thinking man, in his Promethean recognition of knowledge gained through suffering, is obliged to strive for the mind's loftiest and most artistic aspirations, since in no other way can he transcend inherent limitations.

That visionary abstractions did not meet with unanimous endorsement among contemporaries is also evident from Thomas Love Peacock's *Nightmare Abbey* (1818), which burlesques some of the extravagances of Romanticism through the jaundiced eyes of a classicist. At the time of its composition many of the nympholeptic works had not yet appeared; but its satirical author, as an old friend of Shelley, had many biographical details upon which to draw, so that he actually advertised the new vogue in advance of its greatest popularity. Scythrop Glowry (Peacock's name for Shelley in the novel) is the melancholy victim of almost constant dedication to reform and theoretical love. When his cousin Marionetta deliberately baits her lures for him, he capitulates without the slightest reflection because "romantic dreams" have filled his consciousness with "many *pure anticipated cognitions* of combinations of beauty and intelligence."[2] Though his beloved does not exactly coincide with his vision, he becomes "distractedly in love" just as she turns cold. For in her own callow manner she is also nympholeptic, finding him attractive only so long as he is beyond her grasp yet uninteresting when once secured. Scythrop's response to such vacillation is a retreat into a world of chimerical reverie, where he imagines the attainment of his ideal through illusion and thereby precludes success in real life. When the incurable visionary meets a young lady of more intellectual and revolutionary inclinations than his cousin, the new amatory fancy gradually impinges upon the old, taking possession of his heart. To justify the seeming inconstancy, Scythrop assures himself that his soul has a greater capacity for love than Marionetta is capable of filling. Consequently he finds himself enamored of two ladies, unable to choose between them or to part with either.

To expose further the psychological illness of nympholepsy, Peacock travestied the Egeria stanzas from *Childe Harold's Pilgrimage.* Though Byron's marital rupture, as well as his celebration of it in verse, comes under Peacock's scrutiny, the lugubrious Mr. Cypress (a caricature of his lordship) is most notable for pontificating on mankind's futile hopes. When he paraphrases Childe Harold's denial that merit, love, or beauty can exist outside of mental hallucination, Mr. Hilary (the Peacockian voice of rationalism) responds: "Ideal beauty is not the mind's creation: it is real beauty, refined and purified in the mind's alembic, from the alloy which always more or less accompanies it in our mixed and imperfect nature. . . . To rail against humanity for not being abstract perfection, and against human love for not realising all the splendid visions of the poets of chivalry, is to rail at the summer for not being all sunshine, and at the rose for not being always in bloom."[3] And after Cypress, unconvinced, renews his harangue, Hilary accuses him of arguing like a Rosicrucian, "who will love nothing but a sylph, who does not believe in the existence of a sylph, and who yet quarrels with the whole universe for not containing a sylph."[4] As Peacock interpreted this variety of nightmarish love, nympholepts discard the substance in order to chase its shadow. Such unsympathetic criticism may indeed disclose the absurdity of Romantic excesses, but it also reveals how ill attuned its author was to the visionary rhapsodies of his own age.

More indicative of prevailing taste is the fact that William Hazlitt, who often served as spokesman for his intellectual milieu, identified love with hallucination when analyzing his own grievous disappointment. His self-punitive but presumably cathartic exposé, *Liber Amoris: or, the New Pygmalion* (1823), describes how in 1820, while estranged from his first wife, he became hopelessly enamored of his landlord's daughter, Sarah Walker. Part of his desire for her companionship no doubt stemmed from desperate loneliness, in which state he could easily imagine her as the embodiment of ideal love. Also partly responsible must have been his lifelong devotion to Rousseau's *Nouvelle Héloïse* and *Confessions*, as proclaimed by both style and subtitle of the amatory memoir, for like his mentor he fell in love with a projection of his own mind. The opening section of *Liber Amoris*, a dialogue entitled "The Picture," emphasized the disparity between a rather plain girl and a stunning portrait that the artist-lover fancied to be a close resemblance of her. From studying masterpieces of extraordinarily beautiful women he had formed his own concept of perfect beauty but had not believed the ideal to be realizable on earth until he met Sarah. In an obvious reflection of nympholepsy, he confessed to the young temptress: "My faculties leave me: . . . thy sweet image has taken possession of me, haunts me, and will drive me to distraction."[5]

The remainder of this self-flagellating confession records the author's attempt to liberate himself either by winning her or flushing her image from his consciousness. Once the first method was recognized as futile, his depiction of himself as a fumbling middle-aged lover humiliated at the feet of a vain little tart undoubtedly aided the eradication. As he awoke to the painful truth, he discovered that she was an accomplished tease, who encouraged attentions only up to a point. Since she did grant him innocuous liberties, he refused to believe that, contrary to her unequivocal admission, she could never love him. But her illusory openness merely engulfed him deeper. At times she seemed an angel, a goddess, even "a vision of love and joy, as if she had dropped from the Heavens to bless" him (IX, 123). But in other moments she tormented him as a witch or a lamia might have done, so that the whole affair became a nightmare. When he finally discovered that she had been equally generous with her charms to another lodger, his erroneous portrait of her completely disintegrated. Having

2. *Nightmare Abbey, The Works of Thomas Love Peacock,* ed. H. F. B. Brett-Smith and C. E. Jones (London and New York, 1924–34), III, 21.

3. Pages 107–8.

4. Page 108.

5. *Complete Works,* IX, 99. Subsequent references to this edition appear in the text.

originally likened her to a tender flower blossoming in his heart, he decided that she was only a weed; and with that analogy he consoled himself, assuming that the rank growth would disappear in the ocean of time.

One of his final literary efforts to banish Sarah Walker from his mind is embedded in the essay "On Dreams" (1823). According to his associationist interpretation, there exists in sleep a general stupor once our ordinary faculties of thought and sense perception have been allayed; in this state of partial consciousness the brain, deprived of logical direction, permits ideas to emerge without rational continuity or sequential links. "The bundles of thought," he asserted, "are, as it were, untied, loosened from a common centre, and drift along the stream of fancy" (XII, 20). Imagination is thereby granted the means of superseding reason — as it does in the mind of the creative poet, the madman, or even the lover. The oracular quality of dreams lies in their ability to reveal what we would banish from our waking thoughts. All secret hopes, fears, and "almost unconscious sentiments" arise like revenants from the grave when we can no longer exorcise them. Under such circumstances repressed truth is often divulged, for we cannot be hypocritical when the "curb is taken off from our passions" (XII, 23).

This observation led Hazlitt to what must have been a comforting conclusion. According to its rationale he had never been truly in love with a real woman since he rarely dreamt of one to whom he had been attached. Despite the persistence of Sarah Walker's image in his conscious thoughts, she had appeared only once or twice in his dreams and then indistinctly. What he had erroneously attributed to love therefore must be ascribed to humbled pride or a desire for abstract good because "involuntary passion" would certainly have predominated "over the fancy in sleep" (XII, 23). Though he was by his own acknowledgment an excellent Pygmalion for having thought himself into love, he remarked upon being an impossible Endymion, since his occasional dreams, instead of further entangling him in unrealistic devotion, had actually liberated him from it. That his slumbering thoughts, however, were occupied by what he loved most intensely seems evident from descriptions in the essay of recent, vivid dreams concerning the Louvre, where he had reached the zenith of his painting career, and the unforgettable *Nouvelle Héloïse*.

Whereas Solomon in his Song of Songs had been content to eulogize a passion "strong as death" (8:6), the idealistic natures of many Romantic authors required a love that persisted not just during life but, as with Goethe's king of Thule, even beyond the shadows of the grave. Though Byron might praise mortality as Don Jose's liberator from a marital stalemate, it was much more common during the period to treat an unexpected demise as a threat to genuine affection. The apparently insurmountable barrier which Thanatos laid upon Eros might conceivably be overcome, however, through a devotion so uncompromising that physical impediments would be shattered by the most daring of spiritual aspirations; and writers especially sensitive to the plight of those whose happiness had been abrogated by involuntary separation often employed post-mortem reunions to effect a literary solution. Ever since Sophocles' *Antigone*, tragedians had found the motif of the bride who met not her expected lover but death a pathetically moving one. Composers of medieval ballads, many of whom were interested in passion transcending earthly existence, contributed to that tradition by enriching the circumstances with theological problems that beset their own times. For example, was the bereaved survivor justified in questioning divine providence, perhaps even to the extent of impugning God's justice? Or how could the deceased possibly free himself of alleged infidelity, particularly if his death was unknown, unless he returned as a revenant? How also could his soul rest quietly until he ascertained his beloved's faithfulness even during long absence? If love was truly immortal, what then could be wrong in trying to effect a marriage of souls in the hereafter? Yet since this solution required the death of the remaining lover, would voluntary renunciation of life be tantamount to suicide and therefore invite eternal damnation?

Many of these questions are at least implied in the most famous ballad of the spectre bridegroom — Bürger's "Lenore," which Walter Scott gave a distinguished rendering into English as "William and Helen" (1796).[6] According to this adaptation, Helen grieves that her beloved William is not among the returning Crusaders, who are unable to tell her whether he is slain or faithless. Rejecting the possibility that he is a "perjured lover" and despairing of any future joy, she yearns only for death. To her, "William's love was heaven on earth,/ Without it earth is hell." In fact, she arraigns the very judgment of heaven and, in so doing, unconsciously invites eternal damnation. Shortly before midnight William's ghost appears in her chamber and, without revealing precisely his spectral state,

6. *Works*, XLVI, 3–15.

promises to take her to their bridal bed. Through the moonlight they ride at incredible speed, as he invites all the unhallowed spirits to join them in a ghostly bridal procession — a synthesis of nuptial and funeral that Helen as yet fails to comprehend. Shortly before dawn they reach the haunted churchyard where his burial place lies open, and there his armor and flesh fall away, leaving only a skeleton emblematic of death itself to be embraced by Helen. Their love is consummated in the grave, as the pale spectres join in a macabre prothalamion.

From a young girl doomed for excessive devotion to her beloved, Scott, in his only original ballad involving a spectral liaison, turned to a woman punished for marital infidelity. The ghostly visitant in "The Eve of St. John" (1801) [7] is the adulteress's paramour, who, having been murdered by her husband, returns not to claim her in death but to fulfill a divine mission. Though his own future is uncertain, he offers admonition to the living:

> Who spilleth life shall forfeit life;
> So bid thy lord believe:
> That lawless love is guilt above,
> This awful sign receive.

In token of ominous hellfire he burns an indelible hand print upon an oaken beam in her chamber and another upon her wrist. Since the severe penances thereafter undertaken by the contrite couple indicate that they will at last atone for their sins, the spectre knight becomes not only a preacher of morality but also, in a manner especially typical of Scott, an instrument of salvation.

An entirely different treatment of the amatory revenant occurs in a ballad from M. G. Lewis's *The Monk* (1796) entitled "Alonzo the Brave and Fair Imogine." [8] Therein elements of ghoulish horror seem to have been created more for their own sake than for ethical betterment, partially because the author, though preoccupied with faithlessness in love, was not didactically inclined and also because the poem was incorporated into the Gothic romance chiefly to produce the appropriate atmosphere for a ghost's appearance. The terrifying conclusion of the poem is prefigured by Imogine's own rash hope to be claimed as a sepulchral bride should she ever prove unfaithful to her betrothed, Alonzo. Her punishment seems more poetic justice than moral expiation, for emphasis in this ballad is upon the vivid details of her fate. At her wedding to another, Alonzo's spectre appears as a skeleton in sable armor, with worms crawling in and out of the eye sockets, to disappear into the ground with the shrieking lady; and as if death alone were insufficient retribution, her ghost must reappear four times a year to re-enact with her spectral knight a ghastly wedding celebration.

Since many Romantic writers were susceptible to the Gothic spell in adolescence, it was inevitable that even those who did not choose it as a major ingredient of their mature work should sometimes dabble with spectral subjects, often as a means of effecting supralegal justice. Byron's youthful tale "Oscar of Alva" (1807), partially influenced by Schiller's *Geisterseher*, concerns a murdered bridegroom whose ghost appears at the nuptial feast of his former bride-to-be and his younger brother to expose the latter as his assassin. Also through German inspiration, Shelley, in his "Ghasta; or, the Avenging Demon" (1810), created a female wraith who haunts her false lover and finally claims him in death.[9] Coleridge, who in early days had been a qualified admirer of the Gothic, could in "Kubla Khan" (1798) evoke an image of consummate horror by depicting a "deep romantic chasm" as

> A savage place! as holy and enchanted
> As e'er beneath a waning moon was haunted
> By woman wailing for her demon-lover! (ll. 14–16)

And certainly the enchanting Geraldine in "Christabel" behaves like an amatory spectre of uncertain gender when she captivates both Christabel and Sir Leoline.

But themes of this sort, even when employed by the most accomplished writers, could not fascinate indefinitely. After the close of the eighteenth century, Gothic poets and novelists, stimulated either by German examples or the ghostly fare of Allan Ramsay's *Tea-Table Miscellany* (1724) and Thomas Percy's *Reliques of Ancient English Poetry* (1765), could do little more with the threadbare situations than add terrifying details. It was questionable whether they actually succeeded in frightening the covetous or potentially unfaithful back onto the path of rectitude. Though much later the morbidly inclined Thomas Lovell Beddoes wrote poetry on such

7. *Works*, XLVI, 59–68.
8. *The Monk*, ed. Louis F. Peck (New York, 1952), pp. 306–8.
9. In "Sister Rosa: A Ballad," from *St. Irvyne* (1811), a monk who has wronged a nun is finally united with her skeleton in the grave.

topics, his abnormal obsession with macabre moods and charnel worms, particularly in a work like "The Phantom-Wooer" (1851), was contrary to the spirit of Romantic Gothicism, since for him death became in itself man's desired objective rather than his emancipator from physical confines. As it grew more difficult for imaginative artists to handle supernatural themes seriously, only parody remained for the phantom lover. Indeed the phenomenon received its most inglorious exorcism from the anonymous author of the satirical American ballad "Clementine." However devastating the charms of the gold prospector's daughter may have been during life, her California admirer was willing to call a halt to their passion when she drowned, frankly declaring:

> In my dreams she still doth haunt me
> Clothed in garments soaked in brine.
> Though in life I used to hug her,
> Now she's dead, I draw the line.

Logic such as that no doubt signaled the pall of American realism descending upon Romantic vision.

It remained for the novelist-poet Emily Brontë to give the spectre motif its most solemn and, in many ways, most striking treatment. Indeed nowhere in literature is love transcending the grave dealt with more convincingly than in *Wuthering Heights* (1847). Despite its composition during the Victorian age (though admittedly in an area of Yorkshire somewhat behind the times), it epitomized much of what the Romantics believed about the visionary experience.[10] The complex and highly ambivalent relationship between Heathcliff and Catherine — which has an analogue in some of the author's finest Gondal poems expressing an impatient longing for assimilation into God — produces a grotesque, otherworldly passion on earth. Throughout most of the novel it eludes the comprehension of all the characters, including the lovers themselves, who suffer the agonies of psychological hell and are ultimately driven to the only suitable habitat for its resolution — the realm beyond death. Since the spiritual bond defies strictly rational analysis, the author was compelled to focus on the perceptible evidence of its mundane failure — an anguish driving the lovers relentlessly to distraction. Not until the conditions for mystical union are satisfied is the peace of ideal love achieved.

To understand this extraordinary devotion one must trace its development, particularly after Catherine Earnshaw becomes conscious of her strong affinity for Heathcliff, the dark intruder of mysterious, almost diabolical, origin, whom she has grown to love like her own soul. Despite acceptance of Edgar Linton's marriage proposal, she knows instinctively that such a union will be wrong, and this intuitive wisdom is corroborated by her dream of heaven. So miserable was she there that angels angrily flung her out and permitted her spirit to return to the wild heath. Her concept of the hereafter evidently envisions not a world separated from this one but rather an existence of the soul freed from the limitations of human life though unalienated from the physical universe.[11] Catherine realizes therefore that she has no more right to marry Edgar than to be in an orthodox heaven removed from what she has intensely loved on earth. Even so, she asserts with heartfelt resolution defying rational logic that, since her love for Heathcliff is actually a spiritual identity, the two of them can never be separated no matter what she does with her physical substance. Therefore her irrevocable attachment to him is as permanent as "the eternal rocks beneath"; it will survive despite all obstacles, while the pleasant feelings associated with Edgar will, like arboreal leaves of one season, pass away.

Yet three years later in the delirium of brain fever after the violent quarrel between her husband and her beloved, she confesses to the housekeeper Nelly Dean that giving up Heathcliff to become Mrs. Linton had made her an exile and that her only way home lies through Gimmerton Kirk. Like a ballad heroine who longs for death when earthly hopes are shattered, Cathy wills her own destruction. But she knows that she can never rest in the churchyard until Heathcliff is there with her. In what seems merely idle speculation, she wonders whether the man for whom she feels such passionate devotion will himself remain constant twenty years after her death. Or will he by then prefer to stay with his living children rather than allow his spirit to join hers? Certainly she is confident

10. No better evidence of Emily Brontë's affinity with her Romantic predecessors could be adduced than her poem "To Imagination" containing the lines: "So hopeless is the world without,/ The world within I doubly prize." See *The Complete Poems of Emily Jane Brontë*, ed. C. W. Hatfield (New York, 1961), pp. 205–6.

11. Cf. Emily Brontë's poem "Shall Earth no more inspire thee," in which a speaker whom Charlotte's note identifies as "the Genius of a solitary region" asserts of his votary's heart: "Yet none would ask a Heaven/ More like this Earth than thine." *Complete Poems*, pp. 163–64.

that her own soul, after casting off the shackles of mortality, will return to where it ever aspired to be on earth. In almost delirious weakness she laments the "shattered prison" of her physical existence, from which she longs "to escape into that glorious world, and to be always there: not seeing it dimly through tears, and yearning for it through the walls of an aching heart; but really with it, and in it."[12] Though she denies any tranquility for herself until they have achieved the spiritual union impossible during mortal life, Heathcliff accuses her of wishing to torment him after she is at peace. Prophetically, he vows that without her he will have no life whatever because his own soul will lie buried in her grave. Upon learning the following day of her death, he vehemently demonstrates the selfishness of embittered passion by a rash invocation:

> Catherine Earnshaw, may you not rest as long as I am living! You said I killed you — haunt me, then! The murdered *do* haunt their murderers. I believe — I know that ghosts *have* wandered on earth. Be with me always — take any form — drive me mad! only *do* not leave me in this abyss, where I cannot find you![13]

What might ordinarily be regarded as hyperbolic raving in a demented lover must, in view of subsequent events, be interpreted not metaphorically but literally. For after Catherine's demise Heathcliff incessantly tries to make contact with her. Yet so long as his straining against their physical separation manifests itself negatively as hatred, she capriciously tantalizes him with only a hint of her presence and a vague prospect of re-establishing the connection. When in his madness immediately following her death he first digs into the grave and is about to raise the lid of her casket, he hears repeated sighs and feels a warm breath despite the chill wind. Though no living creature is near, his consciousness of Catherine's spirit consoles him, and he returns to Wuthering Heights assured of her continued existence "on the earth." Later, however, he is additionally tormented by awareness that he can almost perceive her but never be positive she is actually there. Even when he tries to sleep in her chamber, there is something ubiquitous and yet elusive about her spirit, which perversely tortures him "with the spectre of hope." Hovering outside the window, sliding the panels of the old oak closet, entering the chamber, or resting her head on the pillow, she always remains just beyond his sensory grasp.

All these weird occurrences — and the author has been careful to cloak psychic phenomena in an ambiguity that would not offend disbelievers —

might well pass for hallucinations were it not that Lockwood, the tenant at Thrushcross Grange, experiences a most alarming encounter with a ghost when compelled by a snowstorm to spend the night at Wuthering Heights. Under conditions such as these, when nature violently assails the bulwarks of civilization, even the sophisticated Lockwood returns to a primeval attunement with the supernatural. The servant Zillah speaks of "queer goings on" and warns him that Heathcliff has "an odd notion" concerning the chamber in which she lodges him, but he knows nothing of its association with the dead Catherine until he retires and reads inscribed in the paint of the window ledge her Christian name combined with three different surnames — Earnshaw, Heathcliff, and Linton. His subsequent drowsing fantasies, culminating in the frightening image of Catherine begging outside the window to be admitted after twenty years of wandering, causes him to cry out so that Heathcliff rushes into the chamber. Despite Lockwood's attempt to rationalize the experience as just a nightmare, one brought on by reading what Catherine had written and then by imaginatively fusing her with the realities of somnolent perception, Heathcliff is not deceived. Absolutely convinced that Cathy's ghost has been there, he tears open the lattice symbolically dividing the material world from the spiritual and implores her to come in. As usual, however, she shows only "a spectre's ordinary caprice" and gives "no sign of being."

Not until both Heathcliff and Catherine have atoned for their respective guilts and made themselves receptive to love can their desired union be accomplished. For more than twenty years Heathcliff, being deprived of his soul, has experienced death in life, but when he begins to anticipate actual death, he rediscovers the significance of love. He loses the sadistic desire to wreak vengeance on the two families that wronged him when he realizes that destructiveness has not gained him Cathy. Consequently, he becomes reconciled to the inevitable affection between Hareton Earnshaw and the younger Catherine. In the uncouth Hareton he sees himself, and in the mutual affection of the young couple he recognizes what he and his beloved had not attained on earth — a sympathetic understanding enriched by respect. Only then is he ready to achieve what he has longed for during many unhappy years. Orienting himself increasingly toward the spiritual world, in which he and his own Catherine have never

12. *Wuthering Heights*, ed. H. W. Garrod (London, 1960), p. 198.
13. Pages 206–7.

been unfaithful to one another, he perceives her immanent presence "in every object." Yet this very reminder that he has lost her in material form causes him to strain against the bonds of mortality.

By detailing the external signs of change in Heathcliff's personality, the novelist convincingly suggests the internal transformation. After a night on the moors, where he apparently met Catherine's spirit, his countenance becomes radically altered: he is reanimated and strangely transported. He explains only that, having been on the threshold of hell, he now is within sight of heaven. So preoccupied does he in fact become with the other-worldly that alimentary sustenance ceases to interest him. After spending a night in Catherine's chamber, he again displays the same excited, distracted expression, as though he had beheld an unearthly vision; and the next evening while pacing the lower floor, he is overheard addressing Catherine as though she were there beside him. During a rainy night he dies in his own bed, the open casement above signifying liberation of a hitherto imprisoned soul; and long after death the wild exultation with which he obviously departed lingers in his eyes.

Survival of the lovers' spirits on earth, though never irrevocably stated, admits of little doubt. Unsophisticated country folk staunchly claim to have seen them walking together on the moors. Even Nelly and Lockwood, who regard themselves as too enlightened to accept such ghost lore, know enough of what the lovers have been in life to make absolute disbelief impossible. Though declaring that the dead rest in peace, they seem to sense that for tempestuous creatures like Catherine and Heathcliff the supernatural plane is indeed more real than the irrefutable material world. Whereas young Catherine and Hareton guarantee a continuity of physical life, the union of Heathcliff and the elder Catherine assures a triumph of the soul. Freed at last from barriers that divided them and from impediments they could not overcome, they achieve their goal beyond the grave, for their passionately intense love proves stronger than either hatred or death.

PART FIVE

Love of Mankind

CHAPTER IX

Universal Love and the French Revolution

W HEN BYRON asserted that Rousseau's inspired "oracles" had "set the world in flame,"[1] he did not exaggerate, for Jean Jacques Rousseau had codified much that in England, as elsewhere, had already become the basis for revolutionary Romantic ideology. Despite his quizzical paradoxes designed more for shock value than detached citation, his philosophy appealed to the spirit of the new age because it offered a constructive design for amelioration. Significantly, his morality for perfectible civil man rested upon an ethic of love. Just as Christ, in an effort to supersede the largely negative attitude of the Mosaic decalogue, had enjoined an inquisitive scribe to love his God and his neighbor as much as himself, Rousseau tried to counteract the overemphasis of both Hobbes and Helvétius upon self-interest by advocating instead a more positive approach to the dilemma of his hypothetical "natural man" in a social state. Without completely rejecting the likelihood of opportunism, he postulated that humanity would, when acting in accord with its inherently good disposition, unite in bonds of affection. Granted that certain instincts were unavoidable, the problem was chiefly one of directing natural drives toward commendable goals.

1. *Childe Harold's Pilgrimage*, III, 81:3.

According to Rousseau, man is born with two innate feelings — love of oneself (*amour de soi*), which in *Émile* (1762) is defined as merely the desire for necessary self-preservation, and sympathy (*pitié*), the inclination to aid those less fortunate. Without the one our species would passively have become extinct; deprived of the other humanity would aggressively have exterminated itself. Either one indulged to excess ultimately becomes highly pernicious. Vainglorious self-love (*amour-propre*) induces a proud man to establish sovereignty over others, regardless of detriment to those whom he deprives. Largely the product of corrupt civilization, it grows in proportion to the diminution of one's fellow feeling for the miserable. On the other hand, excessive sympathy defeats its own purpose. Consequently humanity has developed a special mechanism for keeping the two instincts in proper equilibrium — a conscience governed by the faculty of reason. As Rousseau had propounded human conduct in his *Discourse on the Origin of Inequality* (1755), man's behavior is distinguished from the purely animalistic by a rational ability to choose between good and evil. He retains this freedom of will so long as he acts according to reason; but since rational prowess has no catalytic agent of its own, feelings alone must be relied on to impel him to moral action. Lest man corrupt his own instincts, he must be educated to recognize the valid necessities of life.

Love of anyone beyond oneself, as Rousseau analyzed it in *Émile*, is an attempt to fulfill some essential need. Human affection is therefore a compound of the two basic instincts — the emotional hunger urged by love of self and the obliteration of selfhood required by sympathy. Once the correctly educated youth, such as Émile was conceived to be, combines a responsible love of self with devotion to his beneficent creator, he becomes sufficiently mature to fulfill his social obligations without stimulating egotistic ambitions that would endanger his natural goodness. Should he ever doubt the benevolence of his creator, he has only to consider as proleptic evidence the perfections manifest in external nature. But self, God, and nature are not enough for man; he must also share his emotional experience with his own kind. The most common means of transforming love of self into an altruistic social affection without inviting transfigurational death is, of course, through marriage. For the man who establishes a home inevitably grants hostages to society as well as fortune. Therefore love, the first of innate passions, must lead Émile into a holy and inviolable union that confers ineluctable obligations of citizenry upon him. Since Rousseau himself deposited his five children by Thérèse le Vasseur at a foundling hospital, as he admitted in the *Confessions*, it may seem extraordinary for him to assert in *Émile* that the man who best fulfills familial duties is most likely the best citizen. Yet perhaps one must remember, as Johnson's Imlac warned Rasselas, that philosophers, though they sometimes discourse like angels, are after all only human. Ideally, at least, devotion to one's social group or homeland, despite obvious functional differences between them and the family, should be nothing more than an enlargement of the spirit pervading a well-constituted home.

A love of humanity might well have emanated quite impulsively from the uncorrupted "natural man," Rousseau believed, but in the lapsed condition of artificial society, that phenomenon is no longer spontaneous. In our culture the propensity must originate in friendship and gradually expand into universal love. First man must refuse to tolerate the suffering of all sentient beings; for, as Rousseau warned in *Émile*, anyone hardened to others' distress is "incapable of tenderness towards his fellow-creatures and ignorant of the joys of pity" so that he becomes a "very monster among men."[2] The prerequisite to fellow feeling, then, is one's own vivid comprehension of suffering, and sympathy is developed as projected love. But not only does the man susceptible to others' misfortunes and capable of empathic understanding gain compassion for abject individuals; he is led, through imaginative excitation carrying "him outside himself," to love humanity in general.[3]

Rousseau even averred that self-love (*amour-propre*) might be turned to advantage rather than imperfectly repressed. If its energies were favorably directed, private vice might indeed be converted into public virtue. To achieve this end, the wise individual, realizing that his own well-being depends upon the general welfare, channels his efforts toward the greater goal — one at least congenial with the object of the "general will." And society must, to minimize the conflict, encourage such public spirit. In fact, whenever the selfish impulse is counterbalanced by concern for social health, a respect for justice will prevail. In this manner, claimed Rousseau, retailoring Christ's two commandments to his own philosophy, rational self-love among those already sensitized by pity should "compel us to love mankind even more than our neighbour."[4] Affection for humanity would

2. *Émile*, tr. Barbara Foxley (London, 1966), p. 51.
3. *Émile*, p. 184.
4. *Émile*, p. 215.

serve, in turn, as the cornerstone of virtuous conduct. Hopefully it would provide an intuitive morality characterized by wisely controlled passions and guided not by external authority but, more reliably, by conscience, over which enlightened rationality would preside. The reformation of the human heart, though it might not restore the *saturnia regna*, was expected to heal the breach between nature and civilization, permitting man to be virtuous by being true to himself.

Though rarely with unqualified endorsement, many of the Rousseauistic ideals of fraternal love were imported into England, where some had earlier been promulgated by Locke, Shaftesbury, and Pope. A group of English writers who more or less deservedly earned the soubriquet of "Jacobins" flourished during the last decade of the eighteenth century, enunciating their own varieties of Gallic benevolence. Denounced by Tories for disloyalty, humorless didacticism, and a naïve concern with abstract suffering, they were granted spurious immortality by the satirical lampoons in *The Anti-Jacobin* (1797–98). Among the poets so ridiculed were Robert Merry, founder of the so-called Della Cruscan school, John Thelwall, whom Coleridge tried to persuade that the ideals of "patriotism" and Christianity were compatible, and Richard Payne Knight. Other liberals preferring narrative prose as a vehicle for revolutionary doctrine used the novel to convert theory into concrete exemplars; their number included Thomas Day, whose life offers ironic commentary on his *Sandford and Merton*, Henry Brooke, Thomas Holcroft, Robert Bage, William Godwin, Charlotte Smith, and Elizabeth Inchbald. Some like Thomas Paine, Mary Wollstonecraft, and Godwin — indeed those whose writings had the greatest effect — preferred to declare their polemics in rhetorical disquisitions.

The most influential of Jacobin works was, of course, Godwin's bold and powerful *Enquiry Concerning Political Justice* (1793), which not only flayed existing social ills but offered drastic recommendations for reform. Since scientists had deduced laws to explain natural phenomena, Godwin, like other ethical philosophers of his time, assumed that human behavior might be reduced to a set of theoretical principles which would elucidate man's responses to external stimuli. If physicists and chemists might control the functions of inanimate nature, why should humanity allow itself to remain passively subject to the evils of society? Ever since Locke's ascendancy over English empiricism, the intellectual community had generally supposed that the power of man to improve his circumstances rested squarely on reason and that a desire for pleasure or a fear of pain would induce him to choose correctly. As a corollary, it might be said that the rational individual, being constrained by a propensity to do good, had no free will except in choosing badly, and at the moment of such foolish choice he abrogated his reason. Hume, on the other hand, had tried to account for such lapses by dogmatically asserting that man is moved less by thought than by emotion, that morality is governed by sentiment, and that reason is the slave of passion. Consequently it was against Hume's unacceptable postulates that Godwin was conspicuously rebelling in his determination to liberate humanity from such tyrannies. His exaltation of reason must therefore be seen not only as opposition to the mounting tides of feeling in prevalent doctrines of sensibility, which often implied avoidance of thought, but also as refutation of Hume.

While few liberals caviled at the exposé of social ills in *Political Justice*, most of its admirers came to believe that Godwin had erred in idolizing reason as man's savior. Whether he overstated his argument out of naïve obliviousness to the pitfalls of exaggeration or out of eagerness to carry an oversubtle rhetoric beyond the brink must remain a moot question. One of his most faithful apologists, William Hazlitt, writing *The Spirit of the Age* (1825) when Godwin had sunk into obscurity, chose to defend *Political Justice* on the latter grounds. According to Hazlitt, Godwin was especially concerned with showing the limitations of human will, the illusions of sense, man's ability to withstand the lures of affection, and the possibility of freeing society from the inertia of habit. Hence it was necessary to demonstrate the fallibility of "reason as the sole law of human action"; and to prove his case the ethical philosopher had to "pass the Arctic Circle and Frozen Regions, where the understanding is no longer warmed by the affections, nor fanned by the breeze of fancy!"[5] What Godwin may well have assumed (but certainly did not elucidate in the first edition) was that emotion and reason should be complementary rather than antithetical principles. In the second and third editions he tried to restore the proper balance by acknowledging the valid role of human feeling.[6]

Even so, he continued to deprecate pleasures of sense as compared to delights of rationality. In his view, passion of even the most voluptuous

5. *Complete Works*, XI, 23.
6. Quotations from *Political Justice* in this chapter cite the London edition of 1798. For variants in the editions of 1793 and 1796, see Priestley's edition of *Political Justice*, III, 81–100, 137–232.

sort could easily be overwhelmed by ratiocination because the power of sensual gratification was inferior to that of pure thought. His belief in man's perfectibility rested primarily upon a gradual (never a revolutionary) improvement of reason in its practical application to life. As his key to amelioration he postulated an unemotional love of man for man that strongly suggests the two cardinal virtues of Swift's Houyhnhnms — friendship and benevolence — a kind of utilitarian *agape* pervading behavior. Like Rousseau, he averred the inherent goodness of man, though Rousseau's golden age had been one of unsophisticated innocence in the pre-governmental past and Godwin's was to be one of enlightened rationalism in the post-governmental future.

To describe the achievements he hoped his new morality would effect, Godwin inevitably had to refute numerous principles and redefine various terms used by his predecessors. First of all, it was essential to analyze the inherent nature of human beings as individuals. With one foot squarely in the sensationalist tradition and the other on the banana peel of Platonic rationalism, Godwin denied that man is born with either innate principles or instincts to action (I, 31–44). Each man, having entered the world with nothing but potential, is at all times the product of his education, environment, and experience. Whereas Hume had accounted for sympathy as a consequence of associationism by which one perceives another's pain so vividly that he puts himself in the sufferer's place, Godwin explained pity as the individual reaction to recollection of one's own earlier suffering (I, 35). Although most previous rationalists had seen the conflict in the human condition as basically one between self-love and reason, Godwin reduced self-love, that inescapable *bête noire* of motive psychology, to little more than the desire to achieve pleasure and avoid pain (I, 34).

Reason had traditionally been subdivided into two different though related functions, and all literate people were familiar with the distinction Milton made in *Paradise Lost* (V, 486–90) between the discursive, identified with man, and the intuitive, associated with divine faculties. When Godwin modestly defined *reason* as "merely a comparison and balancing of different feelings" capable of regulating conduct, he was admittedly interested in its human application (I, xxvi; II, 341). In his perfectibilian hopes, however, he was frequently more concerned with its intuitive capacity. In the lofty function to which Godwin (like his friends Price and Paine) often consigned it, reason is less the plodding form of discursive comprehension demeaned by Blake and Keats than it is an incisive perception akin to Romantic imagination in its ability, as by a flash of lightning, to illuminate a world of darkness. Truth, when cogently expressed, must inevitably strike the rational mind with immediate conviction; and, obversely, vice becomes merely an error in judgment or a miscalculation that an electrifying discharge of enlightenment can rectify. All rational conduct, then, must be based upon a thorough understanding of truth (II, 120) — hence the extraordinary importance attached to comprehension as the human analogue of divine providence (I, 318). But for thoughts to be translated into deeds, they must be actuated, as Hume had suggested, not by reason but by feelings or passions, which are governed by anticipations of pleasure or pain.

Nevertheless, Godwin acknowledged that man is rarely capable of acting in accord with his true nature because environmental factors have corrupted him. Believing as he did that man would behave altruistically if given the opportunity (I, 422), he was obliged to show that the most desirable individual interests are congruous with social betterment. Since evil is not intrinsically part of man's nature, it presumably arises from artificial society, which must assume complete responsibility for its existence. Therefore a criminal cannot be presumed guilty or entitled to punishment since he has been molded by his ethos. Contrary to Rousseau, who asserted that "to pity the wicked is to be very cruel to other men,"[7] Godwin maintained that the offender needs to be reasoned with and sympathetically rehabilitated lest he continue to transgress. But the system of retaliation, whereby each punitive effect becomes the cause of further reprisal, must be gradually disrupted by an objective benevolism. Only those extraordinarily good individuals actively determined to benefit mankind can break the strangle hold which necessity exerts on all phenomena; yet once man is convinced that the greatest pleasures derive from the pursuit of virtue, moral problems will be resolved. In this connection, of course, one must remember that to Godwin, whom Hazlitt perceptively termed "the metaphysician engrafted on the Dissenting Minister,"[8] morality is "nothing else but a calculation of consequences" (I, 342, 121, 228). This utilitarian computation must be determined, however, by something nobler than "hedonistic calculus"; ideally it should be governed by concerns for the greatest general benefit, irrespective of personal obligations or private affections. There-

7. *Émile*, p. 215.
8. *Complete Works*, XI, 27.

fore virtuous action, of which the highest species is voluntary fulfillment of duty, depends not only upon good intention but also upon the actual results accruing to society. When man realizes that there can be no legitimate divergence between public welfare and his own, then universal and individual benevolence will be established.[9]

Like most reformers of his day, Godwin optimistically assumed that in the ameliorated state these improvements will become antecedents of even more desirable consequents. For example, someone prompted to good actions less from a disinterested wish to relieve another's suffering than by eagerness to eliminate unpleasant effects on himself will receive such gratification merely from reflecting on his kindly act that through the establishment of habit he will in the future perform similar deeds from totally admirable motives. A "disposition to promote the benefit of another" can indeed become a "passion," which in this usage signifies "a permanent and habitual tendency towards a certain course of action" (I, 424). Refuting La Rochefoucauld's cynical maxim about the pleasure one derives from a friend's misfortune, Godwin asserted that the good man cannot help being genuinely pleased by the happiness of others. Thus benevolence will beget benevolence just as evil has propagated evil; the trend can be self-perpetuating in either direction. Social reform will also proceed from one advancement to another until in the future blissful state special privileges, ranks, outmoded institutions, monopolies of wealth, most private property, wars, violence, punishments, and all forms of compulsion at variance with rational liberty will cease to be. Even governments, as the need for them decreases, will wither away.

That Godwin's work, despite its aridity, kindled many a young liberal into revolutionary flame is beyond question. Henry Crabb Robinson especially credited *Political Justice* with having "directed the whole course" of his life and recorded its effect in his diary: "No book ever made me feel more generously. I never before felt so strongly . . . the duty of not living to one's self and that of having for one's sole object the welfare of the community."[10] Though this was the reaction Godwin hoped to evoke, he himself feared, even after emendations in two subsequent editions, that the work did not accurately represent his ethic and still needed a corrective to be entitled "First Principles of Morals." In his notebook for 1798 he recorded how the contemplated treatise was intended to rectify "essentially defective" portions of *Political Justice* that had not allowed "proper attention to the empire of feeling." Thereafter much of his writing strove to do retrospective justice to previously slighted emotion and often, notably in his novels, put him back into the current of sentimental fiction just when the reading public was growing weary of that dwindling stream.

In his preface to *St. Leon* he tried to forestall the charge of inconsistency that readers of his "graver productions" might bring because in this narrative "the affections and charities of private life" are enthusiastically praised.[11] Therefore he publicly recanted with disarming frankness: "I apprehend domestic and private affections inseparable from the nature of man, and from what may be styled the culture of the heart, and am fully persuaded that they are not incompatible with a profound and active sense of justice in the mind of him that cherishes them." He further observed, quoting his own comments from the work memorializing his first wife, that every facet of human existence contributes to a "sound morality." Hence "the man who lives in the midst of domestic relations" has "many opportunities of conferring pleasure" that will kindle his sensibilities and "render him more prompt in the service of strangers and the public." Indeed the novels of Godwin became a means of translating abstract theories into flesh-and-blood reality. *Caleb Williams* (1794) and, more conspicuously, *St. Leon* (1799) and *Fleetwood* (1805) emphasize the absolute necessity of human affection as a concomitant of universal love.[12] Whereas philanthropy is treated as the commendable norm, misanthropy becomes a short-sighted and ultimately destructive threat to the moral order. Hence Godwin exalted domestic affections as much as the simple life and, like many previous advocates of sensibility, equated emotionalism with tenderness of heart or the ability to respond favorably to human suffering. Both St. Leon and Fleetwood (the latter actually designated "the new man of feeling") are plagued by their alienation from society, and both

9. Hazlitt, in his earliest venture into philosophy, "An Essay on the Principles of Human Action" (1805), argued that man is naturally concerned with others' welfare for the same positive and direct motives that urge furtherance of selfish interest. See also his lecture "On Self-Love" and two conversational essays on "Self-Love and Benevolence." Keats's concern for disinterestedness, shown most notably in his correspondence (*Letters*, I, 293; II, 79–80, 129, 279), Book III of *Endymion*, and the induction to "The Fall of Hyperion," stems partly from Hazlitt's.

10. *On Books and Their Writers*, I, 2–3.

11. London, 1799, I, viii–xi.

12. See B. Sprague Allen, "William Godwin as a Sentimentalist," *PMLA*, 33 (1918), 1–29.

learn through suffering that brotherly love is the only successful means of reintegration.

So confident was Godwin of his philosophical rectitude that he was not seriously ruffled by Malthus's rejoinder to *Political Justice* in 1798. Replying in 1801 to several attacks on his utopian system, Godwin categorically denied that vice and misery are necessarily the only checks on population or (judging, quite obviously, from personal experience) that sex and hunger are the strongest human drives. Instead he contended that as men are elevated above poverty their conduct becomes decent and sober, so that they desire prestige more than bestial gratification. When in possession of happiness and comfortable existence, they will not destroy their good life "by thoughtless excess." The Malthusian impasse, whereby overpopulation will always create poverty and obviate perfectibility, can never come about, according to Godwin's reply, simply because under the guidance of individual reason

> Every man will understand the interests of the community. . . . He will love his brethren. He will conceive of the whole society as one extensive hous[e]hold. He will feel his own happiness so entirely dependent on the institutions which prevail, as will remove far from him all temptation to touch the ark with a sacrilegious hand.[13]

And though Godwin's second reply to Malthus, after the *Essay on Population* had undergone five editions, is less confident than the first, it still clings assuredly to his original hopes.[14] The dreary conjectures of a political economist could make little headway against an idealist determined that, when the chains of degrading penury were rent, prudence and virtue would limit population.

In one of his final publications, *Thoughts on Man* (1831), Godwin reiterated many of his favorite speculations about human regeneration, though, as usual, with shifted emphases. Much of the calculation associated with his earlier utilitarianism had waned: the man of benevolent disposition was no longer expected to weigh consequences but to be moved spontaneously by goodness of heart. Furthermore, this last collection of essays published during his lifetime reveals increased stress upon the function of imagination and the extraordinary power of love. The essay "Of the Liberty of Human Actions," for example, extols affections not only as the cohesive force in all social ties but as "the luminary of the moral world."[15] Clearly he still clung to his original expectation of a rather bloodless intellectual union of reason and emotion. Defining true love as "a passion of the mind,"[16] he assumed that it could exist only through an imaginative going out of oneself for the sake of another; and he ultimately postulated as the noblest kind of affection the sentiment binding parent and child. He even extended his prototype of love to the entire relationship between husband and wife, which should be grounded in selfless concern rather than absolute equality. However much egalitarianism might be the desideratum of social justice, it seemed, in Godwin's mature judgment, the bane of true love and ardent friendship since in all valid relations each individual must be willing to serve, exalt, and benefit the other. Therefore love — either personal or social — binds one who needs and another who provides, uniting protector and protected. If views such as these demonstrate how abstract theory had been tempered by profoundly moving experience, they also reflect the desires of a lonely, sensitive individual still yearning for reciprocal affection binding man to mankind.

After Napoleon attacked Switzerland in December 1797 and proceeded to subjugate that most democratic of European nations, only the most intransigent English Jacobins could have nurtured any further illusions about the ideals of once revolutionary France. In a sonnet made additionally famous by a parody of its two voices, Wordsworth in 1807 fulminated, as he often did when provoked by egregious injustice, against the ruthless suppression of the federated Helvetian commonwealths, whose traditional freedom he associated with their mountains as he did that of England with the indomitable sea. His lament for the overthrow of Alpine liberty, however, derived more from theoretical principles than from personal admiration for the Swiss people.

His only firsthand acquaintance with the Swiss prior to that time had been disillusioning because, in his opinion, they had not lived up to their

---

13. *Thoughts Occasioned by the Perusal of Dr. Parr's Spital Sermon* (London, 1801), pp. 74–75.

14. See Godwin's *Of Population* (London, 1820).

15. *Thoughts on Man, His Nature, Productions, and Discoveries* (London, 1831), p. 234.

16. See the essay "Of Love and Friendship," p. 273.

extraordinary environs. His own sublime experience "among the more awful scenes of the Alps" during a walking tour in 1790 had led him to assume that the inhabitants would be more amiable than he actually found them.[17] For, according to associationist psychology, the grandeur of Swiss landscape should have ennobled its people beyond all others. But despite their respect for democratic liberty, the Swiss impressed him negatively by the "severity and austereness" of their character, as well as an inhospitableness except where mercenary gain was involved. While admitting that his lack of rapport stemmed partly from his own inability to speak German and from contact almost solely with innkeepers, he was nevertheless forced to contrast them unfavorably with the ingratiating French and Italians — those products of corrupt, aristocratic societies.

By the time Wordsworth made poetical use of his recollections, his attitude toward the Swiss had undergone radical enlightenment. Since most of the poem *Descriptive Sketches* was composed during walks along the Loire in 1791–92, it is not surprising that his verses reflect the revolutionary ardor then suffusing his thought. No doubt his association with Michel Beaupuy had meanwhile strengthened his attachment to idealistic French philosophers such as Condorcet and Rousseau. The latter's work in turn heightened his identification of Switzerland with freedom and a life in accord with nature. Furthermore, his reading of Ramond de Carbonnières's annotations to a translation of William Coxe's *Lettres* (1788) awakened the poet's mind to features of Swiss society that presumably had escaped his outward eye. Ramond, a most enthusiastic exponent of Rousseau, contended that Switzerland represented the closest approximation to the legendary pastoral age — in fact, the only European survival of primeval society. Wordsworth thereupon projected onto the Swiss an alpenglow that he himself had overlooked, enriching his travelog with random political observations. In his customary way of grounding the abstract in the concrete, he turned a poem of melancholy impressions into a polemic advocating the feasibility of Rousseauistic social goals.

In *Descriptive Sketches* Wordsworth yearns for the irretrievable golden age when early man, as a free child of nature, "Confess'd no law but what his reason taught,/ Did all he wish'd, and wish'd but what he ought" (ll. 520–25).[18] Of special anthropological interest to the poet is the local tradition among Swiss mountaineers recalling "days more bless'd in times of yore," because it unquestionably links them with a higher state of human perfection. Though the lost Eden can never be restored, the Swiss, relying not upon a materialistic civilization but upon unfallen nature, are capable of simulating a pastoral life in which unaffected virtue, justice, and human love can flourish. This is not to assert, however, that they have escaped the hardships of postlapsarian humanity such as poverty, labor, and calamity, but rather that they seem happier with their lot than those farther removed from nature. Though their struggle for survival is often difficult, the simplicity of their rude existence (a kind of "plain living" conducive to "high thinking") is worthy of esteem. Wordsworth especially cites as extant models of the most primitive occupations the Alpine chamois hunters and herdsmen, who are allegedly "Unstain'd by envy, discontent, and pride" (l. 583) and whose ambitions do not require the subjugation or exploitation of others.

Such men, living close to "Nature's pristine majesty," particularly impressed the poet with their fierce independence, for he considered the stubborn determination to maintain one's freedom essential to the eudaemonic ethic. Where tyranny ruled, as in Savoy, he observed that both virtue and pleasure languished; but where liberty prevailed, general happiness flourished, and personal, domestic, and social love could prosper. The republican Swiss, having been long acquainted with the inestimable value of political freedom and having fought valiantly to protect this cornerstone of well-being, had preserved a proud tradition of liberty (dramatically exemplified in the poem by a boatman's song of William Tell) that not only revitalized the bravery of free men but also inspired the oppressed to rebel. In imaginative retrospect they provided Wordsworth with useful illustration of what mankind everywhere could achieve. Certainly in 1791–92 they served him as irrefutable proof that French idealistic goals could be attained in his own day, and he envisioned a regenerated society which the tricolored waves of liberty would establish throughout Europe.

When Wordsworth realized that cloudy theorizing toward which his earliest poems inclined would not produce the edification he sought to effect, his apprentice years were over. Certainly by December 1798 he knew that nebulous abstractions such as those marring *Descriptive Sketches* had to be avoided. In a fragmentary essay on morals composed at that time, he declared ethical treatises by Godwin, Paley, and "the whole tribe

17. Letter of 6 September 1790 to Dorothy, *The Early Letters of William and Dorothy Wordsworth*, ed. Ernest de Selincourt (Oxford, 1935), pp. 33–35.
18. All quotations from *Descriptive Sketches* cite the 1793 text.

of authors of that class" to be "impotent to all their intended good purposes" because, instead of being preoccupied with the habits on which human behavior is based, they were concerned with prescribing rules for conduct.[19] Speculations divorced from applicable imagery could not correlate formulized wisdom with the very sources in human life from which those principles were drawn. Lacking "sufficient power to melt into our affections," they neither moved people to eradicate noxious habits nor provided examples of proper action because they were unfortunately detached from human nature and had overemphasized discursive reasoning. The philosophers seemed particularly to overlook the importance of established habits of feeling, which cause individuals to react automatically, yet differently, to the distress of others. The "affectionate and benevolent man" offers aid from genuine goodness; the vain, proud, and avaricious give from ulterior motives, assuming that good deeds yield rich rewards. Wordsworth firmly believed that truly kind acts follow from properly developed habits. Further, since they are intuitively, even instinctively, felt to be good, they require no reference to a touchstone of abstract morality.

Assuming that a poet had more effective means of improving society, Wordsworth incorporated some justification for his beliefs in the preface to *Lyrical Ballads* (1800). Unlike the philosophers, he did not feel compelled to proselytize his reader by "*reasoning* him into an approbation." He did feel obliged to explain poetry as a higher order of knowledge than history, science, biography, and philosophy. The poetical medium he deemed far superior to that of prose since metrical language produces immediate delight; because of this exalted pleasure — an aesthetic counterpart of social happiness — poetry is a better vehicle for engendering sympathy. It can also be relied upon to convey "general and operative" truth without the aid of "external testimony" since its import "is carried alive into the heart by passion." In this connection Wordsworth defends his choice of rustic circumstances on the grounds that "elementary feelings" are least likely to be falsified in the lives and language of humble people. The most effective poet, then, is the one best able to present genuine human sympathies in the phraseology of those actually experiencing unvarnished emotions. Yet he must serve as more than just a recorder of the common language; he must possess the ability to conjure up previous situations and emotions so vividly that they take on present mental existence. Above all, he must be aware that his primary function is to bind "together by passion and knowledge the vast empire of human society." Sensitive readers, by becoming more conscious of their kinship with the rest of humanity and by nourishing "feelings connected with important subjects," will establish mental habits that, in turn, promote mankind's improvement.

That Wordsworth himself had not always succeeded in these lofty aims, especially in his most labored initial efforts, he readily admitted. "Guilt and Sorrow," from which "The Female Vagrant" was extracted, he acknowledged as a disappointment chiefly because he had not transfixed the subject steadily with his poetic eye.[20] But the reasons for its failure go much deeper. His avowed desire "partly to expose the vices of the penal law and the calamities of war as they affect individuals" predicated an unusually diffuse target for narrative attack.[21] While his melancholy depictions do arouse the compassion and horror designed to awaken public responsibility toward the downtrodden, his assessment of guilt is not clearly focused. The poor are utterly helpless victims of a social machine over which they have no control and which grinds them down most ruthlessly during wartime. The real culprits are presumably those with power to avert war, financial distress, and physical suffering, but who ignore others' hardships while bettering themselves materially. Hence the principle under attack — the *absence* of philanthropic love — is a negative, amorphous one. On the other hand, the poverty-stricken sufferers, while buffeted by the ruthless winds of hostility, cannot uphold their inherent virtue. And when they violate laws designed to maintain the possessions of those who *have*, the "rigidly righteous" heap further punishment upon transgressors in the name of legal justice. Thus society pronounces sentence upon those whom it has most shamefully abused, and the individual who has betrayed his own ideals readily submits, thinking that through additional sorrow he will atone for sin. To this quagmire of despair, produced by the peculiar interrelation of guilt and sorrow, the poet wished to alert his readers. Yet the inextricable blend of pity, revulsion, crime, and exoneration — one that sociologists are still trying to solve, usually by eliminating poverty — was too abstruse for interlocking narratives to convey as an ethical problem.

It is nevertheless clear that "What man has made of man" stems from

19. See Geoffrey Little, "An Incomplete Wordsworth Essay upon Moral Habits," *REL*, 2 (January 1961), 10–20.

20. See the letter of 9 April 1801 to Miss Taylor, *Early Letters*, p. 270.

21. See Wordsworth's letter of 20 November 1795 to Francis Wrangham, *Early Letters*, p. 145.

the subjugation of kindly natures to overwhelming evil. Particularly appropriate to the principal characters in "Guilt and Sorrow" is the poem's setting on Salisbury Plain, which because of Stonehenge the poet associates with Druidical human sacrifice, for the miserable creatures have been alienated from society by circumstances largely beyond their control. The weary sailor, after enduring long years of impressed maritime service, has been cheated of his earnings so that to acquire money for his impoverished family he has robbed and murdered — only to become an embittered fugitive. The soldier's widow has suffered especially from the aggrandizement of the rich, who defrauded her father of his small property, and from the agonies of war that claimed the lives of her husband and children. Ironically, they meet while seeking shelter in a decayed spital, the emblem of man's good intentions fallen to mocking ruin. The fatally diseased woman whom they find in a cart is also a victim of social oppression, and her dying story identifies her as the sailor's wife. The grief-stricken husband is so overwhelmed with guilt that he seeks retributive justice and, trusting in his Savior, surrenders himself to the gallows.

The final stanzas of the poem in "MS. 2" and "MS. 3," which describe the criminal dying in chains while insensitive human beings watch nonchalantly, may well have been deemed too macabre for artistic comfort.[22] Yet it is a striking parallel to the Druidical practice of conciliating the gods by sacrificing one life, usually that of a criminal, for another considered more desirable by the Gauls in power. Indeed the conclusion of "MS. 1," like its opening stanzas, makes unmistakable Wordsworth's determination to force the similarity of primitive and sophisticated savagery. It thus constitutes one of his most caustic attacks on contemporary society and its false gods. Furthermore, it undermines the complacent attitude toward justice in a nation that degrades the poor beyond their ability to exert rational control over animalistic impulses — in effect forcing them to violate mores of the established order just to survive — and then sanctimoniously punishes them for refusing to be passively tormented.

An interest in social integration was particularly strong in Wordsworth, possibly because he understood it as a healthy corrective to his own retiring nature. Like the preacher who warns convincingly against sins to which he himself has succumbed, Wordsworth is often impressive deploring an individual unable to achieve organic unity with mankind. In his early play *The Borderers* he investigates a sophisticated form of alienation — one in which mental powers are perverted into implements of evil. The setting for the action easily parallels the anarchic conditions of the French Revolution through absence of established law. Amid such confusion, Wordsworth knew, conventional doctrines crumble under the impact of social upheaval; at such times men are most likely to sanction wrongdoing with specious logic. Such degeneration he had observed during his sojourn in France when the Revolution lapsed into the Terror and many inherently good people, lacking nothing more than well-established dedication to humanity, deteriorated through repeated wickedness into an unredeemable hardness of heart. The perpetration of great evil in the name of virtue, Wordsworth declares in the play's introductory essay, springs from a distorted use of reason whereby men betray themselves and seduce others into false ethics.[23] Such rationalism is hardly that of Godwin's *Political Justice* or even *Caleb Williams*. Certainly the discursive reason by which the main character of the play lives has not the slightest chance of leading him to the perception of truth; instead it becomes the *modus operandi* for his "mind diseased," which Wordsworth presents from the criminal's own viewpoint.

Oswald is initially a man of great intelligence, though dominated by the passion of self-love, as is the egocentric character in Wordsworth's early poem "Lines Left upon a Seat in a Yew-Tree."[24] But, whereas the latter merely becomes so content with his own presumptive goodness that he lapses into self-intoxicating solipsism and fails to render positive good, Oswald, lacking "any solid principles of genuine benevolence," perpetrates evil. Having been inadvertently betrayed into crime through unfortunate mischance, he gradually rationalizes his own acts into a philosophy of malevolence. Rejecting human benignity as weakness, he blurs with his prodigious intellect the distinction between right and wrong, blots out memory of his misdeed, and eliminates compunction. To suppress his guilty recollections, he plunges into vigorous action — not into good deeds which, being "silent and regularly progressive," fail to provide sufficient self-gratification to divert his troubled mind from remorse, but into an exercise of dominion over others which feeds his pride and

22. For manuscript variants see E. de Selincourt's notes to "Guilt and Sorrow," *Poetical Works*, I, 94–127, 330–41.

23. This prefatory essay, which was not published until 1926, is reprinted in *Poetical Works*, I, 345–49.

24. George Wilbur Meyer, in *Wordsworth's Formative Years* (Ann Arbor, 1943), p. 208, contrasts this aesthete's sin of pride and Marmaduke's in *The Borderers*.

love of distinction. His destructive manipulation of power is further stimulated by a paranoid conviction that society opposes him and that its moral code is hypocritical.

His contempt for mankind is particularly dangerous because it is the product of careful reflection. He constantly directs his energies toward planning and executing new crimes either to erase or justify old ones, and in the course of his behavior, every successive act is vindicated by the previous one, creating an illusion of free will and choice. Disguising his malignity even from himself, he assumes the character of an honest "speculator in morals." One of his greatest pleasures derives from convincing others of his own sophistry, particularly since repetition of his fall in another gives it plausible sanction and, according to his way of thinking, liberates that person from "the soft chain" of human affection.[25] Such a zealous bigot as Oswald therefore finds conversion of a naïvely amiable young man like Marmaduke a fascinating challenge. By misleading his victim into unintentional wickedness, he expects to produce a replica of himself. But Marmaduke's loving nature, though it may permit him to be more easily duped, ultimately aids him in casting off evil. Despite his commission of a crime, there is still hope for him because the passion of benevolence has been too firmly established to be permanently overwhelmed.

Of far greater lasting concern to Wordsworth than the disruptive forces threatening society were the emotions tending toward unity. He would probably have been less aghast at a modern critic's assertion that his "genius" was essentially "his enmity to man, which he mistook for love"[26] than by modern psychologists' denial that love depends in any way on compassion. For example, a distinguished phenomenologist, Max Ferdinand Scheler, has staunchly denied, contrary to Wordsworth's fundamental beliefs, that fellow feeling (*Mitgefühl*) is identical with affection and, moreover, that sympathy such as eighteenth-century idealists extolled can ever serve as the basis for social ethics.[27] Among Romantics, Coleridge alone would likely have concurred with this modern tendency to separate love from other emotions generally identified with the heart. Refuting a glib definition of love as friendship accidentally compounded by sensual desire, he maintained that sympathy rather than desire should serve as the differentiating feature. "Sympathy," he observed in one of his mealtime illuminations, "constitutes friendship; but in love there is a sort of antipathy, or opposing passion."[28] Later he twice declared Wordsworth to be lacking in genuine compassion, to be a *spectator ab extra* capable of feeling *for* but never *with* his characters.[29] Indeed many critics have chuckled at the paradox of an Olympian devotee of the humble man — one who loves only from afar and remains all the while sublimely uninvolved. As Herbert Lindenberger has stressed, there was something in the Wordsworthian reserve closely akin to that of the lonely solitaries who visit his desolate landscapes, wandering out of nowhere like emissaries from a higher realm and passively working extraordinary goodness in others.[30]

Counterbalancing this proclivity, however, was a conscious determination to overcome the barriers separating men from one another. Both in Wordsworth's own eyes and those of his most ardent enthusiasts the young Coleridge, Keats, Arnold, and Mill, to name only a few — his chief distinction as a practical philosopher was a profound insight into the complex emotional interactions of the human heart. With or without Hartleian associationism, he was always aware that miserly pleasure, like love hoarded up for the enrichment of only one individual, could not be justified as a goal in itself and that sympathy was needed to elevate man above self-love. In the 1794 additions made at Windy Brow to his manuscript of *An Evening Walk*, for example, he interpolated a passage recommending cultivation of a heart whose extensive compassion would embrace the entire sensible world and, through the agency of some "secret power," would be conscious of creation's underlying unity.[31]

Since the inherited tenets of benevolence seemed to rest impregnably secure on the premise that all kindly emotions were variants of love, it probably never occurred to Wordsworth to question either the identity

25. See *The Borderers*, l. 1841.
26. David Ferry, *The Limits of Mortality* (Middletown, Conn., 1959), p. 173.
27. Love, as Scheler defined it, is "a movement of the heart and a spiritual act," sympathy a "responsive function." Though the two are by his definition complementary in some ways, sympathy must be based on love. See Scheler's *Wesen und Formen der Sympathie*, translated as *The Nature of Sympathy*.
28. Entry for 27 September 1830, *The Table Talk and Omniana of Samuel Taylor Coleridge*, ed. T. Ashe (London, 1884), p. 112.
29. Entries for 21 July 1832 and 16 February 1833, *Table Talk*, pp. 171–72, 193. Cf. also *Biographia Literaria*, ed. J. Shawcross (London, 1958), II, 122–23.
30. See *On Wordsworth's "Prelude"* (Princeton, 1963), pp. 205–31.
31. *Poetical Works*, I, 10n. G. W. Meyer makes much of this passage in *Wordsworth's Formative Years*, pp. 163, 167–68, 176, 190, 208, 220, 239.

of affection and sympathy or the desirability of fellow feeling. But there were those who saw a marked distinction between the empathic involvement of sympathy and the detached condescension of pity. Blake and Godwin, with their disturbingly blunt views on Christian virtues, even deplored the effect of pity and charity upon both donor and recipient; and Blake further pointed out in "The Human Abstract" that such dubious virtues were actually dependent on perpetuation of social inequities. More cold-bloodedly, the utilitarians also opposed charity; for it upset their sacrosanct doctrine of *laissez faire* and trapped the lethargic poor in perpetual indigence. Such political economists preferred to eradicate poverty by refusing to encourage its existence. Those actually in want were to be herded into "houses of industry," more accurately called "workhouses" or "Bastilles of the poor," and forced to labor productively.

It was against such hard-bitten economic theory that Wordsworth wrote "The Old Cumberland Beggar." To counter the unsympathetic arguments of utilitarianism the poet rhetorically outpragmatized the pragmatists by showing how a seemingly useless individual renders service to humanity. To the superficial observer the elderly beggar would appear to have less contact with mankind than with nature. So slow are his movements, in fact, that he seems to be the link between animate and inanimate being. But contrary to popular belief, this man deserves considerable respect. Having been created in the divine image, he cannot sink so low as to be justifiably scorned, for according to Wordsworth's interpretation of "Nature's law," even the humblest creature remains within that spirit of goodness connecting all existence. The beggar's assimilation into the natural scheme of life is superbly illustrated through his inadvertent feeding of the birds. While he eats his scanty meal donated by the charitable, these companions of his loneliness pick up the crumbs and become his beneficiaries, thereby continuing the cycle of giving and receiving.

Even beyond this, Wordsworth is concerned with the salutary effects of charity upon the giver. The obvious dependency of the Cumberland beggar causes those who encounter him to become more thoughtful and sensitive. From such a mendicant, eminent philanthropists may have derived their "first mild touch of sympathy and thought" relating them with want and sorrow. Certainly the comfortable members of society profit from comparison of themselves with the beggar, becoming more content with their present lot and aware that his misfortune could befall them. To the villagers he is a living summation of their past charities, and his periodic return, prompting them to spontaneous "acts of love," establishes the habit of giving more successfully than reason alone could impel. Even "the poorest poor" long to feel they have bestowed blessings since we all have "one human heart." Such an individual the poet himself knew — a woman who, as the result of providing the aged pauper with a handful of meal every Friday, was momentarily exhilarated and convinced of salvation. In addition, anyone who gives experiences, through recollection of good deeds, an "after-joy/ Which reason cherishes" (ll. 101–2); and those who repeatedly know this unsought pleasure become unconsciously inclined to virtue. The Cumberland beggar, then, far from being a "burthen of the earth" because he produces nothing marketable, is a heavenly instrument of good who deserves his natural freedom to beg.

A different perspective on love's efficacy is championed in "The Idiot Boy." Critics, generally diverted by its somewhat misleading title, have been hard-pressed to explain why the poet should have told Isabella Fenwick that he had never written "anything with so much glee" or why it remained such a perennial favorite with him. But Wordsworth provided some insight into his attachment when responding to the youthful John Wilson, who had seriously doubted the poetical fitness of the subject since, in his opinion, it excited neither sympathy nor interest.[32] Wordsworth's reply of June 1802 denies any intention of catering to the established prejudices or tastes of most readers. A great poet, he thought, should do more than represent only those emotions endorsed in genteel circles; he must "rectify men's feelings."[33] The repugnance most people feel toward idiots he attributed not solely to human nature but to "false delicacy" and insensitivity, neither of which exists among the lower classes. Whereas gentlefolk conveniently relegate the subnormal to asylums, poor parents, by accepting the direct obligations imposed by idiot children, display "the strength, disinterestedness, and grandeur of love." Also, their neighbors, purged by close contact from any aversion, develop a proper sense of responsibility toward those less fortunate than themselves. Wordsworth pointed out that in the Alps idiots are even regarded as blessings to their families, and he himself applied to them the Scriptural assertion "that *their life is hidden with God*."[34]

32. For Wilson's letter see the edition of *Lyrical Ballads* by R. L. Brett and A. R. Jones (London, 1963), pp. 331–36.
33. See *Early Letters*, pp. 295–97.
34. See Colossians 3:3 — "For ye are dead, and your life is hid with Christ in God."

These were obviously the ennobling sentiments Wordsworth wished his poem to convey, though his narrative did so rather obliquely. Even Coleridge, by conceding the two most common objections to the poem — the idiot's repulsiveness and his mother's folly — implied, like most critics, that Wordsworth should have been more seriously concerned with "maternal affection in its ordinary workings." [35] But such a conventional portrayal would never have inspired Wordsworth's exuberance. Far beyond showing motherly attachment in a senile woman, the poet extols her ability to sacrifice herself for someone ostensibly unloving and unlovable. Betty Foy's devotion is even more self-effacing than that which Kierkegaard considered the most disinterested and faithful form of love — remembrance of the dead, which asks no requital. Hers demands all her energy without returning any satisfaction except that inherent in doing good, for Johnny will always be a burden. Nor does he evince the slightest fondness or appreciation for the life that has been subsumed into his inexplicable and disjunct existence. The true sentiment Wordsworth had in mind was not just maternal instinct, which might be expected even in a female adder, but the ability to give endlessly with a love that is complete fulfillment in itself. Betty Foy knows that she is blessed, as shown by her childlike happiness with what appears to be providential deliverance, and this ebullient joy permeates the entire poem.

It is Betty's characteristic desire to aid where service is most needed that leads to the climactic anxiety of the poem, for she with almost foolhardy abandon entrusts to her beloved son a mission beyond his capability. While she remains with an ailing neighbor, Susan Gale, Johnny is placed on horseback at night to fetch a doctor. Were the situation less serious, it might be taken as ludicrous; yet the narrator prevents both melodrama and maudlin sentimentality by his tone of sympathetic laughter. Indeed a dominant mood of joviality suffuses the poem, indicating implicit trust in divine guidance even amid painful distress. Genial Betty, even while commiserating with her suffering patient or searching anxiously for her lost son, never quite loses her inherent joy, which stems from the pleasure of alleviating others' distress. When Susan is able to demonstrate a similar concern for others, she is miraculously healed. It is of course the two women who test their own capacities for selflessness; the idiot boy serves only as the divine touchstone.

As Wordsworth focused more upon the intrinsic goodness of each individual and abandoned hopes of reforming society *en masse*, his philosophy acquired increasingly vital significance. If the *cul de sac* into which he had been led by the nebulous abstractions of his early poems inhibited further progress, it at least forced him to plot a new tack. Not until he could evolve a positive system or surrogate religion by which men might live would he become the poetical prophet he aspired to be. The basic solution to his quandary appeared to be identification of human affection with the universal life-force. Having himself found nature's lore gratifying, he believed that the assimilation of wisdom from that undefiled source would provide more knowledge of man than intellectual analysis could. Recollections of unforgettable scenes, as he claimed in "Tintern Abbey," had not only restored him psychologically but stimulated "acts of kindness and of love." Quite logically, Wordsworth's affection for nature culminated in worship — a self-transcendent yearning for a more desirable entity. According to his view of synergistic benevolence, the "holy plan" deducible from nature's evident success made human deviation from its perfect accord highly reprehensible. Particularly on an early spring day such as that described in "To My Sister," when exuberant rejuvenation of life demonstrated what should transpire in society, love assumed a "universal birth" intensified by reciprocal emanations. As this "blessed power" pervaded all creation, those conscious of its effectiveness would presumably attune their souls to its harmony.

Wordsworth's resolute belief in love enabled him to reunite what Alfred North Whitehead has analyzed as the lamentable "bifurcation of nature" into subject and object, dividing mind from material world and humanity from its original environment. As Whitehead observed in *Science and the Modern World*, materialistic thinkers had previously striven to anchor all acceptable knowledge to the course of nature, frequently to the exclusion of both God and man. Wordsworth, who opposed scientific and ethical inquiries divorced from humanity, was eager to reintegrate all life into an enduring organism and to bestow human values upon even inanimate reality. The necessary interchange of life he expressed as an unconditional rule in *The Prelude* (XI, A333-34).[36] Though time might compel man to disrupt that unity with the exterior world which an infant takes for granted, the monistic ability to go beyond oneself and continually assimilate his environment compensated

35. *Biographia Literaria*, II, 35-36.
36. All citations of *The Prelude* are from the 2nd edition of Ernest de Selincourt revised by Helen Darbishire (Oxford, 1959).

for the loss. Using the marriage metaphor, he stated in his "Prospectus" to *The Recluse* that Elysian fields now lost might be restored when the "discerning intellect of Man" is "wedded to this goodly universe/ In love and holy passion" (ll. 52–54).

His approach to nature also differed markedly from that of the materialists, who merely sought to exert supremacy over natural forces. Wordsworth, instead, assumed the role of a wise lover desiring an agreeable relationship with his mistress, who when treated with proper admiration, as he asserted in "Tintern Abbey," grants inviolable happiness. Though she may never have betrayed the heart that loves her, she is not obliged to suffer mistreatment or affirm unilateral constancy. That rough handling would be detrimental not only to her but to the remorseful lover is superbly illustrated by the poem "Nutting," which recounts both the poet's selfish exploits as though they constituted sexual ravishment and his chastisement by a guardian "spirit in the woods." As "an impassioned nutter," he discovered an arcane sylvan bower, a "virgin scene" adorned with "tempting clusters" of hazel nuts. "Fearless of a rival" and yet "with wise restraint voluptuous," he first intoxicated himself in sensuous delight. But since innocent enjoyment did not satisfy his rapacity, he with "merciless ravage" broke off a bough, forcing nature to yield up her treasures for his momentary benefit — only to become painfully conscious of having defiled what he should have treated with "gentleness of heart." Originally designed as part of *The Prelude*, "Nutting" was at a very early stage detached from its matrix — perhaps because it was thought too suggestive of pubescent fantasies or because, as too blatant a confession of love gone awry, it did not fit into the plan of the poem.

The true lover's attitude, Wordsworth maintained in Book IV of *The Excursion*, characterized Greek mythmakers, who had animated and humanized the powers of nature in order to make her mysterious ways more comprehensible. The shift from trepidation before hostile forces to admiration for them not only reflected a new rapport between man and his environment but also signaled religious and social advance. As early man ceased to feel that nature was at war with him, his primitive distrust gave way to sympathetic understanding — the first step toward love.[37] By thinking deeply and fondly about his surroundings, he became imbued with a piety linking him not only to the natural but also to the transcendental; and so inspired, he maintained unbroken communion with spiritual presences. Wordsworth, in the tradition of Winckelmann, therefore saw the Olympian gods as the products of artistic imagination embodying supreme affection. His analysis of pagan myth is especially relevant to the misanthropic Solitary, who, having isolated himself from both human society and nature, has no positive credo in which to believe. Indeed it becomes the rhetorical basis for dispelling the skeptic's despondency as well as instituting a redemptive social movement. For the sagacious Wanderer predicts that one who achieves an imaginative involvement with natural forces will ultimately seek the same principle of love in "fellow-natures" (IV, 1207–17). With "holy tenderness" stimulated and reason awakened, he will be so concerned with goodness that his antisocial passions ("abhorrence and contempt") cease to exist; he will become one of the regenerated whose influence will transform the world.

Wordsworth correlated love and nature most impressively in *The Prelude* since he was able to draw from the irrefutable experience of his own life a singularly immediate depiction of the creative mind's development. Throughout the autobiographical poem he emphasized the vital function of love in the education of a poetic soul, though prior to Book VIII its most exalted stage — the spiritual or intellectual — is obscured by absorption into other themes.[38] As Wordsworth understood the progression, maternal affection served as the first catalytic agent in forming the inchoate mind. This "awakening breeze," enabling the child to feel the unity of creation, subjected him to "the discipline of love" (II, A251) and caused his infantile imagination to function poetically by apprehending more than the senses conveyed. Only through strong emotion could this power of creative perception, having no generative impulse of its own, be brought into being. Without prodding from the "energy of love," as Wordsworth's Pastor in *The Excursion* defined life (V, 1012), the world beyond self could have no vital significance. But once this paradigm of stimulus and response had been inculcated, it could, through careful nurture, be repeated on more advanced levels.

In early boyhood Wordsworth unconsciously identified nature with the exhilaration of outdoor diversions. Through this "extrinsic passion," he

37. As St. John wrote, "Perfect love casteth out fear" (1 John 4:18).
38. The A text of 1805–6 is used throughout this discussion of *The Prelude* because it is much more concerned with social love than the B text of 1850, in which Wordsworth occasionally converted affection for mankind into love of God. Presumably as he grew older he had less faith in humanity than in divinity, less in imagination and intuitive reason than in a well-developed sense of moral obligation.

later recalled, nature had "first/ Peopled [his] mind with beauteous forms or grand,/ And made [him] love them" (I, A572–74). The verb "peopled" accurately represents the animism he felt in the material world and suggests that at a primordial stage affinity with the seemingly lifeless foreshadowed his later affection for humanity. What he Platonically called "Wisdom and Spirit of the universe" educated him not with "mean and vulgar works of Man" but rather with "high objects, with enduring things" that purified his thoughts until he recognized "A grandeur in the beatings of the heart" (I, A436–41). Though often the impressions left by his loving mentor remained dormant until "maturer seasons" evoked them, he sometimes remembered exactly his exuberant response to nature's indelible images. Though at times the mysterious and incomprehensible frightened him, the "discipline of fear" working through his conscience, allied even those recollected feelings to his affections. As the delight of youthful existence became inextricably associated with nature, he developed a moral aestheticism based largely upon sensuous appreciation of beauty in its own right. Especially in the difficult period of adolescence, solitary communion with the external world produced inner strength and a visionary perspective. Whereas his childhood responses had included no thoughtful reflection, he became aware at approximately seventeen of analytical reasoning's disjunctive effect compared to imagination's unifying capacity. This cohesive power was even then dimly perceived as the analogue of the "social principle of life,/ Coercing all things into sympathy" (II, A408–9). Thereupon "In all things" he "saw one life, and felt that it was joy" (II, A430). In this interchange of vitality he not only received nature's impetus; he bestowed upon the sensory impressions creative powers from his own active mind.

Even amid surroundings dominated by the powers of man, he never forgot the normative habits of his early training. Though Cambridge did nothing to strengthen either his imagination or his philanthropic love, periodic reacquaintance with nature increased his maturing sensibilities while revealing the shallowness of his social and educational endeavors. As affection for inanimate objects broadened, understanding of "plain-living People" deepened into compassionate admiration (IV, A181–246). His solicitousness in finding shelter for a discharged soldier whom he met on a mountain road proved, for example, how his reawakened sympathy with humanity might lead him back to virtuous action even after the pursuit of vapid amusement. Continued adherence to nature's guidance also enabled him to judge, despite polished verbalism and rhetoric, the validity of ideas encountered in his reading (VI, A118–34). Thereafter, as his summer vacation on the Continent proved, it was impossible, even when transported by Alpine scenery, to forget social concerns. His subsequent experience in London's "Vanity Fair," with its dazzling raree-show of human specimens, revealed to his discerning intellect the festering sores just beneath the painted surface. Especially in the instance of the blind beggar wearing a written account of himself, Wordsworth had to concede how little man comprehends about his own species (VII, A609–22). Abjectly humbled by commiseration with the unfortunate creature, he felt "admonish'd from another world." Only his "early converse with the works of God" sustained him in the city, for the spirit of nature, with its "Soul of Beauty and enduring life," remained with him even there.

Before proceeding to the emotional crux of his development, which seriously shook his faith in humanity, Wordsworth felt obliged to reaffirm his philanthropy. Though some idolatrous admirers have actually denied the premise — "Love of Nature Leading to Love of Mankind" — on which this recapitulation in Book VIII rests, to attack the assertion that the two loves are necessarily related seems to accuse him of delusion or at least confused terminology.[39] Since the earlier text specified "mankind" rather than particular "man," as the later revision read, the poet's original claim was not so extravagant. For someone of his characteristic aloofness, distance lent enchantment to the view — whether the prospect was landscape or manscape. His reference to the Cumbrian shepherds, those first acquaintances outside his family, as "purified,/ Remov'd, and at a distance that was fit" (VIII, A439–40) seemed to reflect his customary attitude. Probably discreet remoteness operated like the imagination in abstracting and reshaping the truly essential. At some remove, the flaws of humanity were so inconsequential as to have no adverse bearing on his affinity with his own species.

For Wordsworth, the shepherds who blended into the mountain landscape and assimilated much of nature's goodness were the essential bridge between the animate and the inanimate. Unlike the fictitious shepherds of artificial Arcadias, they were part of material reality; they were rugged,

39. Even Raymond D. Havens thought that Wordsworth had not proved his case but merely confused "reverence" with "love," "man" with "mankind." See *The Mind of a Poet* (Baltimore, 1941), pp. 108–13, 585.

independent men engaged in productive labors. Moreover, they suggested to the young Wordsworth the link between man and God. At times — when fog made a shepherd seem gigantic, when the setting sun "glorified" him, or when his position against the sky suggested an aerial cross — such a man seemed to be imbued with supernatural powers. Since Wordsworth first saw humanity thus ennobled, belief in man's inherent virtue was firmly established before he learned of moral deformities. But strangely enough, it was in the city, more than elsewhere, that he recognized "the unity of man" and grew convinced of the human soul's divine origin (VIII, A824-36). Against the corruptions of urban life the qualities of tenderness and patience were eminently set off; amid the crowded, often sordid, conditions the need for collaboration and understanding became more obvious. Though he had not yet found so much to love in man as in nature, nothing he saw of wretchedness or vice could overthrow his idealistic faith in humanity.

During his residence in France in 1791–92 love of man actually took precedence over his affection for nature. He hailed the outbreak of the French Revolution not as cataclysm but as inexorable progress. Having been reared in a poor district known for its "Manners erect, and frank simplicity" (IX, A219), he had never been accustomed to false respect paid to either wealth or blood. At Cambridge he had learned to admire an academic republic practicing equality and brotherhood while encouraging intrinsic worth. It was logical, therefore, that he should have been drawn to Michel Beaupuy, an artistocratic "patriot" capable of loving mankind with tender respect devoid of condescension. Beaupuy not only stirred Wordsworth's hopes for the regeneration of humanity but identified those aspirations with French republicanism, and certainly much of the poet's excitement stemmed from a realization that in France theories were being translated into immediate reality. Hence the emotional climax of Wordsworth's development resulted from putting his loves, both for the individual and the multitude, to irrefutable tests. His basic problem might be phrased as a question also revelant in our day: can a passionate love for another human being or an optimistic philanthropy serve as the basis of a new morality overriding all other considerations?[40] Though the Vaudracour and Julia episode, reflecting his own unhappy affair with Annette Vallon, answers negatively for naïve young lovers pitted against a hostile world, Wordsworth still hoped that active benevolence might

236

reform society. With the failure of his personal love, he relied even more heavily upon the success of his humanitarian aspirations.

It was undoubtedly true that Wordsworth, like many another youth, had usually approached the shield of human nature from its golden side. He had felt domestic affection and social benevolence deeply, but he had not thoroughly understood them, much less the complexities of evil (X, A658–79). So with blissful optimism he enthusiastically joined the revolutionary movement in the hope of ushering in the millennium. Even when compelled to return to England in 1793 he believed that "if France prosper'd, good Men would not long/ Pay fruitless worship to humanity" (X, A223–24). His own country's declaration of war against France seriously disturbed him; it divided his affections and undermined the old loyalties on which his morality was based since his fidelity to mankind transcended nationalistic bounds and his hopes depended on French victory. This distressing schism in allegiance, by corrupting his old sentiments, threw him "out of the pale of love" (X, A761–63). In fact, it upset his equipoise even more than did the Reign of Terror, which could somehow be explained as a temporary purgation of accumulated guilt and ignorance. As actions of the extremist Jacobins grew more irrational, however, he began to wonder when the anticipated reign of wise love would succeed that of the guillotine. Yet even after France embarked on imperialistic campaigns he clung to his revolutionary tenets, stubbornly refusing to judge the tree of French liberty by its fruit.

Finally compelled to admit that this experiment in fraternal love had not succeeded, he reached the nadir of disillusionment and easily fell prey to false intellectual notions. Highly distrustful of feelings, he was drawn to philosophical speculations that grounded human aspirations in reason. With his intellectual scalpel he strove to dissect the "living body of society/ Even to the heart" (X, A876–77); but instead of basing moral conclusions on specific realities, he tried to formulate arbitrary rules for determining right and wrong. In the end he became a complete skeptic, abandoning moral questions for the comfort of an absolute science — mathematics. The main obstruction to recovery was a perplexing civil war within himself, for he had foolishly severed his heart from the source of its former strength by banishing "Those mysteries of passion" that make "One

40. The preoccupation of modern writers like J. D. Salinger, Leslie Fiedler, and Norman Mailer with philanthropic and passionate love invites frequent observations on their similarity to English Romantic writers.

brotherhood of all the human race" (XI, A74–92). Under his coldly logical scrutiny both man and nature appeared to be stripped of their spiritual meaning. Whereas love and imagination had always been constructive means of apprehending truth, analytical reasoning served him only in a negative capacity, proudly advertising itself as "The enemy of falsehood" (XI, A136). Succumbing to the spell of destructive forces, he allowed "the eye" to become "master of the heart" and to tyrannize over his mind.

From this severe psychological crisis he was resuscitated by a number of favorable circumstances leading finally to emotional and intellectual maturity. His beloved sister and Coleridge, by establishing a "saving intercourse" with his "true self," reunited the desires of his heart with those of his head (X, A905–16). Dorothy, particularly by urging him to fulfill his obligations as a poet, imbued him with a sense of mission whereby he lived not merely for his own but for humanity's improvement. Bucolic nature, the guardian of his sensitivity, in collaboration with the dynamics of human love, revived those feelings she had once nurtured, granting him "strength and knowledge full of peace" (X, A926) that continued to sustain him ever afterward.

In the process of restoring his impaired faculties, Wordsworth discovered that his responses to unaltered stimuli were considerably changed. During youth he had unquestioningly loved whatever he saw; he "felt, and nothing else" (XI, A238). Since that had been a noncognitive perception, he did not comprehend love as such, any more than he could know God directly from beholding His works. Only later did he begin to enrich his experience with thought, which in retrospect he knew to be essential to the highest form of affection. Because he had once passionately responded to "imaginative power" (XI, A253), he could throw off the mortifying pall of disillusionment by recalling those "spots of time" when mind exerted masterful control over sense. Often his thoughts returned to desolate places not especially memorable in themselves, yet tinged ineradicably by emotions (not always associated with them originally) which ever after were superimposed upon any recollection of them. Such scenes, liberated from their time-space location and then riveted by strong feeling to a mental infinity, became more useful to him as poet than the experience itself. Long after the fervor of youth had passed, he could still draw upon an accumulated reservoir of emotion.

A man who could recognize nature's stable powers working toward maturation and find in them his own source of excitation and tranquility could not long be insensitive to social problems. With the restoration of "that wiser mood," Wordsworth again found "Man an object of delight/ Of pure imagination, and of love" (XII, A45, A53-55). He once more resorted to his "intellectual eye" for comprehension of great truths and trusted those feelings that had withstood severe trial; but this time his hopes for humanity became firmly grounded in a realistic appraisal of man's discernible goodness rather than in any utopian system. He was especially curious to discover why, granted man's inherent capabilities, so few individuals fulfilled their potential. Presumably hard labor alone did not obviate intense feeling or sound judgment unless toil was so excessive that it blotted out all spiritual considerations. And since he had found virtue to be in no way correlated with education or social status, he could not believe that love required artificial refinements for its cultivation. Instead he felt that mankind had been misled by doctrinaire philosophers, whose emphasis on superficial differences had "parted man from man" to the neglect of "the universal heart" (XII, A205-19).

For the concluding book of *The Prelude* Wordsworth reserved not only his ultimate tribute to the mind's loftiest functions but also a clear statement of his final maturation. To achieve the former purpose he focused on the visionary scene from Snowdon, which provided the physical equivalent of a "mighty Mind" that "feeds upon infinity" and so transforms "the outward face of things" that it compels others to perceive and feel. The cultivation of such imaginative power Wordsworth considered prerequisite to achieving self-sufficiency and ethical rectitude. Moreover, at all stages in this psychological development he found human affection to be absolutely essential; and he once more acknowledged this primal ingredient of life in asserting that from love "all grandeur comes,/ All truth and beauty" (XIII, A150-51). Beyond maternal affection and sexual passion he also discerned a "higher love" that could exist only after the imagination had reached complete maturity. This supreme variety enters "the heart/ With awe and a diffusive sentiment" (XIII, A162-63), permeating and embracing all within its range. It originates in "the brooding Soul, and is divine" (XIII, A165).[41] The term "brooding," which suggests a creator moving "upon the face of the waters" before molding the formless void, emphasizes not only love's kinship with plastic powers of imagination but also its function as the human equivalent of God's affinity for the

41. Cf. Milton's "with mighty wings outspread/ Dove-like sat'st brooding on the vast abyss/ And mad'st it pregnant" (*Paradise Lost*, I, 20-22).

world. Indeed several of the mental faculties at this pinnacle of achievement become virtually inextricable from one another, and each supports the others in apprehending truth:

> This love more intellectual cannot be
> Without Imagination, which, in truth,
> Is but another name for absolute strength
> And clearest insight, amplitude of mind,
> And reason in her most exalted mood. (XIII, A166–70)

On this highest plane of "feeling intellect," when the mind is filled with "gentlest sympathies," the distinction between morality and aestheticism becomes as imperceptible as that between heart and head.

To this enviable condition of poised harmony and full realization of poetical powers, Wordsworth was brought in 1797–98 during the most productive period of intimacy with Coleridge and his sister Dorothy.[42] To the latter he attributed most of the tenderness in his character. "Even to the very going out of youth" (XIII, A222) he had admittedly been preoccupied with the sublime love and beauty associated with terror; and had it not been for Dorothy, he might have continued as stern as nature originally fashioned him. Since external nature had retreated into the background of his interests, presumably content to be superseded by God's nobler handiwork, it was Dorothy's sensitivity that caused him to respect the humbler cares in human relations. Nor did he fail to acknowledge that Coleridge, whose chief purpose on earth was to "shed the light of love" (XIII, A250), had ministered to his disturbed psyche in its utmost need. Consequent awareness of the common life and unity of all creation, especially under Coleridge's guidance, made Wordsworth more kindly disposed toward his environment, which included all human concerns. The rapturous joy he had once associated with nature was gradually tempered by duty, reason, and personal grief.[43] Furthermore, the concept of man, with his obvious limitations, was for practical purposes distinguished from the idea of God. Such a realistic dichotomy by no means undercut the ecstatic vision that occurred under rare circumstances "when the light of sense" was extinguished and the human soul felt a mystical union with the Divine Spirit (VI, A534–36), but it was essential to his recovery since his psychological crisis had been largely the product of man's inability to arrogate to himself the role of God on earth.

Despite its acknowledgment of human frailty, *The Prelude* became, by

Wordsworth's own assertion, gratulant and "centring all in love" (XIII, A384). Hence its conclusion appropriately enunciated an apocalyptic hope for a reign of universal love yet to come. "Prophets of Nature," as he addressed Coleridge and himself, "what we have loved,/ Others will love; and we may teach them how" (XIII, A442-45). Since the mind of man, when properly cultivated, more nearly resembled God than nature, there was no need to doubt its ability to become more beautiful than the earth. Man might never remake the world in his own image, but he could at least see it in its true light — as splendidly divine as at the time of creation.

42. For precise dating, see Francis Christensen, "Intellectual Love: The Second Theme of *The Prelude*," *PMLA*, 80 (1965), 69–75.

43. In his "Elegiac Stanzas Suggested by a Picture of Peele Castle," Wordsworth asserted that "deep distress" wrought by his brother John's drowning had increased his sympathies — even "humanised his soul."

CHAPTER X

Philanthropy: Hopes and Limitations

D URING WHAT may have been only a passing moment of dyspepsia, Coleridge on 14 August 1833 delivered the following *obiter dicta*:

> I have never known a trader in philanthropy who was not wrong in heart somewhere or other. Individuals so distinguished are usually unhappy in their family relations, — men not benevolent or benefi- cent to individuals, but almost hostile to them, yet lavishing money and labour and time on the race, the abstract notion. The cosmo- politism which does not spring out of, and blossom upon, the deep- rooted stem of nationality or patriotism, is a spurious and rotten growth.[1]

Though these observations seem caustic from a man usually termed "gentle," they must be considered an attack on professional beneficence practiced merely as compensation. As such, they reveal a strong convic- tion that love of mankind, if it is more than veneer, must, like all charity, begin at home. That man is a fraud who makes a public display of affec- tion for humanity in general while rejecting his own social community. Moreover, Coleridge's psychological insight into the basic motive for public benevolence was astute, for he recognized the inherent need in man to love something — if not those close at hand, then others at some remove. Sometimes, he implied, a spurious affection might indeed be a reaction against or an attempt to overcome latent antipathy. Just as bravery in battle may stem from a compulsive fear of being thought a coward, so too a barrage of calculated benevolence from afar may be the result of hostility at close range.

Concealed in Coleridge's attack is also a justification of himself, especially in his last year of life, as a lover of select individuals whom he had found worthy of enduring affection. Despite serious disillusionment in many personal relations, he had as much right as Leigh Hunt to regard himself as an Abou Ben Adhem who loved humanity, though he might have balked at Hunt's overfacile identification of philanthropy with devotion to God.[2] If in old age he was forced to concentrate on a narrowing circle of friends, he may have been consoled to think that love emanating from a particular human heart was, like the light to which he often compared it, strongest when closest to its source, growing weaker the farther it was diffused in the outer world. Proximity also enabled him to savor the concrete act of kindness, which he preferred to the sweeping gesture of cordiality. The man whose affection for the miserable rarely went beyond abstract principles he had, even in halcyon days, belittled as "My benefactor, not my brother man!"[3]

Specious benevolence he associated with "cosmopolitism," a term that had long rankled in his breast because a note in *Beauties of the Anti-Jacobin* (1799) accused him, while he was studying in Germany, of deserting family and country to "become a citizen of the world."[4] Prior to the French Revolution that phrase had connoted the sophisticate who was above parochialism, but in the last decade of the century it was derogatorily applied to English Jacobins whose national loyalty had become suspect. Though in *France: An Ode* (1798) Coleridge had publicly recanted any former assumption that mankind's hopes depended upon French victory and had declared unequivocally in *Fears in Solitude* (1798) his devotion to homeland and an indwelling English God, he still felt obliged in the second issue of *The Friend*, on 8 June 1809, to clear his name of defama-

1. *Table Talk*, p. 244.
2. See Coleridge's *Aids to Reflection* (London, 1825), p. 9.
3. "Reflections on Having Left a Place of Retirement," ll. 51–59.
4. The note charging Coleridge with "Theophilanthropism" is to lines in "New Morality" (p. 306).

tory charges. Though he felt that internationalism in its ideal condition was, like true philanthropy, "at once the nurseling and the nurse of patriotic affection," he well knew that in practice it too often meant rejection of one's own country.[5] Hence only fraudulent philosophy or mistaken religion would assert that cosmopolitism was "nobler than nationality, the human race a sublimer object of love than a people."[6] Convinced that general benevolence was "begotten and rendered permanent by social and domestic affections," he declared in an attack on Godwinian distrust of emotion that a philosophical system recommending humanitarianism while denouncing "home-born feeling" was deceptive.[7] Paternal and filial duties, like intense private attachments, were necessary to discipline the heart for patriotism and, subsequently, a love of all mankind.[8] For philanthropy to become "a necessary *habit* of the Soul," he wrote to Southey, it must assimilate "every congenial Affection," developing and progressing as "a thing of *Concretion*" (I, 86).

The characteristics of a benevolist, as Coleridge envisaged him, in no way differed from those of a practicing Christian. Though he once defined "benevolence" rather unsentimentally as "Natural sympathy made permanent by enlightened selfishness,"[9] his application of that principle had a decidedly religious cast, combining extreme sensitivity and compassion with firm rectitude and reformational zeal. Urging the genuinely sympathetic to translate righteous indignation into deed, he in one of his most rousing Bristol lectures, that "On the Slave Trade," ridiculed "a false and bastard sensibility" concerned only with removal of those evils that, being forced on the attention, offend overdelicate senses and obstruct "selfish enjoyments."[10] True benevolence, distinguished by gratuitous self-denial, should rather impel one to take action in behalf of whatever needs correction. He lamented (in a way that Jane Austen, with her rationalistic preference for sense over sensibility, would have endorsed) that too frequently, since a kindly disposition is allied with irresolution, sentiment dissipates itself in commiseration without achieving any positive improvement.[11]

While recognizing this inherent pitfall of benevolence, Coleridge assured himself in "Religious Musings" (1794–96) that gradually the individual and barbarous society too would be made subject to the "mild laws of Love unutterable" if, in the process of re-establishing contact with the divine center, both acceded to "all that softens or ennobles Man." Very much in keeping with these views was the first version of his sonnet acknowledging the "soft strains" of William Lisle Bowles's poetry. Though Byron in *English Bards and Scotch Reviewers* would later scoff at the Wiltshire parson's verses of whimpering sentiment, which the satirist deemed best suited to the nursery, the youthful Coleridge in 1794 admired them for thoughtful tenderness and moral sensitivity toward every feature of the exterior world. After reading them, he could never be "callous to a Brother's pains," no matter how insouciant his own life might be. Even when the cares of maturity began to weigh upon him, he attributed to Bowles's sonnets a decidedly therapeutic solace. Functioning very much like the imagination (as Coleridge later analyzed that esemplastic power), they united "lonely pang with dreamy joys" and superimposed meaningful form upon his chaotic substance. The key to this miracle was his own responsiveness. And so irrevocably linked with ideals of humanitarianism was his susceptibility to beauty, love, and sadness that, in Coleridge's youthful mind, an individual's receptivity to moral issues might be measured by his appreciation of aesthetic stimulus.

Like all young idealists of his day, he felt sympathy with the unfortunate many who, as he deplored in "Religious Musings," were denied a place at "Life's plenteous feast" not because the God of nature had failed to provide ample sustenance but because a selfish aristocracy had, through "ruffian gluttony," pre-empted more than its rightful share. To the sufferers, however, all he could offer was the distant hope that more equitable distribution of wealth could be accomplished; for though the French Revolution had taken several disheartening turns, its initial success foreshadowed a new era of social justice. In the same spirit of compassion produced by fellowship of woe he hailed the oppressed donkey of the poem "To a Young Ass" as his brother in misery since neither of them, tyrannized as they both were by unpitying masters, could anticipate well-being until freedom was achieved. Though Coleridge was obviously aware of the ridicule to which this fraternal alliance would subject him, he deliberately

5. *The Friend: A Series of Essays*, ed. Henry Nelson Coleridge (London, 1837), II, 136.

6. *Friend*, II, 134.

7. *Friend*, II, 200–201.

8. For Coleridge's *patriotism* and patriot heroes, see Carl R. Woodring, *Politics in the Poetry of Coleridge* (Madison, 1961), pp. 81–113.

9. *Essays on His Own Times*, ed. Sara H. Coleridge (London, 1850), I, 139.

10. *Essays*, I, 150–51.

11. *Friend*, II, 188–89.

pushed the idea of fellow feeling with the abject as far as it would go (and perhaps a little further) when he wrote to Francis Wrangham: "I call even my Cat Sister in the Fraternity of universal Nature. Owls I respect & Jack Asses I love" (I, 121). In *English Bards* Byron, with a final jibe at Coleridge as an ass's brother, originally had him bray: "A fellow feeling makes us wond'rous kind." Brotherhood notwithstanding, one of Coleridge's most distressing observations in that poem concerned the infectious nature of suffering. Though the ass's master, who was also "Half famish'd in a land of Luxury," should have learned to show pity, he inflicted torments much like those forced upon him. From this cycle of despair only a clean break with the past would serve, and in the giddy anticipation of pantisocratic harmony the earlier manuscript versions of that much maligned poem concluded.

Coleridge assumed, like most ethical philosophers since Artistotle, that eudaemonia was the ultimate goal of moral virtue, and communicated truth the agency for attaining that end.[12] But, in his opinion, this necessary means could be acquired only by an altruist who would humbly seek wisdom rather than contend with opposing dialectics. Just as learning required an opening of the mind, the practice of genuine affection would involve an opening of the heart. The organic interdependence of mankind made this process feasible, for, as Coleridge declared, "There is a one heart for the whole mighty mass of humanity, and every pulse in each particular vessel strives to beat in concert with it."[13] With such views on social cohesion, he endorsed some Godwinian precepts. He felt, for example, that toward legal transgressors society ought to nourish pity rather than indignant vengeance. Furthermore, agreeing that environment (and not human nature) was responsible for vice, he advocated as the cure both enlightenment and eradication of harmful conditions.[14] Perfectibility, as he saw it, entailed a slow process. Masses of humanity could not be suddenly lifted from the morass of barbaric deprivation; but through gradual softening wrought by material plenty and justice, they could be educated to benevolence.

Coleridge was not alone in thinking that French libertarianism, however admirable in theory, had failed in practice because it had been precipitously instituted before the populace was ready. As early as February 1795 he had warned his Bristol audience that an overzealous *fraternité* might easily be transformed into frightful bigotry.[15] Citing the case of Robespierre, who during the previous year had fallen under the blade to

246

which he had sent many opponents (in the name of *liberté*), Coleridge emphasized that exalted ideals might be so fervently advocated that even valid objections to them would be brushed aside or the foulest means be justified in their attainment. "The ardor of undisciplined benevolence," he admonished, "seduces us into malignity: and whenever our hearts are warm, and our objects great and excellent, intolerance is the sin that does most easily beset us."[16] Nor was Coleridge oblivious to the fact that irrational hatred often welded more rapidly than universal affection. There was always the danger that power groups bound together by common enmity would, when the object of their loathing ceased to exist, be obliged to redirect their unifying passion toward some new adversary. Yet the feature of the extreme revolutionary party, the "Mountain," that most repelled Coleridge was its militant atheism. He actually likened Jacobinism in politics to infidelism in religion; both he thought characterized by halfbaked knowledge that acquisition of greater prudence would correct. Despite his early attacks on established privilege and injustice, he declared in the *Morning Post* for 7 December 1799 that "for the present race of men Governments must be founded on property"; later he denied ever having been "a convert to the Jacobinical system" or having doubted that private ownership should be the basis of government.[17] If he was noticeably less shaken than many of his acquaintances by the failure of French revolutionary goals, it was because he had never put his wholehearted faith in them.

There was, however, one last attempt to put some of these ideals into practice. The pantisocracy scheme that inspired Coleridge, Southey, and a few other visionaries was no less realistic than the desire that many nineteenth-century European emigrants cherished of shedding the viciousness of the Old World for the uncorrupted innocence of the New. Like most of the utopian plans actually inaugurated in the American wilderness, it was a cautious approach to amelioration because it strove to realize humanitarian hopes apart from general society. As Coleridge nostalgically recalled, "What I dared not expect from constitutions of government and

12. *Friend*, II, 200–203.
13. *Friend*, I, 126.
14. *Friend*, II, 203.
15. This lecture, revised, was printed twice in 1795 and later adapted for *The Friend* (II, 186–204).
16. *Friend*, II, 190.
17. See *Essays*, II, 331; and *Friend*, II, 28.

whole nations, I hoped from religion and a small company of chosen individuals."[18] Their ideal commonwealth was to be based upon the twin pillars of egalitarianism and aspheterism (community of property), as actually practiced by the earliest Christian communes, for the pantisocrats doubted that social or political equality would ever exist amid wide discrepancies in wealth. In their desire to eliminate "all Motives to Evil," they assumed that the abolition of individual property would eradicate "the *selfish* Principle" which from time immemorial had vitiated social affections.[19] Contrary to Byron's slur in *The Vision of Judgment* that the scheme was "less moral than 'twas clever" and to persistent gossip that Coleridge and Southey rushed into marriage to save the reputations of the Misses Fricker when pantisocracy was rumored to be dispensing with marriage ties,[20] women were not intended to be communal property, for religious tenets were not to deviate appreciably from what the pantisocrats conceived to be the beliefs of pristine Christianity. Initially the group was to have consisted of twelve talented, congenial men and their wives; but later deliberations about including Mrs. Fricker, as well as Southey's mother and servants, show that plans suffered more from overelasticity than inflexibility. Coleridge realized that this experiment in human perfectibility would not reach its goal in one generation, particularly since its founders had already been tainted by corrupt civilization. The real hope lay with the second generation, which was to combine "the innocence of the patriarchal age with the knowledge and genuine refinements of European culture."[21]

It was a typical irony of fate that the desire for increased leisure and freedom from material cares should have contributed, through marital responsibilities, to the scheme's ultimate destruction. One of its most attractive features was that, after the relatively few hours of daily labor required to sustain life, the remainder of their time could be employed in the improvement of their minds and those of their children. Unfortunately, Eden has never been nearby, and for impecunious young Englishmen the Susquehanna Valley was exceedingly remote. But the glowing accounts by European travelers — from the disinterested Girondist patriot Brissot to the realtor Thomas Cooper, who was primarily advertising his Appalachian domain — nourished the dream of a terrestrial paradise in central Pennsylvania. If the fecundity of American nature could eliminate drudgery, then the ingenuity of morally good men and women could produce a superior apostolic society. Their cohesion would depend not upon force

248

or patriotic ties but upon fraternal love cemented through collaborative endeavor. What made the region even more appealing to the pantisocrats was that by 1794 Dr. Joseph Priestley (to whom Coleridge addressed a sonnet), Thomas Cooper, and other republican friends had already settled there. Indeed the attraction of Priestley cannot be minimized since in liberal circles he had an exalted reputation as martyred philosopher, scientist, and the first Englishman who clearly enunciated perfectibility.[22] But the pantisocrats needed wives to achieve domestic tranquility in the cottaged dell; and it was the mundane obligations of marriage, combined with lack of necessary funds and Southey's apathy, that led to the ultimate collapse of their plans.

Even so, Coleridge did not consider the experience a total loss, believing that the concept remained admirable despite failure of execution. In an 1803 letter to his ultraconservative friends Sir George and Lady Beaumont he defended those unrealized ideals as "Dreams linked to purposes of Reason" (II, 999–1000). In addition to being "perfectly harmless" and non-revolutionary, they were in his estimate "Christian" because they had striven for inner reformation of the individual, which in turn would better man's state in eternity. They were "philosophical" as well because they had attempted to improve the entire human race in its earthly condition. As he justified pantisocracy, it was grounded on Christian necessarianism such as Hartley and Priestley had advocated, whereby divine providence working through the chain of cause and effect made man's own endeavors the determinant in both his present and future salvation. Overoptimistic though the scheme might have been it had aided in developing his youthful perspicacity into what was "right in the abstract, by a living feeling,

18. *Friend*, II, 29.

19. For Coleridge's contemporary thoughts on pantisocracy see *Collected Letters*, I, 82–173. See also Sister Eugenia [Logan], "Coleridge's Scheme of Pantisocracy and American Travel Accounts," *PMLA*, 45 (1930), 1069–84; J. R. MacGillivray, "The Pantisocracy Scheme and Its Immediate Background," *Studies in English by Members of University College, Toronto* (Toronto, 1931), pp. 131–69; and Carl R. Woodring, *Politics in the Poetry of Coleridge*, pp. 62–80.

20. See Margaret E. Poole Sandford, *Thomas Poole and His Friends* (London, 1888), I, 128, 98.

21. *Friend*, II, 29.

22. See the opening paragraphs of his *Essay on the First Principles of Government* (1768). From this *Essay* Bentham derived his principle of "the greatest happiness of the greatest number."

by an intuition of the uncorrupted Heart," as well as his determination to project embodied abstraction so that "idea & realities" might coincide. Furthermore, as he declared later in *The Friend*, this passionate interest had saved him from seditious schemes.[23] In reminiscing to the Beaumonts concerning his early flirtation with radical politics, he had been prompted by the recent hanging of a young Irish patriot, for in the latter's fate he saw what his own might have been except for the exhaust valve of pantisocracy. Yet by 1796 he had apparently grown disgusted not only with the democrats but his own inability to live up to "speculative Principles." If ultimately he was spared the lapse into misanthropy that overtook many of his disillusioned contemporaries after pinning their hopes to French ideals, he could attribute his better fortune to a more critical view of man. His concept of perfectibility had never lost sight of human limitations.

Coleridge's most impressive and yet enigmatic imperative to love appears in "The Rime of the Ancient Mariner." For whether one believes with Anna Letitia Barbauld that the poem lacks a moral or accepts Coleridge's equally radical answer that it has too much, the inescapable fact remains that, unless the whole work is regarded as mere fantasy, love must figure prominently in any interpretation of its meaning simply because its concluding section forces that view upon us.[24] If the poem is to be treated as a coherent apologue, rather than a tall tale with appended maxim, the real significance is far more abstruse than the superstitious Mariner is capable of expounding. No doubt the prim Mrs. Barbauld would have preferred an unequivocal pronouncement of its ethical message in the poet's own voice, perhaps as Dr. Johnson wished in the preface to his edition of Shakespeare that the dramatist had expressed a more definite moral purpose, but Coleridge's retort to her stricture suggests that by "moral sentiment" he may have been referring to the supernatural machinery (what he termed "a principle or cause of action") that presumably obtruded too heavy-handedly "in a work of such pure imagination."

Quite likely, because of early adverse criticism, Coleridge felt that the most vulnerable aspect of the poem (and the one most likely to shatter a reader's "suspension of disbelief") was his attempt to make the inexplicable working of divine justice logically comprehensible, especially through a spokesman of limited depth. The prefatory motto rationalizing invisible beings, added first to the 1817 edition, indeed served as proleptic argument against such objections. Presumably the poet realized that, had he made the imaginative any more explicit, he might have fallen prey to the same difficulties to which he in *Biographia Literaria* (Chapter XVII) attributed Wordsworth's failure in "The Thorn." If the moral complexities had been made thoroughly consonant with the speaker, they would have been reduced to a level lower than they deserved. A poet's reverie, as Coleridge from 1800 onward subtitled the poem despite Lamb's objection to stating the obvious, should no more be bound by Sunday school precepts or sequential logic than the *Arabian Nights* tale of the date-eating merchant, which he thought perfectly satisfactory without an explicit moral. This is not to imply that stories of such nature lack ethical import — indeed many a suprarational fairy tale has the same dreamlike character — but rather that they do not comply with the codified didacticism ordinarily expected of fables in Aesop's tradition. Since the ways of God, like those of love, are frequently incomprehensible to man, any rigid attempt to legislate their justification would inevitably have limited their significance.

By common consensus the poem lacks a sustained allegory of one-to-one equivalence for representation of its abstract principles. Even so, in any interpretation of the anagogical meaning deduced by the Mariner himself, the reader must grapple with the possibility that the poem conveys symbolic truths. Though the events are fascinating on the literal plane of the voyage, as well as in the framework of their narration, the moral must be an outgrowth of the fable if the work has artistic unity. Consequently it is difficult to see how the poem can be adequately explained without resorting to symbolic analysis.

An 1805 entry in Coleridge's notebook has since become the invitation for critics to discover arcane meanings in his poetry wherever they can and, furthermore, to connect them with that "inward nature" which, according to his account of divided labors for *Lyrical Ballads*, had been primarily his task to superimpose upon "shadows of imagination" in order to enrich them with "human interest and a semblance of truth."[25] His notebook commentary about the moon indeed compels this identification:

> In looking at objects of Nature while I am thinking, as at yonder moon dim-glimmering thro' the dewy window-pane, I seem rather

23. *Friend*, II, 29–30.

24. For Coleridge's account of Mrs. Barbauld's observation and his retort, see *Table Talk*, p. 87. See also Humphry House, *Coleridge* (Philadelphia, 1965), pp. 90–93.

25. *Biographia Literaria*, II, 5–6.

to be seeking, as it were *asking*, a symbolical language for something within me that already and forever exists, than observing any thing new. Even when that latter is the case, yet still I have always an obscure feeling as if that new phaenomenon were the dim Awaking of a forgotten or hidden Truth of my inner Nature/ It is still interesting as a Word, a Symbol! [26]

That he also championed a more intimate relation of material objects and ethical import than eighteenth-century nature poets had provided can be seen in his epistolary censure of Bowles's moralizing through "dim analogies" between external nature and the inner moral world (II, 864–66). This practice indicated to Coleridge not only "faintness of Impression" but also inferior power of fancy, which aggregated without uniting. The truly imaginative poet, concerned with "the *modifying*, and *co-adunating* Faculty," realizes, as this letter explained, that

> Nature has her proper interest; & he will know what it is, who believes & feels, that every Thing has a Life of it's own, & that we are all *one Life*. A Poet's *Heart* & *Intellect* should be *combined, intimately* combined & *unified*, with the great appearances in Nature— & not merely held in solution & loose mixture with them, in the shape of formal Similies. (II, 864)

Assuming then that nature is capable of suggesting morality, one may well begin an interpretation of "The Rime" with light as a recurrent Coleridgean emblem for both divine and human illumination. Indeed light in Coleridge's poetry has been called "a central symbol, second only to love in its power to bind together disparate strands of his thinking." [27] His scientific inquiries had led to optical speculations, including the belief that both sound and color resulted from an interaction between light and gravitation. [28] His extensive philosophical reading made him well acquainted with the representation of divinity by symbolic radiance. That tradition, to be sure, was so firmly established in Western European literature that it required no explanatory comment when he employed it in "Religious Musings" (1794–96):

> For the Great
> Invisible (by symbols only seen)
> With a peculiar and surpassing light
> Shines from the visage of the oppressed good man. (ll. 9–12)

Not only does the poem conclude with an analogy likening the effect of love upon man to the influence of the sun's joyful, warming rays upon frozen waters, but in a central passage the God of love is specifically located in the sun (ll. 105–13).[29] Thus in Coleridge's own writings — as well as in the works of Dante, Swedenborg, and Boehme — the sun is identified with God as the source of all vital energy.

It followed logically, then, that the reflection or inferior imitation of this power should be represented by the pallid glow of the moon. For such celestial identifications Coleridge found excellent precedent in Emanuel Swedenborg's *Heaven and Its Wonders, and Hell*, which he is known to have read very carefully. Therein, those heavenly beings who respond to Divine Love see God as light and "turn themselves constantly to Him, those in the celestial kingdom to Him as the Sun, and those in the spiritual kingdom to Him as the Moon."[30] Moreover, Swedenborg had associated two specific colors with illumination emanating from these spheres. In the celestial kingdom light received from God as the sun is "flaming in appearance"; that in the spiritual kingdom, radiating from Divinity as the moon, is white.[31] Adapting these identifications to his own purposes, Coleridge in "The Rime" also associated the two empyreal lights with these hues — the sun with redness or the scintillating brilliance of burnished gold (the usual colors of fire), and the moon with whiteness. In addition to the theological tradition linking cherubim and seraphim with redness, he probably was impressed by scientific explanations of why the sun appears red at sunrise and sunset contained in Priestley's *History and Present State of Discoveries relating to Vision, Light, and Colours* (1772), from which Coleridge drew several details of optical phenomena.[32] He may also have been struck by Priestley's exuberant ac-

26. *Notebooks*, II, 2546.

27. J. B. Beer, *Coleridge the Visionary* (London, 1959), p. 52.

28. See letter of 4 July 1817 to Ludwig Tieck (IV, 750–51).

29. For the sun as a symbol of God see also "Religious Musings" (ll. 98–104, 398–401), "The Destiny of Nations" (ll. 13–23), "Fears in Solitude" (ll. 79–86), and "This Lime-Tree Bower" (ll. 40–43).

30. New York, 1911, Par. 123, p. 54. Coleridge read this book in Swedenborg's original Latin and heavily annotated his copy, now in the British Museum. See *Notebooks*, II, 330 §11*n*.

31. Par. 128, p. 56.

32. See John Livingston Lowes, *The Road to Xanadu* (Boston, 1955), pp. 35–38, 74, 77–80.

count of white light as the ideal combination of different colored rays.[33] In that luminous blend the poet may have found an optical equivalent for the desired unity of life — the love by which all things, animate and inanimate, divine and human, infinite and finite, are bound together. At any rate, such identifications were familiar to literate people of his day. It is therefore natural that, granted Coleridge's philosophical and optical knowledge, the two heavenly lights and their characteristic colors should be connected with the lesson derived by the Mariner from his tribulation:

> He prayeth best, who loveth best
> All things both great and small;
> For the dear God who loveth us,
> He made and loveth all. (ll. 614-17)

In view of this injunction, the symbolism can be carried a step farther so that sunlight represents God's love for his creation and moonlight the "one Life" that man is obliged to uphold.[34] Using light imagery as a key, one may read the entire poem as a Coleridgean sermon on love.

Since man apprehends the absolute necessity of love only after losing it, the Mariner must both deny and be deprived of it. His voyage — that trial from which he is destined to learn the significance of Christ's two commandments — begins auspiciously amid increasing solar intensity until after the equator is passed in mid-Atlantic. From the state in which divine spirit predominates until the ship reaches polar latitudes near Cape Horn, however, there is no mention whatever of light; instead the narration is preoccupied with violent tempests such as disturb human consciousness. In the Antarctic regions shrouded by mist and snow the absence of light (and therefore love) is shown by the frighteningly beautiful but inhospitable cold. Consequently, when the albatross appears in this frigid environment "As if it had been a Christian soul," it is appropriately hailed "in God's name." Its affability toward the men at a time of extreme navigational peril and its decidedly religious propensity toward vespers mark the visitant as a symbol of both human and divine love gratuitously proffered. Yet for reasons that the unthinking Mariner himself never comprehends, he wantonly slays the bird in violation of his ineluctable duty to love it. Presumably he is motivated by the same predisposition to sin that moved our earliest ancestor, for Coleridge in a footnote to "Religious Musings" had justified man's initial departure from God's commands in terms of ultimate good. "In the first age," he wrote, "Men were innocent from ignorance of Vice; they fell, that by the knowledge of consequences they might attain intellectual security, i.e. Virtue, which is a wise and strong-nerv'd Innocence."[35] The killing has apparently been foreordained by God for the greater benefit of those who, having once learned the distinction between right and wrong, will, as Milton put it, "see and know, and yet abstain."[36] The Mariner, however, through his misdeed — which is a breach of the imperative to universal love — separates himself from both God and man, becoming thereby an outcast like Cain.

Before alienated man can re-establish contact with divinity, he must atone for guilt through unforgettable suffering. Despite the fair breeze propelling the Mariner's ship into the Pacific (a new ocean symbolizing a hitherto unknown realm of human consciousness), the natural phenomena signal estrangement from all varieties of love. Divine disapproval is first manifest by the rising of the once glorious sun in an unnatural light — neither dim nor red (as might properly be associated with divine fire) but in a garish copper hue. At the equator in the Pacific — the antipodal counterpart of their fortunate position in the Atlantic — the Mariner and his crew are helplessly held captive in a burning luminous mist that hides from them the direct radiance of God and demonstrates that excessive heat, without illumination, expresses hostility. "The bloody Sun, at noon," emblematic of the Lord's vengeance, is from the perspective of the guilty "No bigger than the Moon," indicating that their perception of God's love is negligible. By night the only illumination is that of ghostly, fragmented "death-fires" suggestive of mortality. Indeed all of nature appears utterly repugnant to them amid physical and spiritual drouth.

The phantom ship that serves as an instrument of providence further emphasizes their separation from God; arriving at sunset, when the divine fire seems to rest upon the waves, it drives symbolically between the sun and the men. The image of the sun "flecked with bars" and the "dun-

33. London, 1772, p. 258.
34. For interpretations that have contributed to mine, see Robert Penn Warren, *A Poem of Pure Imagination: An Experiment in Reading* (New York, 1946); Humphry House, *Coleridge* (Philadelphia, 1965), pp. 84–113; J. B. Beer, *Coleridge the Visionary* (London, 1959); and Elliott B. Gose, Jr., "Coleridge and the Luminous Gloom," *PMLA*, 75 (1960), 238–44.
35. *Poetical Works*, I, 116n. Cf. Milton's definition of positive virtue in *Areopagitica*.
36. For Coleridge's unequivocal belief in original sin, see letter of 10 March 1798 to his brother George (I, 396).

geon-grate" clearly suggests that the seamen are incarcerated within themselves, totally incapable of loving, though the sun continues to transfix them "With broad and burning face." The solitary female crew of the spectre vessel commanded by Death becomes, as the bizarre Night-mare Life-in-Death, a demonic burlesque of the divinity guiding human destiny. Instead of leading mankind to the great desideratum, life beyond death, she grants only a living death; and when the Mariner becomes her prize in the dice game that symbolically decides the fates of all his crew as well, she casts him into such a chilling state that he is absolutely cut off from God and mankind. Death, of course, wins the more fortunate sailors. (It is true, as Edward E. Bostetter has observed, that the dice appear to be divinely loaded;[37] but the Mariner still has a function to perform for humanity, and a chance misroll might have defeated the purpose.) The Mariner's subsequent isolation, so complete that he cannot communicate with God through prayer, torments him as much as do the corpses of his crew, for whose deaths he feels responsible. No punishment more condign that this could be inflicted upon one who has violated the cardinal injunction to love.

Before God can intercede to restore the relationship, the estranged individual must demonstrate his ability to respond. In the extreme brightness of the moon, representing that condition under which man is made most intensely aware of his obligation to love all creation, the Mariner's redemption begins; and it is his positive reaction to the water snakes as seen in moonlight that initiates his eventual release. Within the shadow of the vessel, where the waters are "A still and awful red" (suggesting the immanence of God), the snakes appear in brilliant colors and leave tracks of golden fire; beyond the ship in the moon's full light they reflect only her white radiance. So beautiful do they appear in these circumstances that "A spring of love" spontaneously gushes from the Mariner's heart and he blesses "them unaware." Realizing that he is able to pray, he knows that his contact with God, though still impaired, has been re-established. The ensuing movement of the ship by supernatural forces, as well as sleep and refreshing rain, are signs of heavenly grace; and when the vessel has traveled around the Cape of Good Hope to the equator in the Atlantic — that position of unconscious rectitude from which the Mariner fell — he becomes reconciled with his Creator. At this point God's presence rests squarely above him in the sun. Even though his return to home port is by moonlight, the bay is appropriately flecked with the colors red and white, suggesting both kinds of love by which the universe is bound. The inspiriting angels leave "in crimson colours," and on each dead shipmate stands a seraph, an angel of the highest order traditionally associated with divine love and a redness produced by habitual nearness to God's throne."[38]

In order to maintain his restoration, the Mariner, as a redeemed Everyman, must also re-establish contact with mankind and constantly reaffirm the unity of all life. Since he must reconcile himself to religion, a "holy man" is necessary to shrive him of sin. Yet the Hermit can relieve only part of the onus; the Mariner himself is obliged to atone by a periodic retelling of his tale. Vivid reconstruction of his plight while deprived of love compels him to a functional role in society just as it also persuades others of their need for spiritual re-integration. The wedding guest, for example, by contact with the spellbinding story, absorbs a profound truth about man's duty that the frivolous merrymakers at the nuptial feast have not learned, since, through vicarious suffering that leaves him stunned, he assimilates the doctrine of universal harmony in such a way that it becomes applicable to his own life. Though he is assured by the Mariner that the companionship of fellow Christians in prayer is far better than the convivial festivities he has missed, Coleridge in no way intends to discredit marriage in favor of prayer. In fact, the wedding as an ever-present background has a particularly appropriate significance that has long needed explanation. In *Aids to Reflection* (1825) Coleridge described Christian marriage as "a true and perfect Symbol or Mystery," for he interpreted it as "symbolical of the union of the Soul with Christ the Mediator, and with God through Christ."[39] Christ, of course, was from Coleridge's Unitarian view a man — "the inspired Philanthropist of Galilee," as he once termed him[40] — and marriage, by implanting a divine blessing upon human love, became the amalgamation of the two affections essential to the Mariner's apothegm.

When Shelley journeyed to Ireland in 1812 intending to bring about reforms there, he went as the avowed apostle of what he called "this only

37. See "The Nightmare World of *The Ancient Mariner*," SIR, 1 (1961–62), 241–54.
38. Cf. Coleridge's "Cherubs and rapture-trembling Seraphim/ Can press no nearer to the Almighty's throne" ("Religious Musings," ll. 115–16).
39. Page 55n.
40. *Essays*, I, 150.

true religion, the religion of philanthropy."[41] Since genuine ethics seemed to have deserted church and state, his purpose was to promulgate a faith that would supplant outworn creeds which, if judged by evident results, had proved their worthlessness. His gospel was that of applied love manifested in good deeds; and as he counseled Elizabeth Hitchener in January 1812, its followers should "Doubt everything that leads . . . not to love and charity with all men" (I, 234). Having publicly declared himself an atheist and having suffered the ensuing chastisement from both Oxford and domestic authority, he devoted himself to his adopted faith with a proselyte's zeal. Enthusiastically proclaiming his Irish venture in a letter to Godwin, he conceded "no religion but benevolence, no cause but virtue, no party but the world" (I, 243). Revolutionary rumblings in Ireland, though hitherto unsuccessful, suggested that momentous upheavals might occur there and that, if properly guided, they could succeed for all mankind where French attempts had failed. To further such hopes, he published two pamphlets designed to win converts to his philosophy. The one entitled *An Address, to the Irish People*, expressed in terms he thought the general populace could understand, primarily dealt with recommended reform. In view of several abortive insurrections, he particularly warned his readers against employing force to right their grievances, for his concept of happiness amidst liberty relied on virtue and justice, both of which would be destroyed by violence (V, 224–26). The French Revolution provided irrefutable example of a movement that began "with the best intentions" but "ended ill" because its supporters resorted to despicable crimes. To avoid such mistakes, he urged the Irish to put aside superstition, intolerance, and hatred so that through gradual self-improvement they would achieve an egalitarian society in which "men of every way of thinking" might live "together like brothers" (V, 233).

The other pamphlet, addressed to a better educated public and elaborately entitled *Proposals for an Association of Those Philanthropists, Who Convinced of the Inadequacy of the Moral and Political State of Ireland to Produce Benefits Which Are Nevertheless Attainable Are Willing to Unite to Accomplish Its Regeneration*, was much more concerned with theoretical principles, not because specific programs were irrelevant but because Shelley hoped thereby to eliminate what had been a stumbling block to French success. The murders and despotism following the Revolution were in his view evidence that "doctrines of Philanthropy and Freedom, were but shallowly understood" (V, 264). If the Irish were to

258

succeed, intellectual leaders would have to be so firmly indoctrinated that benevolent precepts would gradually infiltrate all strata of society. Nor were these leaders ever to become isolated from their people, for he advocated establishing an organization that would continually debate and disseminate the ideas of the new philosophy. The society would take whatever action seemed necessary to benefit mankind and, despite anticipated opposition from vested interests, would proliferate by founding other units. Nor did he think any valid government would hinder these plans, since the objective of his association was that unimpugnable aim of political philosophers — the happiness of those governed.

Ireland at that moment provided challenging opportunities for philanthropy because its deplorable conditions could "excite the benevolent passions" and "expand private into public feelings" until individuals became aroused not only for their particular spheres but for the entire world and for posterity (V, 253). Development of this concern for "those unconnected with ourselves" Shelley strongly recommended as the antidote to villainous self-interest; the more a man became actively absorbed in others' welfare, the less he would be preoccupied with his own affairs. Furthermore, this projection of love to embrace humanity could create pleasure within the loving individual; as an example he cited the "benevolent and disinterested feeling" produced in the hearts of non-Catholics usefully engaged in behalf of Catholic emancipation. Such disinterestedness Shelley considered the mark of a true philanthropist who, in contrast to the sycophant, was moved not by hope of reward or fear of punishment but rather by strong virtue.

Even before leaving Keswick for Ireland in early 1812, Shelley had grown disillusioned with Southey's apostasy from the liberal cause, and particularly galling was the elder writer's rather condescending view that all sensitive men passed through Shelley's youthful phase in their progress toward maturity. At a time when the first generation of Romanticists had largely turned conservative, Shelley felt a strong need to establish contact with a revolutionary leader who, having kept the faith beyond middle age, remained relatively uncorrupted by the world and still longed to achieve the untarnishable goals. Consequently in writing to William Godwin, whose works had been the major influence on his thinking during the two preceding years, Shelley introduced himself as a young man

41. *Letters*, I, 255.

"ardent in the cause of philanthropy and truth" (I, 220). Though Godwin was no longer a fire-eating radical, Shelley was greatly consoled that time had wrought upon him no "soul-chilling alteration"; rather, "the unmoderated enthusiasm of philanthropy still [characterized] him."[42] Envisioning the elderly philosopher as the author not only of *Political Justice* but also of *The Enquirer* and sentimental novels, Shelley did not associate him (as Wordsworth, Coleridge, and Southey did in their early years) solely with cold rationality. Nor did he feel repugnance toward Godwinian atheism. But it was primarily *Political Justice* that served as entrée to the acquaintance, for in his next letter he wrote Godwin of its profound impact upon him. Like Coleridge's stunned wedding guest, he "rose from its perusal a wiser and a better man" (I, 227). His willingness to bear the world's wrath for dissemination of its principles was a further measure of his devotion.

It was logical then that Shelley informed Godwin of his Irish plans, particularly since the impetus for them had come largely from *Political Justice*. In late January 1812 he wrote of his address to the Catholics in Ireland, which he thought could produce no other impressions than "those of peace & harmony" (I, 243). Godwin's ensuing efforts to curb Shelley's overoptimistic zeal and self-righteousness probably caused the young idealist no offense; yet the former's shrill warnings against founding associations that would inevitably lead to bloodshed came as a shock, especially from the man whose doctrines were at the very core of the plan. Godwin, in fact, asserted that, since the pervading concept of *Political Justice* posited association as "a most ill-chosen and ill-qualified mode of endeavouring to promote the political happiness of mankind," Shelley must have had only a superficial acquaintance with that work.[43] Despite acquiescence to his mentor's superior wisdom, Shelley, in his reply, countered that, because *Political Justice* had not been sufficiently militant, it had generally failed to establish its precepts and that in any case the Irish mob was quite different from the English reading public of 1793. Ten days later, however, Shelley apprised his insistent teacher that even the project for philanthropic organizations had been abandoned; the concept nevertheless he stubbornly refused to denigrate since those societies were calculated only to hasten "the progress of human perfectibility" (I, 276).

That Shelley planned a comprehensive treatment of these principles is suggested by his fragmentary manuscript entitled *Speculations on Morals*.

Its prospectus declares the subject to be a *positive* science of morality striving toward enduring happiness — as opposed to *negative* metaphysics, which ascertains only what is false. By Shelley's definition, a moral act is one that, "when considered in all its accessories and consequences," will "produce the highest pleasure to the greatest number of sensitive beings" (VII, 71). He further explains that virtue is the disposition to promote this happiness, that its constituents are benevolence and justice, and that all praiseworthy deeds are governed by these two principles (VII, 72). *Benevolence* he defines as the desire to do good, *justice* as the understanding of how good should be effected. According to a well-worn dichotomy, he interprets *good* as that which causes pleasure while that which induces pain he considers *evil*. In the most primitive state man may well have been concerned only with self-preservation, regardless of any pain accruing to others from his aggression. Advancing, he presumably realized that such myopic conduct would never produce the well-being of any social entity with which he was associated. Yet this enlightened self-interest is not what Shelley means by *virtue*. Neither fear of torment nor hope of reward produces truly moral action, which must derive rather from a natural predisposition.

Sections of this fragmentary treatise entitled "Benevolence" and "Justice," though still unfinished, represent a more sophisticated elaboration involving the development of imaginative sympathy. A small child, scarcely aware of sensations outside himself, is not much troubled with someone else's pains until he recognizes in another's cries and gestures the same feelings that produce such responses in him. Then only does he comprehend others' suffering and allow his selfish proclivities to be curtailed by sympathy. As a counterpart to the child's maturation Shelley saw the evolution of social behavior, for the more civilized people become, the more interested they are in the welfare of the whole community. Those individuals nurtured by the best poetry and philosophy become additionally sensitized to others' anguish, since it is through the supremely important image-making power that man can perceive and abhor evil or can estimate future pain and pleasure. Whereas the imaginations of selfish men, like those of solipsistic children, are narrowly confined, imaginations of the virtuous encompass wide circumferences. Wisdom and virtue are then inseparable, as Socrates had long ago observed; and disinterested benevo-

42. *Letters*, I, 232.
43. *Letters*, I, 261.

lence Shelley postulated as "the product of a cultivated imagination" (VII, 76).

Somewhat less abstractly than his prose, *Queen Mab* depicts lack of benevolence as the culprit in social ills and shows the world as it might become if proponents of universal love are ever heeded. For this purpose Shelley employed the visionary fulfiller of unrealized wishes, Queen Mab, who in his delineation is a cross between racial memory and Cumaean sibyl. As a tutelary guide she assumes her mission by giving the spirit of nature or necessity what, in essence at least, is a nudge in the right direction so that amelioration must inevitably follow. Having chosen the mortal Ianthe as her emissary to mankind, Mab provides visions showing the present as an outgrowth of the past and the future as an extension of the present.

The panoramas of bygone ages — viewed from a superior vantage point that puts all in proper perspective — form patterns of constant flux within the framework of "Nature's unchanging harmony" (II, 257). From the cyclical rise and decline of human affairs it becomes evident that wealth, power, and self-seeking have corrupted what was once peaceful and free; for every great civilization has been corroded through inner decay. Not only does Ianthe become aware of the transience of worldly grandeur and the folly of most human pursuits; she is impressed with the importance of understanding previous mistakes in order to prevent their recurrence. The study of history, such as Godwin had been urging upon Shelley, is thus recommended not as a belletristic or even a moral discipline but, in the light of scientific inquiry, as a utilitarian means of controlling the future.[44] Through pragmatic analysis of cause and effect Ianthe learns which antecedents produce desirable consequents; without resorting to trial-and-error methodology, she discovers what to avoid or encourage. By this means history can be graphically transformed from an undulating pattern of conflict between tyranny and liberty to an ascending linear progression.

Quite obviously, much in contemporary society cries out for immediate improvement. Man's selfish instincts have been accentuated by modes of commerce that exploit labor and idolize wealth. Indeed the worship of gold, which hardens the rich to human suffering while it embitters the poor, has put a monetary value upon everything desirable, so that man is unwittingly sold into the slavery of mammon. Even "the fellowship of man,/ Those duties which his heart of human love/ Should urge him to perform instinctively" (V, 183–185), has become venal. Senseless blood-shed has often resulted from the ambitions of some men to exalt them-selves over others, as groups in power legally persecute nonconformists in the name of justice or righteousness. Especially deplorable is that such existing ills are perpetuated from one generation to another through the inertia of custom or the apathy of ordinary men.

Yet hope should not be abandoned, for to the rescue would come neces-sity, apostrophized by Shelley as the "Spirit of Nature" and "mother of the world." The doctrine of necessity as he adapted it, primarily from Holbach's *Système de la nature*, became less an acquiescence to determin-ism than a utilitarian endorsement of man's ability, however limited, to control his environment and thereby shape his own destiny. Nor did he find Holbach's materialism, which Godwin had abused for "sensuality & selfishness," at all incompatible with "the loftiest disinterestedness"; rather, he asserted that both materialism and immaterialism (the latter assimilated more from Berkeley than Godwin) were indifferent to the conflict "between benevolence & self love."[45] According to Shelley's belief at this time, necessity was an inexorable precept governing all acts and thoughts, which, like the laws controlling matter, could be turned to posi-tive advantage. Through unbiased analysis of nature's laws, of the proper connection between objects, and of "the constant conjunction of similar events," men of virtue could deduce what *needed* to be done and set in motion a chain of events that would culminate in desired results.[46] Trans-lating this concept of necessity to the ethical plane, Shelley in his notes to *Queen Mab* asserted that cause bore the same relation to effect as motive bore to voluntary action. If one judged deeds partly by their consequences, then all moral individuals ought to be concerned just as much with good causes as with right motives. The application of the term "liberty" to the mind he declared as irresponsible as the application of "chance" to mat-ter: both evasions merely admitted that the conjunction of antecedents and consequents was unknown. Free will, as popularly construed, Shelley thought nothing more than a misunderstanding of the power necessary

44. For Shelley's practical approach to the study of history, see his letter of 17 December 1812 to Hookham (I, 340).

45. *Letters,* I, 316.

46. *Poetical Works,* p. 809. Shelley's explanation of necessity in the notes (pp. 809–12), concerned with a philosophical defense of the concept, might suggest a fatalistic attitude toward progress; but the poem itself expounds a much more optimistic, utilitarian view.

to produce a given effect — a failure to accept as dominant that motive which ultimately prevailed — and in this view he was close to modern psychologists who declare volition to be the result of often unconscious motivation.

It was Shelley's fervent hope that thorough understanding of necessitarianism would eradicate religious superstition and alter untenable morality based on rewards and punishments, both of which he condemned as motive lures. Any objective study of nature ought to reveal the universal life-force as completely amoral; and if that principle were a creator, he would, as author of both good and evil, deserve blame as well as praise. Denying that there was either good or evil except as events and their consequences had some pragmatic bearing upon man's existence, Shelley proposed an ethic founded on the criterion of usefulness. Human morality, if it aspired beyond nature's indifferent force, must be guided by utility toward universal happiness. Admittedly vice had to be condemned and, whenever possible, avoided or controlled. But justice should cease to be the instrument for meting out chastisement and vengeance; the method most likely to produce good results would be (in the Godwinian tradition) charitable forgiveness.

What had thus far stymied advancement was man's false notion of his relation to the world's ruling principle. Since Shelley denied that the pervading force was "an organic being," he could admit no legitimate tie with such an invented deity.[47] He did believe, however, in a universal spirit binding all together; for according to Queen Mab's pantheistic view, "Every grain/ Is sentient both in unity and part,/ And the minutest atom comprehends/ A world of loves and hatreds" (IV, 143-46). From these spiritual subdivisions of the world soul arise the generative antitheses that both plague and bless humanity — truth and falsehood, good and evil, pleasure and pain, sympathy and hate. And since man himself is a compound of a once pure soul with corruptible flesh, he is formed either for noble deeds or ignominy. But Shelley could discover no evidence that any supernatural power cares about man's fate, and he found particularly odious the commandment to believe without convincing proof.[48] Whereas in his earlier days he had hopefully longed to associate the world's unalterable law with "the spirit of universal imperishable love," he had by the time of writing Queen Mab abandoned that desire.[49] He could indeed accept "a pervading Spirit coeternal with the universe," but he adamantly rejected the concept of a creative or purposive divinity.

The term *God,* Shelley postulated, was originally "an expression denoting the unknown cause of known events which men perceived in the universe" and not a Platonic demiurge or a prime mover anthropomorphized by analogy with an earthly monarch. As Shelley contended, not only in the notes to *Queen Mab* but again in his *Refutation of Deism,* there could be no benevolence in a divinity that foretold man's fall, tempted his own creature into sin, and then punished him for inevitable transgression (VI, 33). The evolution of intolerant religion as Queen Mab traces it from wonder at natural forces (VI, 72–145) becomes a record of accumulated injustice and the means of promulgating a doctrine antipodal to its actual results. Shelley's most striking symbol of humanity duped by such hypocrisy is Ahasuerus, the Wandering Jew, who staunchly adheres to belief in God — admittedly a vengeful, jealous deity but also an omnipotent one — despite an earlier refusal to practice his Lord's teachings when he might have aided the suffering Jesus en route to Calvary. Here obviously is mankind caught and tortured in the web of its uneasy conscience. For having acted selfishly, Ahasuerus torments himself with excruciating anguish that, far from expiating his evil, fastens a hateful, imprecatory belief upon him. As the prototype of a true believer, he assumes that a certain virtue inheres in bearing up under pain. If humanity were ever to progress toward happiness, Shelley thought it would have to renounce all creeds that condone suffering. Since in practice Christianity had reconciled its followers to the world's evils, helped them tolerate a despotic *status quo,* and rigidly separated some groups of men from others, it was in the poet's view the chief obstacle to equality and universal brotherhood.[50]

When Shelley wrote *The Revolt of Islam* in 1817, he attached far greater significance to man's comprehension of love than to a manipulation of necessitarian laws for effecting social progress. As he also emphasized in the *Essay on Christianity,* universal benevolence would have to be securely affirmed in the hearts and minds of a people before "regulations of precedent and prescription" could be safely abolished (VI, 249). His preface to *The Revolt* asserted that disillusionment in the results of the French Revolution was quite unrealistic. How indeed could Frenchmen, who for centuries had been enslaved, suddenly by miraculous fiat conduct them-

47. *Poetical Works,* pp. 811–12.
48. *Poetical Works,* pp. 812–18.
49. Letter of 12 January 1811 to Hogg (I, 45).
50. See Mary Shelley's note, *Poetical Works,* p. 836.

selves as wise freemen? Lasting improvements in society could be produced only through relentless efforts to uplift successive generations. Since even Malthus (whose theories were generally thought sophisms for reconciling the masses to perpetual depravity) had in revised editions of his *Essay* conceded that "moral restraint" might avert the ills of over-population, Shelley saw no reason for doubting the perfectibility prophesied by Godwin. Hence he confidently strove in *The Revolt* to kindle such enthusiasm for justice and liberty that neither could be extinguished. Throughout the poem he celebrated love "as the sole law which should govern the moral world," while showing the folly of revenge, envy, and intolerance.[51] His avowed method was to be "a succession of pictures illustrating the growth and progress of individual mind aspiring after excellence" and dedicated to philanthropy.[52]

The principal characters, Laon and Cythna, have been revolutionary leaders, first successful in their attempts to oust tyranny, but later defeated and put to death. In recounting their personal histories, Shelley was most concerned with rejecting as "weak and vain" any despair over their apparent failures. For this purpose he employed two series of oscillating events. The first canto begins with fluctuations in nature — as a resplendent dawn is eclipsed by a lowering storm, which in turn is followed by a beautiful calm. This combat between darkness and light, translated from nature to the sentient world, is then re-enacted in the spectacular conflict between the eagle of tyranny and the snake of goodness, from which the former, at least momentarily, emerges triumphant. That successions of this kind were to be recognized as the inevitable pattern of mutability Shelley had firmly come to believe by the time of writing *The Revolt*, and their appearance elsewhere in his works underlines their significance. An early prose fragment, *The Assassins* (1814), describes a Christian sect actually practicing love such as Jesus taught; their beliefs, resembling the Gnostic acceptance of two contending principles, identify virtue, as in *The Revolt*, with the snake (VI, 155–71). Similarly in his clever essay *On the Devil, and Devils*, composed in 1819 or 1820, he endorsed as rationally sound the Manichaean approach to ontology. The supposition that the world was "superintended by two spirits of a balanced power and opposite dispositions" he interpreted as an allegorical projection of the incessant struggle "between good and evil" within the human heart (VII, 87).

Shelley's use of the snake reveals several facets of virtue that he wished to elucidate. Its cyclical revival and skin-shedding after winter somnolence denote regenerative powers affording virtue a distinct advantage over tyranny; but its reclusive habits cause it to be considered inimical by societies extolling gregarious conformity and superficial goodness.[53] Once ophidians have been forced into becoming outcasts, all attempts to reintroduce virtue by rebellion are pronounced wicked in the interests of established order. This inversion of true values has been unavoidable since any ruling hegemony superimposes its code of ethics upon the vanquished. Indeed Shelley saw evil as the codifier of practiced morality; as he asserted in the *Essay on Christianity*, "some evil Spirit has dominion in this imperfect world" (VI, 235).

Confident that oppression could not withstand the resolute opposition of goodness, he was obliged to show that benevolence could be sufficiently strengthened to keep it from being just "a brief dream of unremaining glory" (l. 128). The poem therefore had to demonstrate that occasional frustrations, however distressing, need not be catastrophic if humanity would courageously rededicate itself to championing virtue. Though patient endurance might be endorsed when nothing positive could be achieved, defiant activism, which Cythna recommends to her band of revolutionaries, should be employed whenever possible. Such militancy was, of course, predicated upon the conviction that universal love would unite forces of liberty as solidly as common hatred had mustered the hosts of malevolence. Since evil was boldly rampant, good had to translate its virtue into a power vigorous enough to burst the shackles of custom and insure that every act of life conform to the precept of love.

To embody his most optimistic hopes for the success of the human mind over earthly adversaries, including its own lapses, Shelley in 1818 turned to the myth of Prometheus as Byron (in the altered tradition of late eighteenth-century German writers) had employed it. In fact, Byron's short poem dealing with the archetypal rebel had been written while he and Shelley were most intimate during the summer of 1816 and had declared the heroic Titan to be "a symbol and a sign/ To Mortals of their fate

51. *Poetical Works*, p. 37.
52. *Poetical Works*, p. 32.
53. Greek interest in medical science, according to Shelley, caused the snake to be thought "an auspicious and favourable being," while in Egypt it became "an hieroglyphic of eternity" (*Works*, VII, 103). Shelley's ambivalent use of serpentine imagery, however, reflects awareness of the complex interrelation of good and evil.

and force." In keeping with contemporary depiction, it had dwelt only on Prometheus' obstruction of despotism but ignored the possibility that he might have been tortured into yielding. Yet according to the tradition of Aeschylus, the defiant benefactor of mankind had after prolonged suffering purchased his own release at the expense of maintaining Jupiter's supremacy, thereby making himself essentially a prisoner of war who succumbed to his captors' brainwashing. For Shelley, as for Byron, such a hero would never do. Whereas the Greek viewpoint considered Prometheus' well-meant theft of fire for man as reprehensible since it was tainted by insubordination against Olympian rule, Shelley, denying arbitrary limitations for man, found nothing censurable in such altruistic behavior. When in his preface to the lyrical drama the poet contrasted his hero with the antagonist of *Paradise Lost*, he took for granted that both deserved the highest commendation for opposing authoritarianism.[54] But Shelley's ideal rebel, unlike Milton's challenger, was to be exempt from "ambition, envy, revenge, and a desire for personal aggrandisement" that marred Satan. Prometheus, devoid of all selfishness, was conceived as "the highest perfection of moral and intellectual nature."[55]

Had Prometheus in any way merited his excruciating torment, he would have been corrupted by a self-contempt that Shelley thought conducive, through excessive fixation upon guilt, to acceptance of evil as inevitable. In *Hellas* (ll. 728–732) the poet made this concept even more explicit by his assertion that a guilty mind breeds revenge and wrong, which conscience in turn feeds with despair; and throughout *Prometheus Unbound* he attacked self-reproach as an obstacle to virtuous action.[56] Remorse, by turning thoughts inward, prevents the outward projection necessary to love. Since the mind becomes what it contemplates (I, 450), it must be occupied with the good and the beautiful beyond itself if man is ever "To fear [i.e., *revere*] himself, and love all human kind."[57]

In his most mature stage, Shelley saw the problem of causality in a more sophisticated light than that shed upon it by the oversimplified law of necessity.[58] From a thorough assimilation of Hume's *Enquiry Concerning Human Understanding*, he knew that causality, far less predictable than popularly imagined, could be tested not by *a priori* reasoning but only by experience and, further, that the power making the connection between antecedents and assumed consequents exists not in causes but in the human imagination. What Hume maintained about the prompting of the will by feelings rather than by reason was also compatible with what Shelley believed about the interrelated functions of human affection, sympathy, and morality. Nevertheless, Mary Shelley's commentary asserting that the poet thought "mankind had only to will that there should be no evil, and there would be none"[59] has sometimes been cited out of context as indication of the poet's childlike wishing or as evidence of Mary's inadequate comprehension since Prometheus himself declares good and evil to be "infinite as is the universe" (I, 294). Yet she specified the condition under which that action could become possible — when man would someday "be so perfectionized as to be able to expel evil from his own nature, and from the greater part of the creation."[60]

Basic to human improvement would be the gradual strengthening of the will through freedom from physical and psychological oppression. Man must cease to be the acquiescent victim of fortune's wheel and intensify his determination to be its propelling force. So long as humanity endorsed Pope's injunction to "Submit" and with clouded vision accepted "partial evil" as "universal good," society would permit tyranny in the name of some divine plan imperfectly understood. Prometheus' very name suggested a new kind of foreseeing and forethinking — a providence in which man was largely responsible for controlling his own future. This did not mean, of course, that his will would ever be wholly free from limitations. But through concerted opposition to iniquity, human volition could be sufficiently reinforced to show that, as Mary Shelley phrased it, "evil is not inherent in the system of the creation, but an accident that might be expelled."[61] However, the climb toward virtue has always required unusual fortitude — especially since the lapse from it derives from weakness. As Virgil's Sibyl warned Aeneas, the descent into Avernus is easy; the difficulty lies in trying to emerge from that perilous state.

Yet individual man cannot be solely blamed for the degeneration, as

54. All citations of *Prometheus Unbound* and Shelley's preface to it are from Lawrence J. Zillman's *Shelley's "Prometheus Unbound": The Text and the Drafts* (New Haven, 1968).
55. *Shelley's "Prometheus Unbound,"* p. 37.
56. See I, 429, 510–11; II, iv, 25; III, iv, 134. Cf. also "Reproach not thine own soul, but know thyself," *The Revolt of Islam*, l. 3388.
57. Concluding line of "Hymn to Intellectual Beauty."
58. For his most emphatic denial that cause is explicable, see "On Polytheism" (1819?), *Works*, VII, 151.
59. *Poetical Works*, p. 271.
60. *Poetical Works*, p. 271.
61. *Poetical Works*, p. 271.

Asia's mythopoeic account of human vicissitudes implies. After the first golden age, characterized by an unfallen heaven and earth, as well as spiritual light and primordial love, Saturn instituted the decaying process of time and deprived man of his birthright — intellectual power, self-control, and love. Strangely enough, Prometheus, hoping to free man, "Gave wisdom, which is strength, to Jupiter" (II, iv, 44); but the latter, representing the evil of inflexible man-made institutions that have outlived their original utility, further enslaved humanity. For having heroically restored to man all that Saturn took away, plus scientific knowledge, Prometheus was condemned to his suffering by the Olympian ruler, who is himself the slave of evil. The poet was perhaps closer than he wished to the orthodox Christian view of free will when he implied that only those dedicated to goodness retain their relative freedom of choice. Certainly Shelley had Demogorgon declare to Asia that in a world subject to chance and change only eternal love cannot be subdued.

Demogorgon's theodicy, on the other hand, is both more profound and more ambiguous. Upon demand, the form of "mighty darkness" radiating gloom explains that a merciful God created the living world, the intellect of man, and goodness, though this elusive oracle later concedes in his true Shelleyan voice that he responds only as Asia would have him speak (II, iv, 112–13). His answer concerning the originator of evil — "He reigns" — is even more refractory, since, by later admission (114–17), "the deep truth," being imageless, lies beyond comprehension and communication.[62] Jupiter's authority had unthinkingly been conferred by Prometheus in a moment of weakness and had resulted in a decline from which humanity could not lift itself. As Shelley wrote in his *Essay on Christianity*, mankind, weighed down by a "legacy of accumulated vengeances," have attributed "to the universal cause a character analogous with their own" (VI, 238). And since the degree of perfection in any society is an index to that of its divinity, Demogorgon's assertion confirms the belief that evil presently holds sway.

For three thousand years Prometheus has endured torment without yielding the secret that, if known, would eternize Jupiter's strangle hold over both mortals and immortals. Apparently the only spirit still free from the monarch's subjugation is the good surviving in the anguished Titan, who has never completely succumbed to the dominion of vengeful evil. After centuries of agony have made him wise, even consuming hatred for his oppressor has ceased, and he repents of the terrible curse with which he had originally hoped to achieve the latter's damnation. That imprecation, rather than having minimized Jupiter's power, had actually inflicted pain upon himself and all mankind by demeaning the sufferers to the tyrant's level. It is necessary, therefore, that Prometheus extricate himself from the perpetual cycle of evil, and he succeeds in doing so when at last he is able to put himself imaginatively in the place of a fallen Jupiter, for whom he can feel only pity. In this way forgiveness of his oppressor becomes the initial step not only toward his own regeneration but also toward the dissolution of tyrannical power.

That his animosity has not been completely eradicated, however, is emphasized by the Furies who, plaguing his thoughts with glimpses of universal frustration, attempt the undermining of his resolve with evidences of wasted self-sacrifice. Whereas famines, pestilences, and suppressed insurrections of mankind do little to shake his resolution, there are two magnificent failures that, as Shelley envisioned them, were sufficient to unsettle any reformer. One was the vision of France in the throes of revolutionary turmoil, for even while its people were ostensibly dedicated to freedom and love, they were actually so divided by factional hatreds that to conclude a reign of anarchy they permitted establishment of a new tyranny. The other was the distortion of Christianity. Though Jesus himself was benevolent, his gospel of love had been altered after the crucifixion into a reactionary doctrine of hatred and repression. This perversion of his teachings consequently withered the sentiments they were intended to nourish. In both instances the objective has been lost sight of because it could not be realized quickly enough, and ironically the would-be benefactors have in reality multiplied the anguish they sought to eliminate. In the failure of others Prometheus sees a paradigm of what his own good intentions are likely to produce.

Only through the complete triumph of love over the human mind can a beneficial end be achieved, and to this purpose both Asia and the attendant manifestations of love dedicate themselves. The millennial prophecy that began and ended in Prometheus must be fulfilled, since in the Shelleyan sense he is the alpha and omega of Revelation. Through him the Promethean Age — the equivalent of a Kingdom of God — will be established on earth. A world ruled by brotherly affection will then be

62. In a note to *Hellas* Shelley denied that "the Gordian knot of the origin of evil [could] be disentangled" (*Poetical Works*, p. 478).

as inevitable as the resurgence of spring after the torpor of winter. Through the sympathetic and imaginative aid of Asia's sister Oceanides, Panthea and Ione, Prometheus successfully overcomes despair and directs his aspirations toward absent love in the first positive sign of rehabilitation.[63] Yet before Asia herself can rejoin her long-estranged Prometheus, she must visit the cave of the miraculous *élan vital* Demogorgon, whose "mighty law" impels the universe. Symbolically Shelley is implying that before love can be permanently united with the human mind it must probe the arcane depths of wisdom and thereby expand cognitive powers. It must understand the nature of man, as well as his dilemma, before attempting any constructive action; and the inherent power to translate aspiration into reality must be released through the imagination. For this purpose Asia and Panthea are obliged to transcend worldly illusions to penetrate to the very source of power actuating necessity, the eternal agency that meekness will force to unloose "the snake-like Doom" (II, iii, 97). Once Asia's mission is accomplished, her return to Prometheus must be virtually instantaneous lest man, when restored to rightful power by successful revolution, be deprived of love and lapse into another tyranny.

The reunion of Prometheus with Asia, whom he sees as increasingly brilliant illumination, predicates Jupiter's doom, for once the mind of man has been perfected, the temporal rule of evil must cease. Demogorgon, far from being the "fatal child" whom Jupiter expects to eternize his triumph over mankind, becomes (like the uprising of a determined people) the instrument for the tyrant's dethronement. The cryptic identification of Demogorgon as "Eternity" is accurate, for he is indeed the fulfillment of time, as well as the seed of evil effecting its own destruction, potentiality brought to fruition, and the latent force of humanity carried through upheaval into victory. Consequently he need not be called by any "direr name" such as "necessity" or "revolution."

The triumph of love, which banishes the blind operation of necessity, enables man to establish sovereignty over himself and his environment. In the new Promethean Age mortals and nature achieve perfect harmony, making beauty identical with goodness and attaining that condition described by Shelley in his fragmentary essay "On Love" when "the bond and the sanction . . . connects not only man with man, but with every thing which exists" (VI, 201). Though the inevitable limitations on mundane existence — death and mutability — remain, man has a modicum of control over them. Freed from pain, guilt, and institutional evil, he assumes rational command of his passions. Love, by liberating the human mind from the "painted veil" of imposture, has enabled him to become true to the promptings of his heart and to fulfill his greatest capabilities.

Whereas Prometheus and Asia, as immortals, have achieved their immutable paradise and withdraw from the world of flux, man, being mortal, must always guard against threats to his liberated condition. For even though Destruction seems at present firmly caged and safeguarded by gentleness, virtue, wisdom, and endurance, it may at some future time escape and menace society.[64] In such an event, the poised perfection of eternity (symbolized by the circular position of the serpent with tail in mouth) will be challenged, and reactionary forces of tyranny will unloose the serpent's wrath upon mankind unless the four cardinal virtues subdue it. As Demogorgon's ultimate warning suggests, the paradigm for man's redemption will always be Prometheus, whose refusal to abandon hope or relinquish his will makes him the savior of mankind:

> To suffer woes which Hope thinks infinite;
> To forgive wrongs darker than death or night;
> To defy power which seems omnipotent;
> To love, and bear; to hope, till Hope creates
> From its own wreck the thing it contemplates;
> Neither to change, nor falter, nor repent:
> This, like thy glory, Titan, is to be
> Good, great and joyous, beautiful and free;
> This is alone Life, Joy, Empire, and Victory. (IV, 570–78)

In an age dominated by reactionary forces that became more firmly entrenched than ever through failures to establish liberalism, Shelley clung tenaciously to his belief that universal love would someday prevail. Whereas many of his contemporaries curtailed their ambitions to goals that were immediately attainable, Shelley continued to advocate the revolutionary ideals popular among English intellectuals a generation before

63. Though many critics have identified Panthea and Ione with allegorical abstractions, such identifications are at best tenuous. The exigencies of Shelley's drama required protagonists to further dialogue and action more desperately than to form systematic allegory. Yet Panthea and Ione, as Asia's sisters, could well be associated collectively with the facets of Shelleyan love — sympathy, imagination, hope, beauty, and goodness.
64. In "The Mask of Anarchy" Shelley calls personified Murder, Fraud, Hypocrisy, and Anarchy "Destructions."

him on the assumption that mankind would ultimately be ready for them. Absolute perfection, he realized, was like one of the mathematical limits always approached more nearly but never completely reached. Even so, mankind he thought capable of infinite progress. In contradistinction to the modern phobia that science creates monsters it cannot control, he believed that scientific advancements would, when put to practical use, be accompanied by an equivalent amelioration of humanity. Aspirations such as these prepared the way for acceptance of evolution as the key to all vital improvement. Though they diminished the role of the Creator on earth, they further elevated the divinity in man.

Afterword

T HE LITERATURE of the Romantic movement, characterized by emphasis on individuality and freedom of imagination, is so varied that one does not find broad homogeneity even in the treatment of one of its most basic tenets — its concept of love. But there do appear unifying strands running through the literature which connect even the most diverse treatments. Particularly significant is an orientation toward the natural and, specifically in regard to love, toward a more relaxed association between human beings. This is quite obvious in the comic approach, which ridiculed (sometimes with gentleness, sometimes with complete devastation) both the artificial conventions of literature and the accepted customs of ordinary life. While upholding the lofty position accorded to love *per se* by the spirit of the age, the comic viewpoint did recognize that, in minor aspects at least, love could be defective; consequently it served as a healthy corrective to oversentimentality, with its insipid, often cloying, unnaturalness. This comic attitude might well be termed the Romantic equivalent of eighteenth-century skepticism and negation. Certainly it seems more closely allied to neoclassical approaches than any other facet of Romantic love; and its chief proponents, Burns and Byron, may well be seen as Janus figures looking backward to their predecessors in wit, humor, and irony while also looking forward to their contemporaries and successors in the portrayal of exalted emotion.

The shift toward naturalness also permitted a new focus in the serious attitudes of the period. At a time when the unequal status of women came under severe attack from such reformers as Mary Wollstonecraft and Godwin, it revealed the possibilities for more meaningful relationships between the sexes both within and without the confines of matrimony. And by overruling the artificial divisions of custom that divided groups of people from one another, it pointed the way toward the reunification of mankind. It even lent credence to supramundane phenomena; for, by releasing the imagination from conventional strictures, it permitted the supernatural to be treated as though it were as natural as the material world.

This predilection for naturalness is closely related to a basic premise of my study — that the Romantics did put love above all else — because the love they praised derived from their own experiences rather than merely from inherited traditions, though the latter were sometimes admittedly useful guides in their personal search. That they did seek passionately for new insights seems, in turn, to explain both their wildest aberrations and their most solid achievements. The Romantic movement constituted an exciting half-century of breaking through ideational barriers; and if some of the mental explorations appear to be unbalanced, one must accept them, without undue stress, as unavoidable by-products of the unfettered imagination combined with individuality. The bizarre and irrational elements, which some critics have exploited as most characteristic of the period, are, I think, only to be expected among those relentlessly pursuing truth beyond the limits set by previous ages. In this regard there seems to be a definite parallel between the spirit of free scientific inquiry current in the period and the literary examination of human emotions — between man's external environment and his inner life; and the comparison logically extends to the trial and error method often necessary to search all possible avenues to knowledge.

Certainly the impetus toward freedom of thought and expression had never been stronger than in the Romantic age, but I am convinced that the results of this moving force were, as a whole, both positive and useful. It was the Romantics' intense belief in the overwhelming *power* of love which caused them to explore its potentialities to an almost limitless extent, so that no human relationship escaped their scrutiny. It was their devotion to the *truth* of love that caused them to question, and often defy, any religious beliefs, laws, and social customs which seemed to impede its implementation among men. Finally, it was their conviction in love's essential *goodness* that made them dare postulate mankind's salvation *upon earth* — not merely in some distant, spiritual afterworld. From Burns's declaration of brotherhood in "Is there, for honest Poverty" to Shelley's apocalyptic vision in *Prometheus Unbound*, there was among the Romantic writers generally a profound faith in a better society. One cannot deny that by the time Romantic flights of fancy settled down into the more restrained Victorian age beneficial changes were beginning to occur in education, government, and social relations; and some credit for these advances is surely due to the position of love in the literature of the early part of the century. Indeed the ideas of Western man have never been quite the same since the Romantics began to explore uncharted regions of thought. Their new focus upon old problems and their shifted emphasis among old values shaped fresh points of view that still apply in the modern world.

But the Romantics voiced their recommendations not only in direct terms through their own words or those of fictional personalities; they spoke most impressively through the fundamental character of their literary heroes. Since idealistic movements especially tend to exalt human models who exemplify their beliefs, it is not surprising that hero-worship flourished in the Romantic age; but it seems to have taken a very different turn in England than it did elsewhere. While continental Europeans virtually created a cult by their glorification of the strong man associated with nationalism and worldly power, most English writers were drawn to another kind of personality. Though their willingness to challenge entrenched doctrines contributed to a certain admiration for Napoleon's energy, genius, and eagerness to overthrow dynastic authority, they generally saw his tyranny for what it was; hence, with the exception of Hazlitt, they did not share the extreme fascination with him felt by German philosophers such as Hegel, Fichte, and Nietzsche. If there was indeed any dominant hero among British Romantics, he was not primarily a military leader; neither was he merely a social misfit, an idealistic outlaw, or a malcontent striving for unattainable gratification, though all of these figures received some recognition. Basically he was an aspiring lover who, according to his own receptivity to light from heaven, became the instrument for working out divine will. Keats's Endymion was not atypical in rejecting a life of active leadership in favor of a higher calling — the fulfillment of love. In fact, most of the outstanding literary characters of the age — the poet whose mental growth Wordsworth detailed in *The Prelude*, Coleridge's Ancient Mariner, Byron's Don Juan, Shelley's Prometheus, and Keats's Lycius — achieved the status of great men largely by virtue of being imaginative lovers. Whereas the worldly empires of Napoleon and his twentieth-century imitators have crumbled, the literary dominion of love has survived.

Index

Abercorn, Lady Anne, 100
Addison, Joseph, 6
Aeschylus, 268; *Agamemnon*, 136
Aesop, 251
Agamemnon (Aeschylus), 136
agape, 214
Ahasuerus, the Wandering Jew, 265
Aiken, Robert, 64
Alfieri, Vittorio, 134
Allsop, Thomas, 84, 88
Anacreon, 49
Anti-Jacobin, The, 212; *Beauties of the Anti-Jacobin*, 243; "New Morality," 243n
Arabian Nights, 251
Ariosto, Lodovico, 164
Aristotle, 246; *Nicomachean Ethics*, 171
Armour, Jean, 61–63
Arnold, Matthew, 67, 111, 227; on Burns's humor, 19–20
Arnot, John, 61
Augustine, Saint: *Confessions*, 166
Austen, Jane, 37, 59, 244

Bage, Robert, 212
Bailey, Benjamin, 178, 181n, 187
Baillie, Joanna, 97
Barbauld, Anna Letitia, 250
Beattie, James, 6; "Essay on Laughter and Ludicrous Composition," 6, 7n; *Essays*, 7n
Beaumont, Sir George and Lady, 249
Beaupuy, Michel, 68, 220, 236
Becher, Rev. J. T., 26
Beddoes, Thomas Lovell: "The Phantom-Wooer," 201–2
Belsches, Williamina (Lady Forbes), 98–99
Bentham, Jeremy, 249n
Bergson, Henri, 70; *Laughter*, 5
Berkeley, George, 263
Beugo, John, 61
Blackwood's Magazine, 43, 96–97, 133, 134, 135, 181
Blake, William, 117–31, 214; on chastity as false ideal, 123–24, 126, 129–31; on deceit in love, 127; on fallen senses,

light imagery, 252–57; on virtuous love, 81–84, 92–93; vision of domestic paradise, 85–88; vision of ideal womanhood, 94–95; on Wordsworth's inability to love, 82; on Wordsworth's "The Thorn" and "The Idiot Boy," 71–72, 230, 251. WORKS: *Aids to Reflection*, 243*n*, 257; "The Ballad of the Dark Ladié," 89; *Biographia Literaria*, 72, 230, 251; "Christabel," 201; "Constancy to an Ideal Object," 95; "The Day-Dream," 88; "Dejection: An Ode," xix, 90; "Desire," 83; "The Destiny of Nations," 253*n*; "Domestic Peace," 85; "The Eolian Harp," 86–87; *Essays on His Own Times*, 244, 247; "Farewell to Love," 84; *Fears in Solitude*, 243, 253*n*; *France: An Ode*, 243; *The Friend*, 243–48, 250; "The Hour When We Shall Meet Again," 86; "The Improvisatore," 94, 95*n*; "The Keepsake," 88; "Kubla Khan," 201; "A Letter to ———," 89–92; "Lewti," 91; "Lines in the Manner of Spenser," 86; "Lines: On an Autumnal Evening," 85; "Lines: Written at Shurton Bars," 86; "Love," 89; *Lyrical Ballads*, 251; "On the Slave Trade," 244; "Pantisocracy," 85; "Reflections on Having Left a Place of Retirement," 87, 243*n*; "Religious Musings," xvii, 244, 245, 252, 253*n*, 254; "The Rime of the Ancient Mariner," xvii, 250–57, 278; "This Lime-Tree Bower," 253*n*; "To Asra," 84; "To a Young Ass," 245–46; "To the Nightingale," 86; "To the Rev. W. L. Bowles" (I), 245

Coleridge, Sara Fricker, 83, 84, 86–88, 248

Columbine. *See* Pantomime

Comedy, sentimental (*comédie larmoyante*), xv, 23

Commedia dell'arte, 37–38

Condorcet, Marquis de, 115, 220

Cooper, Thomas, 248

Crabbe, George: *The Parish Register*, 103*n*

Cromek, R. H.: *Reliques of Robert Burns*, 66

Crompton, Mrs. Peter, 94

Cunningham, Allan: "Robert Burns and Lord Byron," 22

Cupid-Psyche myth, 179–80, 186–87

Currie, Dr. James: *Life* (of Burns), 66

Daniel, book of, xv

Dante, Alighieri, 77, 253; Beatrice, 172, 174; *Inferno*, xv, 132, 133, 186; *Paradiso*, xvi, 92

da Ponte, Lorenzo, 38

D'Arcy, M. C., xiv

Darwin, Charles, 116

David, King, 10

Day, Thomas: *Sandford and Merton*, 212

Delpini, Charles Anthony: *Don Juan; or, the Libertine Destroyed*, 37

De Quincey, Thomas, 4; on Wordsworth's domestic arrangement, 75–76

de Vere, Aubrey, 70

Dibdin, Thomas, 38, 41

Dickens, Charles, 31

Digby, Kenelm Henry: *The Broad Stone of Honour*, 79

Dr. Faustus (Marlowe), 23, 38

Don Giovanni; or, a Spectre on Horseback, 41

Donizetti, Gaetano: *Lucia di Lammermoor*, 106

Don Juan (the character): pre-Byronic evolution of, 23, 36–44

Dostoevski, Fëdor Mikhailovich, 168

Drury Lane Theatre, 38, 42

Dryden, John: *All for Love*, xv

Edinburgh Review, 96, 133

Edleston, John, 49*n*

Eliot, T. S., 21

Elizabeth I, 51

Endymion myth, 177, 198

Eros, 73, 95, 162, 166, 199

Euripides, 134

European Magazine, 40, 41, 43*n*

Evans, Mary, 82, 92

Examiner, 39, 40, 42, 43

Fenwick, Isabella, 229

Fichte, Johann Gottlieb, 277

Fiedler, Leslie, 237*n*

Fielding, Henry, 46; comic theory, 23;

134; *"An die Freude,"* 91; *Der Geister-seher,* 201
Schlegel, A. W. and Friedrich von, 79
Scott, Anne, 101
Scott, Charlotte Carpenter, 100–1
Scott, Sir Walter, xix, 21, 97–106, 116; on consequences of unrestrained passion, 103–4; on correlation between behavior in life and in love, 102–4; as exemplar of middle-class morality, 97; on importance of marriage for love, 101–2; on tragedy of unwise attachments, 104–6; on wisdom of overcoming amatory disappointments, 99–100. WORKS: *The Bride of Lammermoor,* 104–6; "The Eve of St. John," 200; *The Heart of Midlothian,* 102–4; *Ivanhoe,* 99–100; *The Lady of the Lake,* 101–2; *The Lay of the Last Minstrel,* xix, 101; *Marmion,* 101; *Quentin Durward,* 99; *Rokeby,* 99; *St. Ronan's Well,* 99; "The Violet," 98; "William and Helen," 199–200
Segati, Marianna, 29
Shadwell, Thomas, 40
Shaftesbury, Anthony Ashley Cooper (third earl of), xiv, 212
Shakespeare, William, 23, 40; *Antony and Cleopatra,* xv; *Hamlet,* 85; *Othello,* 30; *Romeo and Juliet,* 25, 48
Shaw, G. B., 37*n*
Shelley, Harriet Westbrook, 142, 144
Shelley, Mary Godwin, 85*n*, 142, 144, 269
Shelley, Percy Bysshe, xvi, 31, 116, 137, 138–44, 163, 164–76, 193, 195–96, 257–74; on achievement of love in death, xviii, 167, 174–75; on cyclical conflict between good and evil, 266; hopes for applying philanthropy in Ireland, 257–60; on ill effects of marriage, 143; on imagination and sympathy, 261–62, 271, 272; on incest as an acceptable form of love, 138–39; on necessity's function in achieving perfectibility, 262–63; on societal improvement through regeneration of human mind, 268–73; on superiority of free love to marriage, 140–44, 173–74. WORKS: *An Address, to the Irish People,* 258; "Adonais," 175, 176; "Alastor," xvi,

165–68, 169, 170, 177, 182; *The Assassins,* 266; *The Cenci,* 140; *A Defence of Poetry,* 164, 171–72; "A Discourse on the Manners of the Ancient Greeks . . . ," 165; "Epipsychidion," xvii, 170–74; *Essay on Christianity,* 265, 267, 270; "Ghasta; or, the Avenging Demon," 201; *Hellas,* 268, 271*n*; "Hymn to Intellectual Beauty," 168–69; "Julian and Maddalo," xv; *Laon and Cythna,* 138–140; "Lines Written among the Euganean Hills," xvii, xix; "Lines Written in the Bay of Lerici," xviii; "The Mask of Anarchy," 273*n*; "Ode to the West Wind," xix; "Oh! there are spirits of the air," 85*n*; "On Love," 167, 170, 174, 272; "On Marriage," 141; "On Polytheism," 269*n*; *On the Devil, and Devils,* 266; *Prometheus Unbound,* 167, 268–74, 277, 278; *Proposals for an Association,* 175, 258–59; *Queen Mab,* 143–44, 262–65; *A Refutation of Deism,* 265; *The Revolt of Islam,* 140, 167, 265–67; "Rosalind and Helen," 144; *St. Irvyne,* 140; "The Sensitive Plant," 169; "Sister Rosa: A Ballad" (*St. Irvyne*), 201*n*; *Speculations on Morals,* 260–62; "To Jane: 'The Keen Stars Were Twinkling,' " xviii; "To ——— (One word is too often profaned)," 192–93; "To St. Irvyne," 165; "The Triumph of Life," xvii, 175–76; "Una Favola," 174–75; "The Witch of Atlas," 169–70; *Zastrozzi,* 140
Sillar, Davie, 62
Smith, Charlotte, 212
Smollett, Tobias, xiv
Socrates, 162, 164, 261
Solomon, King, 7, 10; Song of Songs, 198
Sophocles, 134, 171; *Antigone,* 199
Southey, Robert, 87, 116, 247, 259, 260
Spenser, Edmund: *The Faerie Queene,* 163–64, 179
Staël, Mme. de, 79; *De l'Allemagne,* xv
Steele, Sir Richard, 6
Sterne, Laurence, xiv, 6; treatment of humor, 23